Manuscript Records of the FRENCH AND INDIAN WAR

IN THE
LIBRARY OF THE
AMERICAN ANTIQUARIAN SOCIETY

Charles Henry Lincoln

HERITAGE BOOKS
2007

HERITAGE BOOKS
AN IMPRINT OF HERITAGE BOOKS, INC.

Books, CDs, and more—Worldwide

For our listing of thousands of titles see our website
at
www.HeritageBooks.com

A Facsimile Reprint
Published 2007 by
HERITAGE BOOKS, INC.
Publishing Division
65 East Main Street
Westminster, Maryland 21157-5026

Copyright © 1909 Charles Henry Lincoln

— Publisher's Notice —
In reprints such as this, it is often not possible to remove blemishes from the original. We feel the contents of this book warrant its reissue despite these blemishes and hope you will agree and read it with pleasure.

International Standard Book Number: 978-1-55613-739-6

PREFATORY NOTE.

The manuscript records of the French and Indian war exist only in very incomplete form and are widely scattered. Such official records as survive are largely in British and French archives or have remained in American state collections. The correspondence of prominent individuals is found in widely separated localities if the writers continued to be men of note in their later years, and the equally important manuscripts of many temporary leaders have been buried because their writers soon fell from their position of leadership. To the student of history it is extremely helpful to have the location of all important manuscripts of any given period known. It is for this reason that the Society issues this calendar of the manuscripts in its collections relating to the French and Indian war.

The first portion of this volume centers about the personality of Sir William Johnson, one of the most notable of American Colonial leaders. Although it summarizes but a small portion of the correspondence of a man of wide influence and of long continued authority, it contains letters nowhere else available. For this reason if for no other it is a worthy contribution to American historical research.

In the second division are manuscripts throwing further light upon the war with France and the work of John Bradstreet throughout that war. Again no pretence is made that the collection calendared is all-inclusive but it well illustrates the difficulties attendant upon the duties of a Colonial quartermaster and the experiences of a leader of frontier expeditions during the war. Born in England in 1711 John Bradstreet spent the greater portion of his life in America. From 1745 when he participated in the Louisburg campaign he was active in maintaining British control in America. His death in 1774 obviated the necessity of his taking sides on the question of American independence and left him to share with Sir William Johnson, who died in the same year, the credit of a vigorous opposition to French interests. Among the later Bradstreet manuscripts is found also a good example of the arguments and methods used in securing a legal title to lands obtained from the Indians during the stormy period preceding the American Revolution.

Following these divisions is a group of miscellaneous manuscripts throwing additional light upon various phases of the war. In these the conflict in Pennsylvania is touched upon as well as the war in New England and the Northwest. Although the letters center about no one person several notable leaders are among the writers and the list as a whole is worthy of recognition. Where the names of writers have been forgotten the manuscripts furnish many details regarding the period of which they speak and are the more important coming from widely separated sources.

Finally there is the Orderly Book of William Henshaw, a Lieutenant in Capt. Jeduthan Baldwin's company of provincial troops serving under Sir Jeffrey Amherst in the war. The one hundred and fiftieth anniversary of this expedition is an especially fitting time for printing this manuscript in full. It opens to the reader a side of military life which is but partially shown by letters of onlookers or even of participants. It is a description of camp life from May to November 1759, given by a minor officer on his march to Fort Edward and when on duty at that fort, and presents a more enduring picture than any occasional visitor could paint.

It is upon collections such as the one here calendared that writers of our provincial history must rely for many details. States may reprint colonial records, the writings of colonial leaders may be preserved in printed volumes, but unless the owners and custodians of miscellaneous collections of provincial papers open their treasures to the student no comprehensive record can be obtained.

WALDO LINCOLN,
FRANKLIN P. RICE,
NATHANIEL PAINE,
Library Committee.

TABLE OF CONTENTS.

Prefatory Note	3
Abbreviations employed	5
The Sir William Johnson Manuscripts	7
The Col. John Bradstreet Manuscripts	55
Additional Manuscripts of the French and Indian War	133
The Lieut. William Henshaw Orderly Book	179
Index	255

ABBREVIATIONS USED.

A. D.—Autograph Document.
A. D. S.—Autograph Document Signed.
D. S.—Document Signed.
A. L.—Autograph Letter.
A. L. S.—Autograph Letter Signed.
L. S.—Letter Signed.
[ ]—Information Supplied.
[?]—Doubtful reading or information.
***—Omissions.

THE MANUSCRIPTS OF
SIR WILLIAM JOHNSON.

Mr. Allen — Gipsey of Ireland 7br 1st 1773

Please to send me by this opportunity
100 lb of Linseed or Lemon, 1 Dozen of Porter,
1 lb Good, 2 Gallons of Red Spirit, 6 lb Duck
46 pounds of Mothers lot, & 8 pounds of Good
Powder, which charge to Duty of

Y'r Humble Servant

[signature: W. Johnson]

16 Amis — 6.
6 Ill. Jas — 9.
2 G Swiv. —
2 Jug — 3. 14.
Bathos — 1. 8. 6
2 d Pnd

AUTOGRAPH OF SIR WILLIAM JOHNSON. (See page 40.)

THE SIR WILLIAM JOHNSON
MANUSCRIPTS.

1755. Shirley, W[illiam.] Boston. Letter to Gov.
Feb. 25. [Benning Wentworth] of New Hampshire.
Encroachments of the French upon the English
colonies in America and particularly upon New
England; letters received from the home government authorizing measures against the enemy;
steps taken in the past; proposed movements
set forth in [Shirley's] message to [Massachusetts]
Assembly [Feb. 13] and reply [Feb. 18] enclosed;
enlarges upon terms of message and reply;
expects to appoint Col. William Johnson to
command of expedition; by so doing will avoid
Colonial jealousies and obtain aid from Indians;
Massachusetts Assembly bound to secrecy regarding expedition; wisdom of speedy decision on
part of New Hampshire; sends Col. Robert
Hale as Commissioner to explain project further
if desired. L. S. 6 pp.

> Similar letters sent to Governors of other Colonies and
> printed: Penna. Col. Records, Harrisburg, 1851, VI, 310,
> to Lt. Gov. R. H. Morris; R. I. Records, Providence, 1860,
> V, 414, to Gov. William Greene.

1755. Wentworth, [Benning.] Portsmouth. Letter to
Feb. 28. Gov. William Shirley, [Boston]. Acknowledges
letter of Feb. 24 [25?] with enclosures; considers
proposals for Crown Point expedition reasonable
except that Coos should be fortified; agrees as
to excellence of appointment of Col. [William]
Johnson as Commander in Chief but is uncertain

as to manner of appointment [i. e. by Shirley]; is about to summon full Council of Colony and will consider plan in more detail; welcomes coming of Col. [Robert] Hale; "if he can convert the Exeter members * * * he will gain a great point, if not a miraculous one;" fears greatest difficulty will be the want of money and asks advice as to best method of raising necessary amount. Cont. Copy. 2 pp.

1755. **S[hirley,]** W[illiam.] Boston. Letter to Gov.
Mar. 4. [Benning Wentworth,] of New Hampshire. Acknowledges receipt of Wentworth's letter [of Feb. 28] and is gratified at approval of plans against Crown Point; agrees that Coos should be fortified; gives further outlines of plans against the French and Indians; thinks nothing upon which the colonies disagree should be undertaken at the outset; pleased that selection of Col. [William] Johnson as Commander in Chief is well received; will agree to any method of appointment of Johnson if the result is the same; Col. [Robert] Hale will be glad of advice in working a miracle on the Exeter men [See: Wentworth to Shirley Feb. 28]; suggests three methods by which New Hampshire can raise money for expedition; is to ask [Maj]. Genl. [Edward] Braddock for an engineer; hopes New Hampshire will be an example to the New England "Charter Governments." Cont. Copy. 3 pp.

1755. **Franklin,** B[enjamin.] Philadelphia. Letter to
Aug. 11. [Sir William] Johnson, [Johnson Hall]. Acknowledges Johnson's letter of Aug. 1 and has forwarded letter to Capt. [Robert] Orme; [Thomas] Pownall is in New York and letter [to Pownall?] will be forwarded to him; will acquaint Gov. [Robert Hunter Morris] with

record of Johnson's proceedings; hopes money appropriated by Assembly of Pennsylvania may be used in part to aid him against the Indians but fears the provision for taxation of lands of the proprietors will cause the Governor to veto the appropriation measure; "Thus, from petty private Considerations in particular Colonies, general publick good is obstructed;" necessity for union of the Colonies. A. L. S. 2 pp.

See: A Brief View of the Conduct of Pennsylvania for the year 1755. London. 1756 p. 39.

1761. [Johnson, Sir William.] Fort Johnson. Letter to
Dec. 9. William Smith, D[avid] Bostwick, P[hilip] V. B. Livingston, William Livingston and David Vanhorne, [New York]. Expedition to Detroit prevented acknowledgement of their letter of Jun. 22; introduced [Samson] Occom to the Oneidas as an instructor in religion as desired by the Society; approves effort to obtain influence over Indians through religious teachers as French have done; will do his utmost to aid them in their efforts to this end. Draft. 1p.

The men addressed were the American Correspondents of the British Society for propagating Christian knowledge.

1762. [Johnson, Sir William.] Johnson Hall. Letter to
Mar. 30. [Thomas] Fitch, [Hartford]. Sends speech of Mohawk Indians at Johnson Hall [giving their opinion of the claims of the Susquehanna Co. to land in New York and results, if claim be persisted in]; has met Eliphalet Dyer and [John] Woodbridge: warned them as to results of settlement in Wyoming Valley, but they insisted on claim of Connecticut to the country and intention of founding a settlement; declares "that effusion of blood and depopulating of the frontier must inevitably follow" if this intention

is fulfilled; hopes Fitch will intervene in matter. Draft. 2pp.

1762. [Johnson, Sir William.] Johnson Hall. Letter to
Sep. 21. [James] Hamilton, [Philadelphia]. Has been visited by deputies from the Susquehanna Company of Connecticut and has convinced them of the unwisdom of settling in the Wyoming Valley; fears these efforts, with the proclamation of Gov. [Thomas Fitch], will not prevent settlers from Connecticut coming; has laid the matter before the Lords of Trade; if settlement is made, expects Indians to resort to force; outbreak should be prevented if possible. Draft. 2pp.

  The deputies from Connecticut were Joseph Chew and Col. Thomas Fitch.

1763. [Bradstreet, John.] Albany. Letter to [Sir Jeffrey
Nov. 7. Amherst, New York]. Regrets that Amherst is to give up the command of British forces in America so soon; Indians recently at Albany suspected of being spies; they have been sent to Sir William Johnson; hopes they will not be allowed to escape as they deserve death; Indians would despise English if spies were not punished. Draft. 2pp.

1763. [Johnson, Sir William.] Johnson Hall. Letter to
Nov. 17. [Thomas] Gage, [New York]. Can not give full opinions but embraces opportunity of [Henry?] Gage sent by Commodore [Joshua] Loring to write short letter; thinks former has reformed "from the indiscretion to which youth are often subject"; hopes he may receive commission in Commissary Department; friendly Indians fear war from the Delawares; doubts the loyalty of the Onondagas; will write more fully soon. Draft. 1p.

1763. [**Johnson,** Sir William.] Johnson Hall. Letter to
Nov. 23.   [Thomas] Gage, [New York]. Refers to letter
of Nov. 17; describes the attitude of various
Indian tribes; many are apprehensive of resentment of enemies and must be treated carefully
if they are to be held; advice as to an expedition
against the Senecas; proposes movements against
the Delawares and Shawanese; some Canadians
to be taken to dispel Indian hope of French
alliance; has written the Lords of Trade as to
conditions and in regard to enlisting Indians;
asks Gage's opinion; if latter agrees with idea
of enlistment, requests him to give orders on
[John] Bradstreet for supplies of arms as well as
presents for Indians; will report results of conference with Indians as soon as held. Draft. 3pp.

1764. [**Johnson,** Sir William.] Johnson Hall. Letter to
Jan. 12.   [Thomas] Gage, [New York]. Summarizes interviews with Senecas and Indians from the Five
Nations; the enlistment of Indians in colonial
forces; Lieut. [John] Montresor and others have
informed him of proposals made by Indians at
Detroit; distrusts Indian promises and would
have retained hostages if authorized; French will
endeavor to arouse Indians and will supply them
with ammunition; English policy is to arouse
antagonisms between the various tribes; by
continuance of presents would make them look
to English rather than to the French for favors;
encloses accounts of [Thomas] McGee, deputy
agent; they are certified by Col. [Henry] Bouquet;
warrants on paymaster general requested.
Draft. 2pp.

1764. [**Johnson,** Sir William.] Johnson Hall. Letter to
Jan. 20.   [Thomas] Gage, [New York]. Acknowledges
Gage's letter of Jan. 8 with dispatches for Niagara and Detroit; difficulties of forwarding them

but hopes to do so; refers to his letter of Jan. 12, and repeats certain news as to Indian interviews; steps taken against Senecas and a white man with them; latter lodged in Albany gaol; [John] Ellison who was captured in 1762 has obtained his freedom and reports that the friendly Senecas may be relied upon; sends Capt. [Daniel] Claus's account of Indian expenses. Draft, 2pp.

1764.   [**Johnson**, Sir William.] Johnson Hall. Letter to
Jan. 27.   [Thomas] Gage, [New York?]. Acknowledges letter of [Jan.] 12 forwarded by [John] Bradstreet; discusses royal proclamation [of Oct. 7, 1763] agreeing with Gage as to its utility in the "southern acquisitions"; northern lands on a different footing; Indian problems in Canada and in the Northwest; advantages of missionary work among the Indians; recommends Niagara as a fitting place for Indian treaty; has heard from Lt. Gov. [John] Penn regarding the Conestoga massacre: fears the consequence of this act despite Penn's proclamation. Draft. 3pp.

1764.   [**Johnson**, Sir William.] Johnson Hall. Letter to
Feb. 19.   [Thomas] Gage, [New York]. Acknowledges letters of Jan. 31 and Feb. 6; white deserters as well as prisoners among the Indians; expected outbreak of southern Indians following that of the northern tribes; speaks encouragingly of number of friendly Indians whom he can rally to British side; urges a treaty of offensive and defensive alliance with friendly Indians; specifies provisions favored; [Daniel] Claus not able to reach Montreal; asks certificate as to rank of Lt. [Guy] Johnson that latter may obtain land under royal proclamation; case of Christopher Strubble who deserted from [William] Shirley and has been among Indians; returned in 1759 and was forgiven; other notes. Draft. 4pp.

1764. [**Johnson,** Sir William.] Johnson Hall. Letter to
Mar. 2.   [Thomas] Gage, [New York]. Express just
arrived from a party of friendly Indians sent
against enemy; on Feb. 26 party heard of Delawares on way to attack English settlements
and on Feb. 27 friendly Indians attacked them,
took 41 prisoners from Delawares and sent
them under escort to Johnson Hall; writer
expects them in a few days; among prisoners
is "Capt Bull" son of Teedyuscung; asks Gage's
opinion as to furnishing guard for villages of
friendly Indians while latter are on campaign;
will send prisoners to Albany upon arrival.
Draft. 1p.

Friendly Indians were commanded by Capt. Andrew Montour.

1764. [**Johnson,** Sir William.] Johnson Hall. Letter to
Mar. 16. [Thomas] Gage, [New York]. Acknowledges
letters of Mar. 4 and 8; considers it wise to have
troops near when peace treaties are made with
Indians, and June a proper time for meeting at
Niagara; advice for instructions to Maj. [Henry]
Gladwin at Detroit; general meeting of Indians
at Onondaga; ideas as to obtaining tracts of
land from them; news regarding capture and
disposal of hostile Indians; [See letter of Mar.
2.] confessions of Capt. Bull; hostile Indians
increasing and "the sooner some troops move
will certainly be the better"; plans for joint
action of friendly Indians and troops; advances
of money made to Indians; further advances
necessary; needs £5000 at once for presents,
and 100 light shotguns for other uses; advantages
of employing Indians. Draft. 6pp.

1764. [**Johnson,** Sir William.] Johnson Hall. Letter to
Apr. 6.   [Thomas] Gage, [New York]. Acknowledges
letters of Mar. 26 and 29; favorable results of

negotiations with Senecas, Five Nations, and other Indians at Johnson Hall; expeditions against the Delawares; backwardness of provinces in raising troops; advice as to expedition against Western Indians; approves sending one party via Lake Ontario and Erie to Presque Isle, and a second party down the Ohio and up the Muskingum; this would encourage friendly Indians; English parties could join by means of the carrying places of the Scioto [to Lake Erie]; hopes to hear of destruction of French at Detroit; urges need of money; great benefit of enlisting Canadians against the Indians; congratulates Gage on being chosen Commander in Chief in America. Draft. 3pp.

The treaty with the Senecas referred to in this letter is printed O'Callaghan: Documents relating to the Colonial History of the State of New York, VII, 621-623.

1764. Apr. 30. [Bradstreet, John.] Albany. Letter to [Thomas Gage, New York]. Acknowledges letters of Apr. 22 and 23 and has forwarded packet to Detroit as requested; has written Maj. [Henry] Gladwin; arms for troops; has directed Capt. [John] Montresor to order New York levies to Oswego at once; Lt. Col. [Maj. William] Browning urges the forward movement fearing attacks at carrying places; assistance expected from Sir William Johnson. Draft. 2pp.

1764. May 5. [Bradstreet, John.] Albany. Letter to [Sir William Johnson, Johnson Hall]. Has written Maj. [Alexander] Duncan to hold troops at Oswego until [Johnson's] arrival; is expecting last of provincial recruits hourly and will be on march shortly so requests Johnson to await him at Oswego; names men and garrisons to be left at Fort Stanwix and Oneida Lake; Lt. [Cornelius] Cuyler to join Capt. [Ephraim] Lake at Fort

Stanwix the latter to command; requests that Johnson's men be summoned from Fort Schuyler. Draft. 2pp.

[1764.] May 7. Bradstreet, John. Albany. Letter to [Thomas] Gage, [New York]. Acknowledges letter of Apr. 30; reports from various companies of provincial troops assembling for expedition; has been told by Sir William [Johnson] that Indians are to join the expedition and hopes they will do real service rather than watch "according to custom"; requests commissions for two Majors to avoid provincial Majors commanding next Lt. Col. [Alexander] Campbell. A. L. S. 1p.

1764. Jul. 12. [Bradstreet, John.] Niagara. Letter to [Thomas Gage, New York]. Conditions at fort; mortification of British troops delaying an expedition because of Indians, but considers latter, especially the Senecas, untrustworthy; 100 friendly Indians in camp and more on the way; Sir William Johnson considers it imprudent to proceed at present, hopes the enemy will not retire and leave no opportunity for a battle; will send accounts of needs at Niagara. Draft. 3pp.

1764. Jul. 19. Bradstreet, John. Niagara. Proclamation to Indian Traders at Niagara. Proclamation granting, on representation of Sir William Johnson, liberty to trade with distant Indian Nations at Niagara and prescribing regulations under which such trade shall be conducted. D. S. 1p.

1764. Sep. 1. [Johnson, Sir William.] Johnson Hall. Letter to [Thomas] Gage, [New York]. Acknowledges letters of Aug. 15 and 16 but has had no opportunity to write Col. [John] Bradstreet; doubts loyalty of Chenusios Indians; summarizes results of conference with Indians at Niagara; absence of "Pondiac" [Pontiac], the "Powtewatamies" and Ottawas; dangerous positions of small English outposts at long distances from supplies; such posts give Indians the feeling that they have the English at their mercy; important to maintain trade relations; better protected posts if fewer in number should be kept up; expedidition of Col. [Henry] Bouquet not started as yet; Indian news from Lt. Col. [William] Browning; Lt. Col. [William] Eyre about to go to England; encloses accounts of officers in his department and of sub-agent [Thomas] McGee. Draft. 3pp.

1764. Sep. 11. [**Johnson**, Sir William.] Johnson Hall. Letter to [Thomas] Gage, [New York]. Much concerned at news of [John] Bradstreet making treaty with hostile Indians at Presque Isle; thinks Bradstreet must have made treaty not knowing of advance made by Col. [Henry] Bouquet; treaty may be renounced by English but fears enemy will consider this unfair; despite this Johnson considers treaty void; motives of Indians in treating with Bradstreet; advice as to orders to be sent latter; hopes evil results may be prevented; has sent Indian aid to Bouquet. Draft. 3pp.

1764. Sep. 12. [**Bradstreet**, John.] Detroit. Letter to [Thomas] Gage, [New York]. Transmits a copy of his negotiations with various Indian tribes about Detroit; eagerness of certain tribes to be included in the treaty; encloses also (*a*) copies of letters from Capt. [Thomas] Morris on his way to the Illinois country; (*b*) oath of fidelity taken by inhabitants of Detroit; (*c*) instructions to Lt. Col. [John] Campbell and Capt. [William] Howard; (*d*) account of steps taken to prevent debasement of currency, and (*e*) copy of permission to people to trade with Indians; movements about Detroit by Lt. [John] Sinclair. Auto. Draft. 2pp.

See: Bradstreet, John, Proclamation July 19, 1764.

1764. [Bradstreet, John.] Detroit. Letter to [Thomas]
Sep. 12. Gage, [New York]. As peace concluded with various Indian tribes "is agreeable to [Gage's] instructions", concludes that troops "sent [under Col. Henry Bouquet] by way of Fort Pitt are stopped"; if peace is not kept by Indian tribes, will punish them severely; further intelligence will be sent by way of Fort Pitt; writer is obliged to remain at Sandusky; will inform Bouquet and [Lt.] Gov. [John] Penn if events go wrong or if Indian outbreak is renewed. Auto. Draft. 1p.

1764. [Johnson, Sir William.] Johnson Hall. Letter to
Sep. 21. [Thomas] Gage, [New York]. Acknowledges letter of Sep. 16; Delawares and Shawanese Indians continue hostile depredations; expects peace with Indians met at Niagara [Aug. 6] to continue; certain Indians north of Lake Ontario have made peace since then; has explained to the Six Nations the absence of authority in the peace made by Col. [John] Bradstreet with Indians at Presque Isle; thinks Hurons and Six Nations regard that pact as invalid; requests by the "upper" Indians for provisions whenever messengers are sent to Johnson. Draft. 2pp.

1764. [Bradstreet, John.] Sandusky. Letter to [Thomas
Oct. 5. Gage, New York]. Assures him in answer to letter of Sep. 15, that negotiations with Indians ended in a satisfactory peace and not in a truce; is aroused over its infringement and has sent to every tribe demanding satisfaction; as Gage does not mention time for Indians to send deputies to Sir William Johnson he has postponed

the summons until following year; Indian troubles caused by Thomas King, chief of Oneidas and by the Senecas; experience of Capt. [Thomas] Morris confirms this; encloses reply of Five Nations to summons to arms; report of 17th and 46th regiments to be sent by Capt. [Richard] Montgomery. Auto. Draft. 2pp.

In a letter to Bradstreet, dated Sep. 2, Gage had disavowed the peace with the Indians made by the former and explained in letter of Sep. 12. The last named letter, of course, had not been received by Gage when the letter of Sep. 15 referred to above was written.

After the return of the Tuscaroras from North Carolina in 1714-15 the Iroquois Confederacy is usually spoken of as the Six Nations; Bradstreet reverts to the earlier name.

1764. Nov. 4. [**Bradstreet,** John.] Niagara. Letter to [Thomas Gage, New York]. Encloses copies of nine letters giving summary of each in an attempt to justify his conduct during the Detroit expedition and return to Niagara; outlines happenings since leaving Sandusky; efforts to aid Col. [Henry] Bouquet; loss of boats on lake; movements and efforts of Lt. Col. [John] Campbell, Lt. [John] Sinclair, messengers to Indians etc.; difficulties in securing provisions; has received letter of Oct. 15 but three earlier packets were sent on to Detroit; has "some satisfaction" in approval of conduct except making "formal peace"; assures Gage that on receiving his letter by Capt. [Richard] Montgomery he will be convinced that this power was given him [Bradstreet] and the blame, if any, is not his. Draft. 4pp. See previous entry.

1764. Nov. 20. [**Bradstreet,** John.] Albany. Letter to [Thomas] Gage, [New York]. Acknowledges letter of Oct. 26; attempts to explain parts played by various Indian tribes during and after the peace of Detroit; action of Shawanese, Delaware and

Seneca Indians in connection with embassy of Capt. [Thomas] Morris; things done while Sir William Johnson was waiting at Niagara for the Senecas; further justification of writer's acts on return from Detroit; encloses copy of request to return home made by the Five Nations when at Sandusky; they were allowed to go taking hostages of Shawanese and Delawares to Sir William Johnson; complaints against Oneidas. Draft. 3pp

1764. [Johnson, Sir William.] Johnson Hall. Letter to
Dec. 18. [Thomas] Gage, [New York]. Acknowledges letter of Dec. 6 received Dec. 16; satisfaction over success of Col. [Henry] Bouquet; conditions which may now be demanded from Indians; favors mouth of Kanhawa as point for trading post with western Indians; necessity of gaining over "Pondiac" for lasting peace; possession of Illinois country will defeat French interference; suggests an expedition or embassy under [George] Croghan the latter to be present at peace negotiations going thence to the west with troops and with some of the Indians making peace; trade favors to be offered outbalancing those offered by French; has many Indians at his home "full of complaints of wants;" congratulates Gage on succeeding to position held by Sir Jeffrey Amherst. Draft. 3pp.

1765. [Bradstreet, John.] Albany. Letter to [Thomas]
Apr. 25. Gage, [New York]. When setting out for the west [Detroit expedition] in June, 1764, was informed by Sir William Johnson that rum must be provided for Indians "to make good his engagements"; was obliged to clothe those who went with him to Detroit and make presents to chiefs; encloses opinion of Johnson on subject and requests reimbursement for money thus expended. Draft. 1p.

1766. [Johnson, Sir William.] Johnson Hall. Letter
Jan. 7. to [Thomas] Gage, [New York]. Has no
anxiety for safety of Capt. [Thomas] Sterling;
regards with disfavor proposition to abandon
outposts; under upright officers military posts
aid trade, defeat French and Indian machinations
and hold adjacent country to English allegiance;
some Americans wish them abandoned because
they restrain "Republican designs" and prevent
abandonment of "Allegiancy and Dependence
to the British Crown"; reports disturbances
at Albany over sale of stamps for duties; damage
to house of Postmaster "VanScoike" [Henry
Van Schaack.] Draft. 4pp.

1766. [Johnson, Sir William.] Johnson Hall. Letter to
Jan. 30. [Thomas] Gage, [New York]. Sends letter by
[George] Croghan; Croghan has sent [Alexander]
McKee to Fort Pitt and [Thomas] Smallman to
Illinois; hopes latter and Maj. [Robert] Farmar
may aid English cause and restrain French in
the settlement; writer's plans for tiding matters
along until better arrangements are made with
Pontiac; necessity of maintaining frontier posts;
plans for expedition under Croghan; forces
should be sent even if necessary to recall them
later; favors reimbursement of Croghan for
losses of previous year; encloses petition from Lt.
[Andrew] McTavish late of Col. [Simon] Frazers
regt. for land due to reduced officers; considers
himself in same class; if Croghan expedition is
approved, wishes medals etc. for Indians;
encloses accounts of various officers. Draft. 3pp.

1766. [Johnson, Sir William.] Johnson Hall. Letter to
Mar. 15. George Croghan, [Detroit?]. Acknowledges letter and accounts of Feb. 14; has forwarded
latter to Genl. [Thomas Gage] with recommendation for payment; advice as to method of pre-

senting accounts; understands from Pensacola
that the 34th regt. has reached the Illinois
country but this will not interfere with Croghan's
mission; probable expense of mission to be sent
to Gage; negotiations looking to a meeting
between Johnson and Pontiac at Oswego; intends
to appoint [Alexander] McKee Commissary
at Fort Pitt; does not object to [Thomas] Smallman at Detroit unless earlier promises may
have been made to Lieut. [Allen] McDonnell
or Lieut. [Jehu] Hay recommended by Col.
[Henry] Gladwin; other possible appointments.
Draft. 3pp.

1766. [Johnson, Sir William.] Johnson Hall. Letter [to
Jun. 20. Gov. [William] Franklin, [New Jersey]. Acknowledges letter of Jun. 7 with enclosures; favors
establishment of colony [along the Ohio river];
hopes he will use every means to bring to justice
colonial murderers of Indians; conduct of many
frontiersmen unwarranted; expects Benjamin
Franklin will have an opportunity to speak
regarding the erection of a new colony in the
west; [Maj]. Genl. [Thomas] Gage will have no
share in such a colony but thinks Lord Adam
Gordon would; advises consultation with authorities in England. Draft. 2pp.

This letter is printed in full on p. 47 of this volume.

1766. [Johnson, Sir William.] Johnson Hall. Letter to
Jun. 28. Gov. Henry Moore, [New York]. Acknowledges
letter of Jun. 14; pleased that Moore agrees
with [Thomas] Gage and himself in plans for
Indian settlements on frontier; is to meet Pontiac and other Indians at Ontario in summer;
if no more attacks on Indians occur, hopes to
accomplish much at this congress in way of
division of territory; hopes to see Moore soon
and would be glad to have Lady Moore and his

daughter come to Johnson Hall; thanks the Governor for his offers of favors and for his friendship. Draft. 2pp.

1766. [Johnson, Sir William.] Johnson Hall. Letter to
Jul. 8. [Gov. William Franklin, New Jersey]. Encloses plan for colony mentioned in letter of Jun. 20, also letter to [Henry S.] Conway with recommendations regarding the project; is writing Benjamin Franklin respecting the matter and suggests that he do the same; regrets the hostility shown the Indians; is about starting to meet Pontiac and the western Indians at Ontario and does not expect to return within three weeks. Draft. 1p.

This letter is printed in full on p. 47 of this volume.

1766. [Johnson, Sir William.] Johnson Hall. Letter to
Jul. 10. Benjamin "Franklyn", [London]. At request of Gov. [William] "Franklyn" and several Pennsylvania gentlemen encloses a plan for establishment of colony in Illinois country with letter to Secry. [Henry S.] Conway on same; requests Franklin to forward the latter; owing to licentious conduct of frontiersmen fears an Indian outbreak at any time; hopes to be able to satisfy Pontiac and western nations at meeting in Ontario for which he is on the point of setting forth. Draft. 1p.

This letter is printed in full on p. 48 of this volume.

1766. [Bradstreet, John.] Albany. Letter to [Thomas
[Jul.] 21. Gage, New York]. Has applied to the Mayor [of Albany] as to completion and furnishing of barracks for soldiers; one battalion only thus far provided for; demands of Sir William Johnson for boats the reason why more are not available for the troops ordered to march by Gage. Auto. Draft. 1p.

1767.   [Johnson, Sir William.] Johnson Hall. Letter to
Jan. 15.   the Lords of Trade [and Plantations]. Refers
to his letter of Oct. 8, 1766 in answer to theirs
of Aug. 20 regarding petition of inhabitants
of Montreal; mission of [George] Croghan has
resulted in peace with Indians of the west assembled at Illinois; efforts of French and Spanish
to arouse dissatisfaction; frauds of Indian traders
etc. furnish opportunities for French to stir up
the Indians and these can be prevented only by
enlargement of powers of the Indian Department;
cites illustrations of cheating by traders at
Detroit; outlines plan mentioned in letter of
Oct. 8 for controlling this trade; dealings of
Col. [Thomas] Cresap with certain warriors of
the Six Nations: considers such affairs as this
flagrant violations of his own powers and certain
to bring bad results. Draft. 3pp.

   Printed with slight changes: Docts. relating to Col. Hist
of New York, VII, 894; letter of Oct. 8, 1766 ibid 871;
Albany 1856.

1767.   **Wood,** Draper S. Albany. Letter to Col. John
Feb. 3.   Bradstreet, Albany. Twenty-five sleds wanted
for Sir William Johnson's Indians to enable
them to carry provisions from Fort Stanwix [to
Johnson Hall]. A. L. S. 1p.

1767.   **Glen,** John. Schenectady. Order to Commissary
May 28.   Officers [and whom it may concern]. Orders to pass
the bearer, Andrew English, with batteaux laden
with provisions to be delivered to Wallace [Wouter
Dance?] at Caughnawa for the Indians subject to
orders of Sir William Johnson. A. D. S. 1p.

1767.   **Glen,** John. Schenectady. Order to Commissary
May 29.   Officers [and whom it may concern]. Orders to
pass bearer Adam Smith and provision batteaux;
on receipt of goods acknowledgement to be made

and deficiencies to be noted on orders; goods to be delivered to Mr. Wallace [Wouter Dance?] at Fort Stanwix and held for the Indians subject to orders of Sir William Johnson. A. D. S. 1p.

1767. [Johnson, Sir William.] Johnson Hall. Letter
Aug. 14. to [William Petty], Earl of Shelburne. Refers to his letter to Shelburne May 30 on the subject of a Congress with the Six Nations at German Flats and the irregularities in the Indian trade; is about to set out for [Saratoga] Springs for his health; summarizes the methods he (Johnson) has employed in dealing and trading with Indians and good results therefrom; doubts regarding attitude of home government; result from methods of others; Indians becoming restive and consider most of the colonists as poor fighters but sharp traders; young men under little control by the old chiefs; small British garrisons and unwillingness of Americans to do anything but talk; fears that powers granted him are not sufficient to prevent serious troubles from the Indians as he can not redress their grievances against colonists. Draft. 4pp.

Printed with slight changes: Docts. relating to Col. Hist. of New York, VII, 946. Letter of May 30 ibid 928; Albany 1856. Shelburne is sometimes known by his later title, Marquis of Lansdowne, but more generally in America by the earlier one. The letter as printed is from the letter received in England and not from this draft.

1767. [Johnson, Sir William]. Johnson Hall. Letter to
Sep. 22. [William Petty], Earl of Shelburne. Refers to his own letter of Aug. 14 and acknowledges receipt of Shelburne's of Jun. 20; encloses a "Review of the former and present state of the Trade, and Indian Affairs" within his district, which he considers a lengthy but true statement; outlines methods of trade with Indians followed by the French; prefers them to methods now

The Sir William Johnson Manuscripts. 27

in use; they took trade to Canada rather than to New York; will render all possible assistance to Gov. [Sir Guy] Carleton in regard to obtaining information as to early traders; Indian grievances; Carleton obliged to send troops toward Carillon; no willingness shown by the colonial authorities to prevent encroachments on Indians about the Ohio; is about to go among the Senecas and will endeavor to decrease the prevalent dissatisfaction. Draft. 4pp.

Printed with slight changes; Docts. relating to Col. Hist. of New York, VII, 951. Review mentioned is printed ibid VII, 953.

1767. [Johnson, Sir William.] Johnson Hall. Letter to
Oct. 26. [William Petty], Earl of Shelburne. Refers to his letters of Aug. 14, Sep. 22 and review enclosed in latter; has taken trip among the Onondagas and finds hostility of Indians greater than he has reported; Indians anxious for settlement of boundary line between themselves and the colonists, and desire compensation for grievances suffered at hands of whites; are not satisfied with promises or with orders to colonial Governors but wish aid from the king; lacking this Indian chiefs can not restrain their tribes from attacking settlements; French emissaries particularly active at this time; urges necessity for new system of control for Indian relations; sends letter by [John Tabor] Kempe, Atty. Genl. of New York. Draft. 3pp.

Printed with date "Oct" supplied: Docts. relating to Col. Hist. of New York, VII, 985.

1768. [Johnson, Sir William]. Johnson Hall. Letter to
Jan. 8. Rev. [Richard] Peters, [Philadelphia]. Acknowledges letter of Dec. 14; is gratified that he had so little trouble with Indians and regrets that they would not continue line [of boundary

between themselves and colony] so far as he wished; reasons for feeling among Indians; responsibility of French and of English settlers; pretentions of Delawares to lands mentioned by Peters may be disregarded in presence of Six Nations; intrusion of Virginians [upon land north of the Ohio] will cause trouble; hopes they may be removed; will do his best for the interests of Pennsylvania at any time; hopes Indian feeling will not prevent speedy adjustment of boundary line [with Maryland]. Draft. 3pp.

The lands upon which the Virginians settled were along the Monongahela and Red Stone Creek. This land was claimed by the Delawares and the Six Nations of Indians and by Pennsylvania, Maryland and New York of the Colonists. For the settlement with Indians, see: Proceedings of Johnson's Congress with them in Docts. relating to Col. Hist. of N. Y. VIII, 38, (Mar. 2-12, 1768). Owing to Indian feeling, Maryland and Pennsylvania were unable at this time to complete the survey of their boundary line. See Johnson to Thomas Penn, Feb. 5, 1768.

1768. Feb. 5. [Johnson, Sir William.] Johnson Hall. Letter to T[homas] Penn, [London]. Acknowledges letter of Jul. 1767 with postscript of Sep. 12, regarding land which King George granted to Johnson; requests Penn to take out the grant and promise payment of fees; is uncertain whether royal grant will cover his whole purchase from Indians by proper survey or not; expenses of writer have increased since retirement from business and acceptance of official position; hopes king will regard his needs as also his services and reward him accordingly; bad condition of Indian affairs; has heard from [Richard] Penn of a massacre of Indians on the frontier of Pennsylvania; among other bad results is unwillingness of Indians to agree to boundary line between Pennsylvania and Maryland. Draft. 3pp.

Grant of land referred to was an old Indian grant on northern side of Mohawk river. It consisted of 66,000

The Sir William Johnson Manuscripts.   29

acres and was given to Johnson by the Mohawks in 1760, Johnson giving 12,000 dollars in return. The colony of New York would give no patent for the land, holding that the Crown alone could do so and Johnson did not receive his patent until June, 1769, as result of application to King in 1766 and favorable report by Board of Trade, Feb. 1767. See Johnson to John Watts, Oct. 4, 1769 and Johnson's Memorial to Crown Jul. 8, 1766, Docts. relating to Col. Hist. of N. Y. VII, 839.

1768.   [Johnson, Sir William.] Johnson Hall. Letter to
Jul. 28.   Gov. [William] Franklin, [New Jersey]. Acknowledges letter of May 23 by S[amuel] Wharton and is grateful for enclosures; discusses the new plan for regulation of Indian trade; powers of Superintendent of Indian Affairs strongly expressed but management of trade left to the respective colonies; agrees with Franklin as to poor results to be expected; salaries increased but amounts for various services limited; gratified that posts are to be garrisoned by British troops; western boundary to be settled soon; colonies expected to give assurances that white men will not pass the border line; suggests that New Jersey may wish her commissioners to be present at Indian negotiations. Draft. 2pp.

This letter is printed in full on p. 48 of this volume.

1768.   Glen, John. Sch[enecta]dy. Order to Commissary
Aug. 2.   Officers [and to whom it may concern]. Orders to pass bearer with provision batteaux; on receipt of goods acknowledgement to be made and deficiencies to be noted on orders; batteaux in charge of "Wouter Dance" [Walter Dance?] to receive their load from [Douwi] Fonda at "Cagnowagie" [Caughnawa] and to deliver it to Capt. [Lt. John] Galland at Fort Stanwix; latter will hold goods subject to order of Sir William Johnson as they are for the Indians. A. D. S. 2pp.

On verso are Glen's instructions to Wouter Dance and receipt from Lt. Galland to Dance, each an A. N. S.

1768. [Johnson, Sir William.] Johnson Hall. Letter to
Aug. 5. [Thomas] Gage, [New York]. Acknowledges
letter of Jul. 18 to Mr. [Guy] Johnson; information regarding western Indians obtained from "Chipeweigh" [Chippeway] chief; hopes to have large Colonial as well as Indian representation at approaching Congress for settlement of boundary line [Oct. 1768 at Fort Stanwix]; discusses boundary question and asks Gage's advice; long dispute [from 1703 when grant from Queen Anne was obtained] over Kayadarosseras lands settled by payment of 5000 dollars [to Mohawks]; previous efforts by Gov. [Henry] Moore a failure. Draft. 2pp.

1768. Galland, John. Fort Stanwix. Letter to Walter
Aug. 17. Dance. Gives receipt for provisions from store of [Jelles] Fonda for use of Sir William Johnson. A. D. S. 1p.

1768. [Johnson, Sir William.] Johnson Hall. Letter to
Aug. 24. Lt. Gov. [John] Penn, [Philadelphia]. Acknowledges letter of Aug. 6; preparations for meeting of Boundary Congress with Indians at Fort Stanwix; hopes it will meet about Sep. 18; doubts if Shawanese will be present; will be glad to see [Colonial] Commissioners at Johnson Hall before Sep. 15. Draft. 1p.

Printed Penna. Arch. 1st series, IV, 307.

1768. [Johnson, Sir William.] Johnson Hall. Letter to
Sep. 12. [Thomas] Gage, [New York]. Acknowledges letter of Sep. 3; has directed continuance of commissaries to enable the provinces to make some provision for them but doubts if latter will undergo any expense in the matter; thinks additional provision should be made by home government for deputies and interpreters among Indians; matter of having other persons among

Indians is left by government to the colonies and the need of persons to look after trade will soon appear; communications from Govs. H[enry] Moore, [William] Franklin and Lt. Gov. [John] Penn as to Indian Congress at Fort Stanwix; confidence of [Robert] Rogers in success of his expedition although complaining to [Levin] Gale of ill treatment. Draft. 2pp.

1768. [Johnson, Sir William.] Fort Stanwix. Letter to
Sep. 25. [Gov.] John Blair, [Virginia]. Reports arrival of Col. [Andrew] Lewis and [Thomas] Walker, commissioners from Virginia to the Boundary Congress with Indians; has desired them to remain longer than anticipated as Indians are slow in coming; claims of Six Nations; hopes by granting certain of them to obtain a better line than one proposed by Lords of Trade; considers it better to delay treating with Cherokees until settlement is made with northern tribes; hopes Congress will terminate in a fortnight. Draft. 1p.

The treaty was signed Nov. 5, 1768.

1768. [Johnson, Sir William.] Johnson Hall. Letter to
Nov. 18. T[homas] Penn, [London]. Acknowledges letter of Aug. 11; outlines results of Boundary Congress with Indians at Fort Stanwix so far as they affect Pennsylvania; accomplished more than he expected considering the ill humor of the Indians and the opposition of the New Englanders; among latter notes particularly agents of Dr. [Eleazer] Wheelock who wished lands reserved for religious purposes [endowment of missionary school among Indians]; as [Richard] Penn has described Pennsylvania boundary Johnson refrains from repetition but refers him to report to Lord Hillsborough; urges his own claim to confirmation by Crown of early grant

of land in America. [See: Same to same, Feb. 5, 1768.] Draft. 3pp.

1768. [Johnson, Sir William.] Johnson Hall. Letter
Nov. 18. to James Jeffreys [Jeffries?, London]. Death of Mrs. [Grace] Cosby; will be glad to be of any possible service to Jeffries or to Lady Fitzroy [in settlement of estate]; received power of attorney [in matter] Nov. 10; [power dated Mar. 22, 1768;] discusses questions arising in settlement of estate; position of [Oliver] DeLancey; poor title of late Mrs. Cosby to certain lands; possibility of life interest rather than power of absolute disposal; other complications. Draft. 2pp.

See: O'Callaghan, Doct. Hist. of New York, II, 794, note, 926, 934–937.

1769. [Johnson, Sir William.] Johnson Hall. Letter to
Jan. 13. [Thomas] Gage, [New York]. Acknowledges letter of Jan. 2 received since his own of Jan. 4; thanks Gage for vouchers of [George] Croghan's account and packet from [Wills Hill, Earl of] Hillsborough; thinks that lands obtained by Crown by treaty of Fort Stanwix amply justify money spent; colonies would have paid amount altho some delay might have ensued; quit rents or sale will reimburse Crown if it so desires; home government will soon need to take some direction of commerce with Indians and not rely on colonies; would not be justified in diminishing estimates [for maintenance of posts etc.]; asks advice of Gage on this matter. Draft. 2pp.

1769. [Johnson, Sir William.] Johnson Hall. Letter to
Feb. 17. [Thomas] Gage, [New York]. Acknowledges letter of Jan. 23; agrees that a portion of French intrigue among western Indians may be due to trade but thinks another part is the result of

The Sir William Johnson Manuscripts. 33

a deliberate attempt to keep up an enmity between Indians and English in preparation for war; in either case frontier posts should be maintained; defends his conduct and bargain made at treaty of Fort Stanwix; means of reimbursement open to Crown; difficulty of joint action by colonies; reform advocated in management of trade relations with Indians; action in England based on too much confidence in colonies; sends expense account at Fort Pitt by [George] Croghan as also account of expense at Illinois; considers expenses high. Draft. 4pp.

1769. [**Johnson,** Sir William.] Johnson Hall. Letter to
May 26. [Thomas] Gage, [New York]. Has received letters from [Jehu] Hay, "late Commissary at Detroit" and Capt. [Norman] McLeod reporting an intended outbreak by various tribes of Indians in Ohio and west; siege of Detroit anticipated; other news from Detroit and from Capt. [Thomas?] Robinson on Lake [Erie]; forwards half-yearly accounts except those of Capt. McLeod. Draft. 2pp.

1769. [**Johnson,** Sir William.] Johnson Hall. Letter to
Jun. 12. Gov. [William] Franklin, [New Jersey]. Acknowledges letter of Apr. 10; will discuss with [George] Croghan matter [of western lands] mentioned by Franklin; hopes for successful outcome; pressure of other affairs in England prevents action; lands for Indian school; regrets that he can not offer his land on the Susquehanna at a lower price but has had offers for parts of it and expended so much that he can not lower original sum; no signs of colonies maintaining proper Indian establishments; commissaries have been withdrawn; has kept interpreters at posts or matters would be in worse condition than they are; hopes to see Franklin in fall after a visit to the Indians.

Postscript notes receipt of Franklin's letter of Apr. 29. Draft 3pp.

This letter is printed in full on p. 50 of this volume.

1769.
Jun. 24. [Johnson, Sir William.] Johnson Hall. Letter to [Thomas] Gage, [New York]. Acknowledges letter of Jun. 12; alarm at Detroit subsided for the present; discusses the situation among the western Indians generally; purposes to take a trip to Onondaga for a month to investigate matters; Guy Johnson will take his place during his absence; news of Detroit by Col. [John] Wilkins; [Gov.] d'Aubry [of Louisiana] has ordered [Louis] St. Ange [de Bellerive] "to send all the Spanish officers and Soldiers"; other war news from "Huron Andrew" and [Jehu] Hay; Indians told that French would return soon. Draft. 2pp.

1769.
Aug. 17. Penn, John. Black Point. Letter to [Thomas Gage, New York]. Has received letter from Col. [John] Armstrong to [Joseph?] Shippen and from contents fears an Indian war; Indians upon the Ohio displeased with sale of their lands at treaty of Fort Stanwix; is about to hasten to Philadelphia to do all in his power to suppress trouble. Cont. Copy. 1p.

This letter was forwarded by Gage to Johnson. See Johnson to Gage Dec. 8, 1769.

1769.
Aug. 23. [Johnson, Sir William.] Johnson Hall. Letter to Gov. [William] Franklin, [New Jersey]. Acknowledges letter of Aug. 11; accident to himself at Onondaga when on his Indian trip; thanks Franklin for news in letter to [George] Croghan; English authorities express discontent with extent of grant from Indians of land beyond the Kanhawa river; writer gives his own views in support of cession and is glad final authority

is given to settle matter; notes of late trip among Indians; latter offended with New Englanders' intrusions into Pennsylvania; hopes to be able to smooth over the disaffection; sends respects from Sir John and Guy Johnson. Draft. 2pp.

This letter is printed in full on p. 52 of this volume.

1769. [Johnson, Sir William.] Johnson Hall. Letter
Oct. 4. to John Watts, [New York]. Acknowledges letter of Sep. 25 and thanks him for promise to forward royal patent to lands [north of the Mohawk river]; land given him by Indians without asking in 1760; has proved expensive since; location of lands etc.; patent under great seal finally granted by Crown Jun. 8. 1769; sends money by [William] Adems [being?] the amount of [Jean?] Cadot's pay; requests assistance of Watts in passage of petition laid before Assembly by Capt. [James] DeLancey favoring [in opposition to measure introduced by Philip Schuyler] division of Albany County. Draft. 1p.

1769. [Johnson, Sir William.] Johnson Hall. Letter to
Dec. 8. [Thomas] Gage, [New York]. Cherokees wish the Six Nations to join them in an attack on hostile southern Indians; Six Nations replied that their enemies were those of the Illinois country but that they would engage in no war without consulting Johnson; Cherokees agreed to come to council with the Six Nations at Johnson Hall; writer is troubled over expense of council which he is in no situation to meet; asks Gage's aid in this matter and his advice as to position to be taken in the subject of the council; benefits and evils to the English and colonists of an Indian war such as the one proposed. Draft. 2pp.

1770. [Johnson, Sir William.] Johnson Hall. Letter to
Jan. 30. Thomas Penn, [London]. Acknowledges letter

of Sep. 13, 1769 and sends money to pay expenses connected with late grant of land from the king; bearer [John] Robberts can give account of relations with Indians; nothing done as yet by local governments for regulation of Indian trade; fears results of this policy; claims of Connecticut persons to land within Pennsylvania limits considered "ridiculous"; respects of Sir John Johnson. Draft. 2pp.

1770. [Johnson, Sir William.] Johnson Hall. Letter to
Aug. 1. [Thomas] Gage, [New York]. Results of Congress [with Indians at German Flats] more favorable than he had anticipated; war proposed by Indians has been postponed until after further council with the "Wabache" [Wabash] nation; Johnson pleased with large attendance at the Congress; will send complete returns of transactions next week. Draft. 1p.

  For report of Congress, see: Johnson to Lord Hillsborough Aug. 14, 1770, in O'Callaghan, Doct. Hist. of New York II, 973-978, or Docts. relating to Col. Hist. of N. Y VIII, 224-244. War postponed appears to have been conflict between Cherokees and Choctaws for which the former claimed the aid of the Six Nations and their white allies. Hillsborough's reply is in Docts. relating to Col. Hist. of New York, VIII, 253, of date Nov. 15, 1770.

1770. [Johnson, Sir William.] Johnson Hall. Letter to
Sep. 21. [Thomas] Gage, [New York]. Trusts Gage will be pleased with results of Congress with Indians [at German Flats]; pleased that they are in harmony as to effect of Johnson's advice regarding possible war between [Cherokee and other] Indians to the south and west; during earlier conferences and at this Congress endeavored to improve relations between Indians and Whites, and to persuade Indians to live at peace with each other; efforts made to oppose his work; because of good results obtained by

[George] Croghan and Capt. [Beamsley] Glazier considers their accounts as worthy of approval and payment; is about to make a month's excursion into Indian country during which time Guy Johnson will act in his stead; congratulates Gage on promotion to Lieut. Generalship; encloses accounts of men at Ontario. Draft. 2pp.

1770. [Johnson, Sir William.] Johnson Hall. Letter to
Sep. 25. [Thomas] Gage, [New York]. Acknowledges letter of Sep. 17 regarding mines near Lake Superior; correspondence with Lord Hillsborough on the subject; thought permission of Indians might be secured and mines worked but doubted the conduct of agents; results of a settlement would be trouble; refused share in Company offered by London agents; thinks that Gage's observations on the question are "extremely just and probable"; considers it unfair of promotors of enterprise to withhold statements as to settlements etc. that might influence judgment of investor; is about to set out on trip among Indians mentioned in last letter [Sep. 21]. Draft. 2pp.

See: Johnson to Lord Hillsborough, Dec. 23, 1768 in Docts. relating to Col. Hist. of New York, VIII, 140.

1771. [Johnson, Sir William.] Johnson Hall. Letter
Jan. 22. to [Jan Baptist Van Epps and the Trustees of Schenectady]. Affairs of the town as presented in the Assembly; cautions the town against giving away power to unsettle early land grant or to divide the township; only extravagant grants should be questioned and in case referees are appointed, men of "strict integrity & disinterestedness" alone should be selected; does not know enough of questions discussed to give detailed advice. Draft. 2pp.

1771. [Johnson, Sir William.] Johnson Hall. Letter to
May 24. [Thomas] Gage, [New York]. Acknowledges
letter of Apr. 15 and refers to his own of Apr.
18; Indian accounts paid to order of [George]
Croghan; thought the account was incurred by
order of Capt. [James] Edmondstone; rumors
of Indian disturbances in south and west; Cherokee and Choctaw nations; hopes for better
news from convention at Scioto but fears war
before long; all well at Fort Chartres. Draft. 1p.

1771. [Johnson, Sir William.] Johnson Hall. Letter to
Jul. 10. [Rev. Thomas Bradbury] Chandler, [Elizabethtown, New Jersey]. Acknowledges letter of
May 30; regrets that document sent with it
became lost; is sure that he agrees in thought with
Chandler in his views of the Church; hopes that
he will yet find Chandler's "farther Defence" and
postpones till then further discussions. Draft. 1p.

> Pamphlet mentioned is the 3rd of the series by Chandler
> and is entitled "The Appeal farther defended; in Answer to
> the Farther Misrepresentations of Dr. Chauncy" N. Y. 1771.

1771. [Johnson, Sir William.] Johnson Hall. Letter to
Jul. 25. [Thomas] Gage, [New York]. Acknowledges
letter of Jul. 15; regards the "Powtewatamies"
as a troublesome tribe; French at the Illinois not
so apprehensive as is pretended; expects return
of Thomas King within a month; mentions
[Francis] Maisonville, who is about to present
his suit for lands at Detroit, as a "useful man
and a fast friend to the English"; is holding a
conference with Indians and will send results
later. Draft. 1p.

1771. [Johnson, Sir William.] Johnson Hall. Letter to
Sep. 29. [Thomas] Gage, [New York]. Sends letter by
his son [Sir John Johnson] and Col. [Guy] Johnson; is preparing to go again among the Six

Nations to confer as to an embassy to the southward; will write in detail on return, meantime refers him to Col. Johnson; encloses account of salaries and disbursements in his department for last half year. Draft. 1p.

1771.   [**Johnson**, Sir William.] Johnson Hall. Letter to
Nov. 16.   [Thomas] Gage, [New York.] Gives account of his trip to the Indian country; Six Nations expressed "detestation" at death of Thomas King and sent word to tribes responsible that such were their feelings; agrees that western Indians have been encouraged by the French; intends making [Francis] Maisonville resident at Post Vincent to watch in these matters; regrets increased expenses at Fort Pitt; does not question [George] Croghan's disposition but recommends frugality. Draft. 3pp.

1772.   [**Johnson**, Sir William.] Johnson Hall. Letter to
[Jan. 1.]   J[ohn] Watts, [New York]. Is sending second petition regarding division of [Albany] County to Capt. James DeLancy; is perfectly satisfied with line of division proposed; people desire the courthouse to be at Johnstown; is willing to contribute more to the building up of the town etc. and requests assistance of Watts that it may be made the County seat of the new County. Draft. 1p.

1772.   [**Johnson**, Sir William.] Johnson Hall. Letter to
Oct. 12.   Thomas Penn, [London]. Delay in answering letter of February due to business undertaken since then; thanks him for kindness to Lieut. [Benjamin] Roberts and will return money advanced altho Roberts was not empowered to use his name; asks if Letters-patent [for Mohawk land] are recorded in England. Draft. 1p.

40   *American Antiquarian Society.*

1773.   [Johnson, Sir William.] Johnson Hall. Letter to
Mar. 19. Rev. [Eleazer] Wheelock, [Hanover]. Acknowledges letter of February; has treated Indians bringing it in accordance with recommendations; hopes a desire for study may be awakened among other Indians and Wheelock's undertaking be marked with success. Draft. 1p.

1773.   Chew, Joseph. Johnstown. Letter to Thomas
Jul. 15. Allen, [New London]. Health of Sir William Johnson necessitates trip to ocean; has recommended Allen's house [New London Coffee House] to Johnson; diet recommended; regards to family. A. L. S. 1p.

1773.   Johnson, [Sir] W[illiam.] Fishers Island. [Long
Sep. 1. Island Sound]. Letter to [Thomas] Allen, [New London]. Orders ammunition and miscellaneous articles to be sent at first opportunity. A. L. S. 1p.

This letter is reproduced in facsimile facing p. 9.

1773.   [Johnson, Sir William.] Johnson Hall. Letter to
Nov. 25. Rev. [Richard] Hind, [London]. Refers to letters from [Daniel] Burton as to religious matters, matters, especially the work of the Society for propagating the Gospel; mission at Johnstown in charge of [Richard] Moseley; religious conditions in general; Rev. [William] Andrews replaced by Rev. [John] Doughty at Schenectady; work of Rev. [John] Stuart among the Mohawks and Rev. [Harry] Munroe at Albany; his own work in behalf of the church and schools of the region about Johnstown. Draft. 3pp.

1774.   [Johnson, Sir William.] Johnson Hall. Letter to
Feb. 17. Rev. [Henry] Caner, [Boston]. Thanks Caner for edition of church service in Mohawk tongue; understands from experience how easily errors

in translation may have been made; is endeavoring to write a short history of the Bible which will contain a brief "historical deduction of facts and incidents in a regular and well connected order"; thinks it will be of much use to the Indians. Draft. 1p.

MANUSCRIPTS
RELATING TO THE
OHIO-ILLINOIS COUNTRY.

Printed in full from the
Manuscripts of Sir William Johnson.

NOTE.

In printing in full certain letters from our French and Indian War manuscripts, two objects have been considered. It has been thought wise that the members of the Society and others interested might know in more detail the nature of the manuscripts in our collection and the manner in which they are being calendared for historical use. These particular letters have been inserted at this point because they form a united group from the Johnson collection concerned with the foundation of an English settlement in what was at that time the far west. They are noteworthy in that they illustrate one stage in the accomplishment of the British and especially the Colonial purpose to contest with the Indians and with France or Spain if necessary, the possession of the territory west of the Allegheny mountains. Other illustrative manuscripts will be found printed in full on pp. 103 and 171, as also the Orderly Book of William Henshaw, the last division of this volume.

Sir William Johnson to Gov. William Franklin of New Jersey.

JOHNSON HALL June 20th, 1766.

Sir:

I have been favored with your Letter of the 7th Inst together with the Enclosures containing a Letter from the Company with the Reasons for Establishing the Colony &c of all which I before gave my approbation & shall chearfully do every thing consistent with my Office for Carrying it into Execution as early as possible;—I have already hinted the Affair in a Letter to the Lords of Trade & I am somewhat of Opinion it would answer better that I recommended it in Gen.[1] Terms, as an Affair I had heard was in Agitation, but as it is deemed necessary to the design that I sho[d]. enclose it I shall not Scruple to lay it together with my recommendation thereof before the Ministry under a flying Seal to your father who will doubtless be consulted on the Occasion.—

I have sounded Gen[l]. Gage on the Occasion, who declines being concerned I apprehend it will not be the Case with Lord Adam Gordon. As to what you say of apply[g] for an Extensive boundary I agree in opinion with you on the Utility of it, but the Government should I think be previously Sounded on that head Least it might obstruct or retard the Design—

I am persuaded you will use all your Endeavors for bringing the Murderers of the Indians to Justice, the Conduct of the frontier Inhabitants in many Colonies being such as gives us great reason to dread a Renewal of that Cruel War from which we are but Just freed, every Week brings me fresh Complaints from the Inds & but Just now I have recd an Acct of the Murder of 4 Onondagas on their return from the South ward with 2 or 3 more tow.[ds] Fort Pitt So that I have great reason to doubt of Succeeding in attempting to Calm the Minds of a Revengefull people to whom we are Giving fresh provocation.

I promise myself great Satisfaction from your friendly Correspondences which I shall be glad to improve by every occasion that Offers as I am—

Gov.[r] Franklin

I shall write to the Compy by next Opp[ty]—

Sir William Johnson to Gov. William Franklin of New Jersey.

JOHNSON HALL July 8th 1766–

Sir:

The 20th. ult°. I acknowledged the receipt of your last favor, & Signified my Intentions of Enclosing the plan for the Colony with my Recommendation to the Ministry which I now send you with a Letter thereon to M[r]. Secretary Conway, wherein I have said all that I could Venture to do from my very slender knowledge of him and the delicacy of the Subject but I hope the Nature of it and the interest of some Gentlemen at home, may render it an Object worthy of attention.

As I have not had the pleasure of your father's Correspondence I just wrote him a few Lines wch you can Explain more fully as I should think it were better that my Letter was put into the Office for the Sec^y of State but this I Submit to his discretion & hope You will write him thereon.

I am sorry it goes over at a time when from the daily Murders & Encroachments complained of we have all the reason imaginable to Expect an Ind^n War. Sev.^{l} other Murders have been Committed Since my last so that I know not where it will end.

As I am Just Setting off to meet Pondiac & the Western Nations who are arrived at Ontario for that purpose I have only time to add that I am with much Esteem, Sir,

Yours Etc

I shall be very Glad to hear from you & shall return in Three Weeks—

Sir William Johnson to Benjamin Franklin.

JOHNSON HALL July 10th 1766—

Sir—

At the Request of your Son Gov-^{r} Franklyn, & sev.^{l} Gent.^{n} of Pensilvania, I now enclose you a Scheme proposed for establishg a Colony at the Ilinois, together with my Letter to Mr Secretary Conway in fav.^{r} thereof, which the proposers denied might be transmitted thro' your hands— I have accordingly sent it under a flying Seal, & must request you to forward it as Addressed—

I daily dread a Ru[p]ture wth the Ind.^{s} occasioned by the Licentious Conduct of the frontier Inhabitants who Continue to Rob, and Murder them.—I am imediately to meet *Pontiac* with the Western Nat.^{s} at Ontario and wish I may be able to satisfy them.—

Altho' I have not had an Opportunity of Cultivating your Acquaintance I shall always be Glad to render you, or yours any Services as I am, &c

To

Benj.^{a} Franklyn Esq.—

Sir William Johnson to Gov. William Franklin.

JOHNSON HALL July 28th 1768.

Sir,

Mr S. Wharton delivered to me your kind favor of the 23d of May with the Several Inclosures for which I give you many thanks.— I hope you will Excuse my having deferred an Answer to it, until my return home which was some days ago, having received it Whilst on a Tour to the seaside for the recovery of my health which was brought very low thro my fatigues etc.—

Tho' I by no means accuse you of neglect of Writing I shall be very happy in your agreable & friendly Correspondence abstracted from any motives arising from the Subject.

The Extracts you were pleased to send me were very Acceptable, as they contain abundance of Judicious Remarks, & Sufficiently shew my much esteemed M^r. Franklin's Experience, attention & knowledge in American affairs.—

You must before this time have been advised of the new arrangement of all these matters, and of the Reform by which the Management of the Indian Trade is Committed to the Care & Charge of the respective Colonies Whereby the Alterations which you wisely foresaw, are in part made, the powers of the Super.Intend.^{ts} are however pretty Strongly tho' Generally Expressed, their sallaries increased, but they are limited to a very Small Annl. Sum for the Various Services & Contingent Expences of their Departments. The Event of which, you seem so Justly Sensible of that I cannot but be intirely of your Opinion, altho' I find that the Lords of Trade think every post that is kept up sho.^{d} be Garrisoned by the Kings Troops, Yet there will be sundry other Expences found necessary for the Colonies to be at for the preservation of the Trade, which may render it impracticable, as a Union of Sentiment on these Occasions cannot be Expected, for the reasons you have Judiciously Assigned.—

The Settlement of the Boundary Line will I believe shortly take place, it is only retarded by reason of the distant residence of the Shawanese & Delawares whose presence I Judge necessary not as Owners of the Land but as Nigh Neighbours to the Settlements, to whom they may easily be troublesome—Your Province does not appear concerned in this Line, but as the Governmt. think the Colonies should give all security to the Transaction by Laws, to prevent their people from Transgressing, which may be a Case Common to every Colony, I thought it best to mention it, and in Case you think the attendance of one or two Commissioners from Your Government necessary to attend the Treaty You will doubtless take measures accordingly—

I have only now to add that I am
with perfect Esteem, Sir, Your Excellys &c

His Excell^{cy}
Govr Franklin

Sir William Johnson to Gov. William Franklin.

JOHNSON HALL June 12th. 1769.

Dear Sir,

Your kind Letter of April 10th relieved me from the Suspence which your Long Silence occasioned and which you have sufficiently accounted for. Indeed my own Situation has been such since we parted, that I can the easier excuse any omission of that nature in another, and this hitherto prevented me from Setting you a good Example, tho' I could not pretend to afford you equal entertainment from the unimportant events of these parts.

I began a Letter near three Weeks ago, but dropped it in Expectation of having something worth communicating in a little time altho' I have waited to no purpose.

I thank you for the Copy you transmitted me, & shall Settle the Matter with Col. Croghan as you desire when he & I has more Leisure than we have had Since his arrival in these parts, and I shall likewise talk fully to him upon the Subject. I hope it will go on with better success than it has hitherto done, but think it will require time and perseverance.

You have doubtless before this time heard from our Friend Wharton, as I expect to do but have not as yet. Neither have I had any account from any person concerning the event of his Voyage, or on the Subject of the Retribution. The Letter from the Sec.^y of State which I have Just received by the pacquet containing very little, and nothing material, and by my other Letters I find that the Whole face of things is much as it was when we heard before. The nature of the dispute about the Rights of Parliament, and the disturbed State of Affairs at home Create so many difficulties that when it will end, or other business be fully attended to must be uncertain—I thank you kindly for the Pamphlet you sent me which is I think a very good performance, and I fancy I could guess the Author of it —in return I send at your desire by this opportunity Evans's Manuscript Journal, I also inclose you Copys of the Two Letters from the Two Clergymen which you wanted, I have since had several Curious & Extraordinary Letters from Parson, Williamson al.^s Johnson one of a Very late date, All on the Subject of Lands & Establishments for the faithfull & desiring to know why I did not make public the boundary that they might take possessⁿ of their lands. There are no New Steps taken for carrying on the pious work and the Oneidas have thro' some disgust withdrawn most of thier Children from the Seminary, I believe all attention is more directed to the Susquehanna Vales, concerning the Settlement of which I hear they have come to Some Strong resolutions in Connecticut.

I wish I could dispose of my right on Susquehanna below the price I mentioned, especially as you Signify an Inclination for it, but really, from the Trouble & Expence it has already put me to, and the price I have been very lately offered for a great part of it, I cannot consistently do it. The Account of its being very hilly & Stony must have arisen from some misinformation, for except where some points of hills happen to Come to the River which occupy but a Very Small part of it, It is perhaps as Rich & Valuable for the Generality as any Land whatsoever, & this is allowed by some who have carefully viewed & are now Sollicitting me to dispose of it. As to Indian Intelligence I cannot say any thing Satisfactorily. The Commissaries are withdrawn, & I don't see any speedy prospects of such Establishments on the part of the Colonies as will Answer the purposes of preserving peace & Extending Commerce, neither can it be expected that they will make an adequate provision, or from their different Interests unite in a matter of that nature so as it may be attended with any Good effects, I have kept Interpreters & Smiths as yet at the posts, without which, affairs would not have gone on so easily as they have done,—Belts however, Said to come from the Southward are amongst the Indians & there has been an Alarm lately at Detroit which Frightened & Stopped the Traders at Niagara, & has induced the Inhabitants of the first mentioned Settlement to fortify themselves on the opposite Side of the River, which will probably alarm the Indians & may have consequences different from what is intended.

I think to go up the Country for a little time & do what little I can under the present restrictions for preventing any Union to our prejudice, and as my health is but very indifferent may possibly go down to the Sea Side in the fall when if I should happen to be near you, you may be Assured that I should Visit Burlington with great pleasure—In the Meantime I shall be happy in hearing from you whenever your Leisure will admit you to write to him Who is Always with great Sincerity D[r] Sir,

His Excell.[cy]
Gov.[r] Franklin

Mess.[rs] Wells & Smith by whom you wrote the 29th April, forwarded the Letter but did not come this way, which deprived me of an opportunity of shewing them those Civilities which your Friends sho[d] Always receive at my hands.

Sir William Johnson to Gov. William Franklin.

JOHNSON HALL Aug.[t] 23[d]. 1769.

Dear Sir
Upon my return from Seneca which was about 12 days ago I had the favor of your kind Letter of the 11.[h] of this Month which till now I could not Answer, & even now I cannot be as particular as I co.[d] Wish, for not being able to Write without much pain tho I have a Great deal of business on my hands, for on my return in the Night from the Hut of a Chief near Onondaga where I held a private Conference My Canoe overset, & I had to make the Shore & get up a Bank in the Dark with much difficulty in effecting which I tore my Swelled Leg very much on a Small Stump, so as not yet to be able to go into my study, or write without great Inconvenience tho' it is recovering much faster than I Expected.

I most kindly thank you for the news communicated in your Letter as well as for the perusal of what you wrote to Col. Croghan who has received it; My Letters from home seem to Express a dissatisfaction, at the Great Extent of the Cession beyond the Kanhawa, tho' it is indisputably the Lands of the 6 Nations, & if it had been denied, the Latter wo.[d] have proved Worse Enemys than the Cherokees can be, besides I believe the Virginians wo.[d] have settled on it at all Events. It is however left to me now, that in case I don't think it good policy to give up that part it will be Confirmed. I wish I could say the same as to the Grant of the Traders to which objections are made.—

I can Just say a Word as to my late Tour. I met near 2500 Ind.[s] at Seneca assembled from the Sev.[l] Villages, & I found them more dissatisfied than I hope I left them. They are greatly discontented at the Withdrawing people from the posts Which it is not in my power to Continue there, & I don't find the provinces inclined to do any thing material on that head.

The Ind.[s] are likewise dissatisfied with the N Englanders Intrusions into Pennsylvania, which they say will involve their people in disputes, They complain bitterly of Ill usage & Acts of Injustice at the posts & frontiers & say that the other Confederacys have invited them to Joyn in Measures for redress, And Indeed from the sev.[l] Discoveries I have Made The belts Constantly passing thro the Nations from the French, The late proceedings on Ohio, & their Speeches at Ilinois, I must have very unfavorable Sentiments of their Intentions.—After a meeting to be held soon at Onondaga I shall know more, In the meantime I use all my endeavors to prevent a Gen.[l] dissaffection, & to keep matters quiet as long as the present State of things will admit of—I persuade myself I have no occasion to Apologize for not being more particular under my present Circumstances, and Wishing to hear from you by every opportunity Convenient to yourself I remain with Great Cordiality & Truth Dear Sir &c

His Excell^{cy} Govr Franklyn—

Sir John Sends his best Compliments, as does Guy who desires me to tell you that he Wrote you a Long Letter last month, & will give you the Trouble of more whenever he has Subjects for them.

THE MANUSCRIPTS OF
COL. JOHN BRADSTREET.

By Colonel John Bradstreet commanding all his
Majesty's Forces on the Western District &c,&c,-

Notice is hereby Given to all Indian Traders, that on a Representation of
Sir William Johnson's, Liberty is granted them to Trade with the distant Indians, who at times come
here and name other for all kinds of Merchandize, except Arms and Ammunition, which they are strictly forbid
to sell, give, or on any wise allow the Indians to get from them on pain of being treated as Enemies to their
King and Country. The Merchandize hereby permitted to be bought and sold, to be at the here after
named prices. And to avoid impositions on either side, an Officer with two Indian Traders will attend the
Tent allow'd for the Trade alternatively, which is to be known every morning and on the 21st in their opening.

A Stroud Blanket 2 yards	2 Beavers	A Stek Pipes tops	ring of pewter	A pair of Silver Wrist Bands	2 m:f Beavrs
A large French Blank.t	2 m:f D°	Bottles of Sm: Scissors		3 Pair Sheer ear Bobs	1 Beavr 1 sp:c
A Laced Type ditto	1 large D°	Gun Flints Common and 40/Mohawk	silk or crot:e bag	12 Silver Broches	1 Beavr
A small ditto	1 m:f D°	Most gun locks with gaiters for gun powr 2 beav		2 large Silver Coppers	1 D°
A Bolt of Gartering	1 ditto	A small Bolts	1 large Beavr	A Silver Hair plate 6 v 5 at	3
A Man's Ruffled Shirt	1 large D°	A Wristband	1 C/k	A sqr: small	2
D° plain	1 m:f: 10		1 m:corn	2 Silver Gorgets	2 m:f a D/c
	1 m:b: 2°	a good Ringo	1 Beavr		
P.'s good Gunge	1 D°	3 q: Gallon of Rum	3 D°		
3/0 Wampum	1 Large Do	H:lov:l silver arm Band	2 D°	Given at Niagara July 19th 1764
4 Cured Vermillion	2 m:f Bells	Green Cups D°		Jn° Bradstreet

(See page 75.)

THE COL. JOHN BRADSTREET MANUSCRIPTS.

[1755.] June.   [Bradstreet, John.] Oswego. Letter to [William] Shirley. Acknowledges two letters brought by carpenters and received Jun. 8; progress in boat building; rough character of the waters of the lake [Ontario]; need of more carpenters; French have passed on way to the Ohio country. Auto Draft. 2pp.

[1755.] [June.]   [Bradstreet, John. Oswego.] Letter to [William Shirley]. Acknowledges letter of June 15; is building boats as directed "with such alterations" as improve them; news of Shirley's coming given out by new arrivals; conditions at Niagara; reenforcements expected; considers himself equal to any exigency as he understands conditions thoroughly. Auto. Draft. 2pp.

1755. Jul. 20.   [Bradstreet, John.] Oswego. Letter to William Shirley. Acknowledges letter of Jul. 12; arrival of three companies from New Jersey; prevalence of the flux in camp; flight of the French to Niagara. Auto. Draft. 1p.

1755. [Jul.] 24.   [Bradstreet, John.] Oswego. Letter to [William Shirley]. Arrival of Capt. [William] Douglass and party on 21st; no Indians come to camp; will strengthen fortifications until Shirley's arrival or until orders to contrary are received. Auto. Draft. 1p.

        On verso of preceding letter.

1755. [Bradstreet, John. Oswego.] Letter to [William
[Aug. 2.] Shirley]. An account of the work done by the
troops at Oswego since June 1, 1755. Auto.
draft. 1p.

1755. Shirley, W[illiam.] Albany. To [John] Bradstreet.
Nov. 28. May grant furloughs to certain men in Shirley's
regt. sending remainder to Schenectady with a
part of their bounty; men at Lake George to be
enlisted under Sir William Pepperrell or in
Shirley's regiment; directions as to barracks and
whale boats; is to settle accounts with Maj.
[William] Hoar for money advanced at Lake
George. A. L. S. 2pp.

1756. [Bradstreet, John.] Albany. Letter to [William]
Apr. 6. Shirley. Has received word from Capt. Laforay
[George Le Hunte?] through Capt. [   ] Bradley
that harbors on lake are "stopt"; need of imme-
diate and energetic movements to forestall the
French; work done and plans for the future.
Auto. Draft. 2 pp.

1756. Alexander, William. [Albany.] To John Brad-
[Jul. 1.] street. Monies received and paid on batteau
account March-June, 1756; balance due Alexander
is £1450, 6s. 6d. N. Y. currency. D. S. 5pp.

1756. Alexander, William. Boston. To John Bradstreet.
Sep. 13. Difficulties with Col. James Otis regarding
accounts of batteau men under Capts. Lawrence
White and James Allen. A. L. S. 1p. Mutilated.

1756. Fairservice, James. [Albany.] To [John Brad-
Nov. 17. street]. Account against "His Majesty's Service" Mar. 4–Apr. 10, 1756. A. D. S. 2pp.

1757. Loudoun, [John, Earl of.] New York. To John
Mar. 8. Bradstreet. Commission as Captain in "His

The Col. John Bradstreet Manuscripts. 59

Majesty's Royal American Regiment." Countersigned J[ohn] Appy, and seal attached. D. S. 1p.

1757. **Kirkwood,** James. Boston. To [John Bradstreet.]
Apr. 4. Account of sundries received on board snow *Diamond* by order of "Col" Bradstreet. A. D. S. 1p.

1757. **Kirkwood,** James. Boston. To John Bradstreet.
Apr. 5. Receipt for stores and provisions delivered on board snow *Diamond.* D. S. 1p.

1757. **Lothrop,** Benjamin, jr. Boston. To John Bradstreet.
Apr. 5. street. Receipt for stores and provisions delivered on board ship *Lyon.* D. S. 1p.

1757. **Cartwright,** Thomas. Boston. To John Bradstreet.
Apr. 6. Receipt for stores and provisions delivered on board ship *Boston.* D. S. 1p.

> Under this date are two receipts similar to the above signed by Bartholomew Killoran and Andrew Newell, each for his own vessel.

1757. **Kirkwood,** James. New York. To [Commanding
Apr. 22. Officer at New York]. A Return of his Majesty's stores on board the snow *Diamond.* A. D. S. 1p.

> See: Kirkwood to John Bradstreet; Apr. 4 and 5, 1757.

1757. **Cartwright,** Thomas. New York. To [John Bradstreet].
Apr. 23. street]. A manifest of the cargo received on board transport *Boston* with an account of provisions for the ship's use. A. D. S. 1p.

1757. **Hallowell,** Benjamin, jr. and five others. Boston.
Apr. 23. To [John Bradstreet]. Mensuration at Boston of following three transports with statement of their time of entrance into his Majesty's service: ship *Two Brothers*, William Wingfield, Master; ship *Sheffield*, J[ohn] Reed, Master; snow *St. Peter*, [Robert] Kennedy, Master. D. S. Ben-

jamin Hallowell, jr., Ralph Hartt, Alexander Hunt, Peter McTaggart, William Welsh, George Wilson. 1p.

1757. **Reed,** John. Boston. To John Bradstreet.
Apr. 23. Receipt for stores delivered on board the ship *Sheffield.* D. S. 1p.

1757. **Kennedy,** Robert. Boston. To John Bradstreet.
Apr. 23. Receipt for stores delivered on board the snow *St. Peter.* D. S. 1p. and duplicate.

1757. **Collins,** James. Boston. To John Bradstreet.
May 9. Receipt for stores delivered on board the brigantine *Mermaid.* D. S. 1p.

> Under this date are eight receipts similar to the above, signed respectively by Patrick Connell, William Davis, Neil Gillis, Patrick James, Zephaniah Pinkham, William Scott, Peter Sinclair, and Ab[raham] Somes, each for his own vessel.

1757. **Gwynn,** Anthony, **Tannott,** Thomas, and Thomas
May 9. **Woodbridge.** Newbury. To [John Bradstreet.] Have surveyed the following vessels with their equipment and certify the date of fitness of service; Snow *Charming Molly,* Joseph Wadleigh, Master, May 5; Brigantine *Antelope,* Jeremiah Stanniford, Master, May 8. D. S. and attested. 3pp.

1757. **Mugford,** James. Marblehead. To John Bradstreet.
May 11. Receipt for stores delivered on board the ship *Hooper* for use of the Crown at New York. A. D. S. 1p.

1758. [**Bradstreet,** John.] Albany. Letter to James
Mar. 13. Abercrombie. Arrival of carpenters from Col. Meservey [Nathaniel Meserve?] including many boys; will not be able to furnish 1200 boats by May 15; needs 100 more carpenters from New Jersey and Philadelphia. Auto. Draft. 2pp.

The Col. John Bradstreet Manuscripts. 61

1758.   [Bradstreet, John.] Letter to James Abercrombie.
Mar. 24.   Acknowledges letter of Mar. 18; 250 batteaux prepared to go with army to Crown Point; has raised 800 rangers for attack on Cadaraque but doubts if all will serve in another quarter; difficult to procure men for general service because of large bounty offered by colonies for provincial enlistments; bounty offered by [William] Shirley; asks Abercrombie's plans and states need for provisions at Albany. Auto. Draft. 3pp.

1758.   Mortier, A[braham.] New York. Letter to John
Mar. 26.   Bradstreet. Has received from [Charles Ward] Apthorp an account of money advanced by order of [Maj. Genl. John Campbell, Earl] Loudoun or of Bradstreet, and from [Maj.] Genl. [James Abercrombie] a warrant for £3000 in payment of account; warrant will serve to repay amounts advanced Col. [Nathaniel] Meserve for carpenters and batteau service; directions as to future accounting of Bradstreet and others; congratulates him on recent advancement. A. L. S. 2pp.

1758.   De Normandie, Daniel. [Albany.] To John
May 4-   Bradstreet. Account of all monies received
Nov. 30.   and paid for the batteau service by Daniel De Normandie under the direction of [Lt.] Col. John Bradstreet, Commander-in-Chief of all the batteau men. 1 vol.

   The volume is in 127 pages and contains in addition to De Normandie's accounts, 165 signed receipts from men in batteau service for monies received.

1758.   Comyn, Pieter. Fort Stanwix. Letter to [John
Sept. 25.   Bradstreet]. Expense incurred for wages and allowances to three officers and company of 71 men enlisted by order of Brig. Genl. [John] Stanwix. D. S. 1p.

1758. Bradstreet, John. Albany. Account for Pilots
Nov. 15.   and Interpreters. Account of monies paid for
pilots and Indian interpreters upon the expedition
to Cardaraque, with receipts for same. In ms.
of clerk except signatures. 1p. and duplicate.

1758. Apthrop, Charles Ward. Boston. Letter to John
Nov. 25.   Bradstreet. Acknowledges letter of Nov. 12,
enclosing [Abraham] Mortier's draft for 10,000
dollars; has credited Bradstreet's account with
draft and paid Capt. [Joshua] Loring £200 New
York currency as directed; will look into matter
of payment of James Otis. L. S. 1p.

1758. [Bradstreet, John.] Albany. Letter to [Sir Jeffrey]
Dec. 31.   Amherst. As desired sends state of batteaux;
reasons for widely scattered location of boats.
On verso is the statement showing number and
location of available boats. Auto. Draft. 2pp.

1759. Amherst, Sir Jeffrey. New York. Letter to [John]
Feb. 4.   Bradstreet. In reply to letter of Feb. 3 sends
warrant for £3000; methods of recourse for the
payment of this amount and low state of military chest at New York; Bradstreet to explain
situation to [Thomas] Gage at once. L. S. 2pp.

1759. Gage, Thomas. Albany. Letter to [John] Brad-
Apr. 19.   street. Directs Bradstreet to pay certain specified accounts amounting to £100, 16s. being the
expenses for entertainment etc. for Indian
scouting party sent out at Fort Edward. On
verso are four receipts to Lt. George Coventry
for various items of above accounts of date
Apr. 21, May 28 and Jun. 24 (2) respectively.
D. S. 2pp.

1759. [Bradstreet, John. Albany.] Account of men at
Apr. 24.   Hospital in Albany. Account with His Majesty's

hospital at Albany for 14 batteau men who were in the hospital at various times between Feb. 25 and Apr. 24, 1759; total is £2.10d. In ms. of clerk. 1p.

1759. May 11. **Glen,** John. Schenectady. To Commissary Officers [and whom it may concern.] Orders that bearers of letter be not "stopt nor hindered on any acct. whatever" as they have provisions on batteaux; commissaries receiving or giving provisions to note same on letter. A. D. S. 1p.

1759. Sept. 2. [**Bradstreet,** John.] Schenectady. Letter to [Thomas Gage]. Acknowledges letter of Aug. 26; provisions accumulated; would have given Major [Gabriel] Christie charge of transportation had his orders from Maj. Genl. [Jeffrey] Amherst allowed him to do so; will report to latter and do as directed by him in the matter. Auto. Draft. 2pp.

1759. Sept. 21. [**Bradstreet,** John.] Albany. Letter to [Sir Jeffrey Amherst]. Regrets that letter of Sept. 15, just received, shows fear of lack of provisions; has no fear himself; sends [Lt. George] Coventry's return of provisions gathered, and states that more can be raised. Auto. Draft. 3pp.

1759. Sept. 21. **Mortier,** Abraham. New York. Letter to [John] Bradstreet. Has sent money to Albany to pay his note for £2500 to Bradstreet, so that he may have cash if he prefers. A. L. S. 1p.

1759. Oct. 16. **Appy,** J[ohn.] Crown Point. Letter to [John] Bradstreet. Acknowledges letter of Oct. 11 to [Maj.] Genl. [Jeffrey Amherst] and refers him to latter's letter of Oct. 10 for instructions as to the sick in the New York regiment; other questions left to Bradstreet's discretion until return of

Amherst; some information from letters of Brig. Genl. [Thomas] Gage. L. S. 1p.

1759.
Dec.
Glen, John. Schenectady. To Commissary Officers [and whom it may concern.] Orders as to passing provision batteaux; names of men engaged in carrying provisions from Little Falls [Whitehall, N. Y.] to Fort Herkimer. A. D. S. 1p.

1760.
Jan. 1.
Stout, Jonathan and 102 others. Elizabeth Town, [N. J.] To Capt. John Riky. Power of attorney to receive and receipt for wages due in the batteau service. D. S. 3pp.

1760.
Jan. 13.
Coventry, George. [Albany.] Draft on John Bradstreet for £206 in favor of John McComb. A. D. S. Endorsed by Bradstreet. 2pp.

1760.
Feb. 4.
[Bradstreet, John.] Albany. Letter to [Sir Jeffrey Amherst]. Sends two sworn waggon accounts to "show what little faith, truth or honor there are in complaints so frequently made"; disputes regarding demands of previous year; urges that preparations be begun at once for any campaign intended in 1760. Auto. Draft. 2pp.

1760.
Feb. 18.
Mortier, A[braham.] New York. Letter to [John] Bradstreet. Regrets his inability to pay balance of Bradstreet's warrant for £12,631.19s. 6d. in favor of [Capt. Daniel] De Normandie but military chest is not able to advance that sum. A. L. S. 1p.

1760.
Feb. 21.
Appy, J[ohn.] New York. Letter to Thomas Hancock. Acknowledges letter of Jan. 16; arrival of dispatches for [Maj.] Genl. [Jeffrey Amherst] and letters for the several governors calling for new levies for approaching campaign; specifies letters to be forwarded. L. S. 1p.

1760.   Mortier, Abraham, New York. Letter to [John]
Mar. 9.   Bradstreet. In response to orders from [Maj.]
           Genl. [Jeffrey Amherst] has endeavored to
           obtain for Bradstreet a credit of £8000 in New
           England; [Charles Ward] Apthorp informs him
           that he has no money at Boston and there is none
           available at New York; small amounts elsewhere.
           A. L. S. 2pp.

1760.   [Bradstreet, John.] Albany. Letter to [Joshua]
Mar. 18.   Loring. In reply to letter of Mar. 13, states
           that "the King's service requires 50 good ship
           carpenters over and above the 50 mentioned"
           to build batteaux at Albany; has acquainted
           the General [Amherst] with his demand "where-
           fore for the Publick and your own sake don't
           fail." Auto. Draft. 1p.

1760.   [Bradstreet, John.] Albany. Letter to [Sir Jeffrey
Mar. 30.   Amherst]. Provisions received from contractors
           and application made to Brig. Genl. [Thomas]
           Gage for troops to move them; no cedar boards
           arrived but 29 of [Joshua] Loring's carpenters
           are at work [on boats]. Auto. Draft. 1p.

1760.   [Bradstreet, John.] Albany. Letter to [Sir Jeffrey
Sept. 14. Amherst, Montreal.] Congratulates him on the
           capture of Montreal and the reduction of Canada;
           outlines work of forwarding provisions; amount
           at Oswego and amount reported by [James]
           DeLancey as being at or near Albany; requests
           a warrant for £10,000 by bearer Capt. [Philip]
           Schuyler. Auto. Draft. 2pp.

1760.   [Bradstreet, John.] Albany. Letter to [Philip
Oct. 23.   Schulyer]. Thanks him for proffered services
           in settling his [Bradstreet's] accounts; hopes
           that [William] Pitt will remember his [Brad-
           street's] service in the subjugation of Canada;

suggests that the command of a regiment or the Governorship of New York would be an appropriate compensation; hopes [Schuyler] will recommend him for such an appointment; "the American world await with impatience" his reward "and if I get nothing they will be no less surprised than myself." Auto. Draft. 2pp.

1760. Clark, Joel. [Albany.]   To John [Bradstreet]
Nov. 11. Sworn lists of batteau men serving under Clark's command Jun. 22 [to date]; first list contains 11 names, second list 7 names, third list 34 names. Two lists are sworn to by Clark. D.S. 3pp.

1760. [Bradstreet, John.] Albany. Letter to [Sir Jeffrey
Dec. 7. Amherst]. By Act of Provincial Assembly [of New York] all persons impressing horses etc. for the war are held personally responsible; trouble occasioned his agents by this law; gives instances; ingratitude of people to British for protecting them; they give nothing without being paid for it "being spurred on by a nest of Harpies"; asks that something be done for the relief of his agents, who are suffering for impressments made in the line of duty. Auto. Draft. 3pp.

1760. Mortier, Abraham. New York. Letter to [John]
Dec. 8. Bradstreet. Acknowledges letter of Nov. 30 enclosing [Maj.] Genl. [Jeffrey] Amherst's warrant for £8000 in his [Bradstreet's] favor with receipts for same; will see that all his bills are paid promptly as those in favor of Capt. [George] Middagh and Col. Van Schack [Capt. Goose Van Schaick?] have been; ship *Dover* brought no money from Great Britain; other military news. A. L. S. 1p.

1760. Amherst, Sir Jeffrey. New York. Letter to John
Dec. 28. Bradstreet. Acknowledges letter of Dec. 21;

The Col. John Bradstreet Manuscripts. 67

has received complaints against Lt. [George] Coventry from Sheriff [Goose] Van Schaick but waits to hear both sides before taking action and will present what Bradstreet has said in Coventry's behalf; is about to apply for commission for [Abraham] Cuyler as Deputy Postmaster at Albany. A. L. S. 2pp. mutilated.

1761. Jan. 17. **Mortier,** Abraham. New York. Letter to John Bradstreet. Acknowledges letter of Jan. 12 by [Cornelius] Cuyler; paid him balance of Bradstreet's account as directed after charging exchange; arrival of the *Fowey* with some money; congratulates Bradstreet on victory of [Frederic] King of Prussia over Count [Leopold Joseph Maria von] Daun [at Torgau, Nov. 23, 1760]. A. L. S. 2pp.

1761. Jan. 17. **Mortier,** Abraham. New York. To John Bradstreet. Statement of account Nov. 19, 1760 to date, showing expenditure of [Maj.] Genl. [Jeffrey] Amherst's draft of Nov. 19 for £8000. A. D. S. 2pp.

1761. Feb. 2. [**Bradstreet,** John.] Albany. Letter to [Sir Jeffrey Amherst]. No unnecessary labor to be spent upon the Hudson river barracks; has investigated claim of Cornelius Buys for batteau service in 1756 and finds it baseless; notes as to condition of service; is obliged that [Philip] Schuyler is to be sent to England on first war ship or packet. Auto. Draft. 1p.

1761. Mar. 9. **Amherst,** Sir Jeffrey. New York. Letter to [Joshua] Loring. Proposes that provisions be moved from Louisburg by traders from Boston to Quebec; Loring is to notify Boston captains through Thomas Hancock and to inform Gov. [Edward] Whitmore [of Louisburg] of names of vessels engaged. Cont. Copy. 1p.

1761. Butler, John. [Canawago.] Letter to Jellis Fonda.
Apr. 26. Certificate of amounts of money given Fonda for payment of various persons and accounts. A. D. S. 1p.

1761. Mortier, Abraham. New York. Letter to John
Nov. 4. Bradstreet. Acknowledges letter of Oct. 31; had packed the money to be sent him in box and put it on board a sloop about to sail; various charges and accounts paid; amount sent. A. L. S. 1p.

1761. Mortier, Abraham. New York. Letter to [John]
Nov. 5. Bradstreet. Encloses warrant of [Lt.] Genl. Sir Jeffrey Amherst for £8000 in his favor; requests that warrant be endorsed and returned with customary receipts. A. L. S. 1p.

1761. Amherst, Sir Jeffrey. New York. Letter to [John]
Nov. 15. Bradstreet. Acknowledges letter of Nov. 9 and is much surprised at the movements of various provincial regiments; reports necessary from officers at Oswego and Fort Stanwix; has heard from Capt. [Joshua] Loring of loss of the *Anson* on Lake Ontario; encloses warrant for £6000; has promoted Lt. [Samuel] Bradstreet to a company in 40th regiment. L. S. 2pp.

1761. Coventry, George. [Albany.] To [John Bradstreet].
[Dec. 7.] Account of monies paid to 45 men [names given] of 55th regiment employed in transportation service at Lake George from Jul. 30 to Aug. 12, 1761, with receipt for same. D. S. 1p.

1761. Mortier, Abraham. New York. Letter to [John]
Dec. 16. Bradstreet. Acknowledges letter of Dec. 11, enclosing order of [Lt. Genl.] Sir Jeffrey Amherst in Bradstreet's favor for £6000; various bills paid and the balance turned over to [John] Glen. A. L. S. 1p.

1762. **Amherst,** Sir Jeffrey. New York. Letter to [John]
Feb. 10. Bradstreet. Arrival of the *General Wall* with letters for the army in New York and Canada; forwards letters with packets of his own for commanding officers at Fort George and the Governors in Canada. A. L. S. 1p.

1762. **Bergstrom,** J [ ] G. Little Niagara. To
"Feb. 29." [John] Bradstreet. Certificate of impressment into the service of horses and cattle belonging to Stedman & Allen, with receipt of latter for wages paid. A. D. S. 2pp.

1762. **Mortier,** Abraham. New York. Letter to [John]
May 17. Bradstreet. Encloses Capt. William Ogilvie's bill on John Stevenson in writer's favor for £1565; asks if bill is accepted. A. L. S. 1p.

1762. **Mortier,** Abraham. New York. Letter to [John]
Nov. 8. Bradstreet. Acknowledges letter of Nov. 3 by [John] Carns, enclosing warrant of [Lt.] Genl. [Sir Jeffrey Amherst] in Bradstreet's favor for £5000; returns warrant for Bradstreet's endorsement. A. L. S. 1p.

[1763.] **Mortier,** Abraham. [New York.] Letter to [John]
[Jan. 9.] Bradstreet. Acknowledges letter of Bradstreet enclosing paper of Maj. [Robert] Rogers; financial dealings with Rogers and Bradstreet. A. L. S. 1p. mutilated.

1763. **Mortier,** Abraham. New York. Letter to [John
Mar. 21. Bradstreet]. Acknowledges letter of Mar. 14, enclosing warrant of [Lt.] Genl. [Sir Jeffrey Amherst]; warrant not so large as order given earlier; expects Bradstreet to make up the difference either in cash from next warrant received or by payment to Capt. [William] Winepress. A. L. S. 1p. and Auto. duplicate enclosed in Mortier to Bradstreet, Apr. 9, 1764.

1763. **Cuyler,** Abraham. Niagara River, Lake Erie.
May 9. To [John] Bradstreet. Certificate that he has taken into the service a boat belonging to John Stedman. A. D. S. 1p.

1763. [**Bradstreet,** John.] Albany. Letter to [Sir Jeffrey
May 23. Amherst.] Calls attention to encroachments made by the city of Albany upon lands which the Crown has used since 1758 for military purposes; claims of others rest on charter from the Governor; considers it a good time to enforce the claim of the Crown; privileges granted the city by new charter; submits a copy of charter for consideration. Auto. Draft. 3pp.

See: Bradstreet to Thomas Gage, Oct. 14, 1765, post p. 86.

1763. **Amherst,** Sir Jeffrey. New York. Letter to [John]
Jul. 28. Bradstreet. Awaits news from Detroit and the South; last reports from Maj. [Henry] Gladwin were favorable and Maj. [John] Wilkins will forward more as received; Havana returned to Spain; most of the English troops in West Indies will return to Europe but some may go to Canada; advises Bradstreet to keep up connections with North and West if those sections are not restored to peace. L. S. 2pp.

1763. **Wilson,** John. Fort Ontario. To John Glen.
Aug. 9. Certificate that John Bone brought load of artillery from Fort Stanwix to Fort Ontario. A. D. S. 1p.

1763. **Amherst,** Sir Jeffrey. New York. Letter to [John]
Aug. 20. Bradstreet. Acknowledges letter of 15th; satisfied with work accomplished; under new arrangement small posts are to be abandoned, so requests names of persons to whom they may be given and who can be relied upon to deliver them to the Crown in case of need. L. S. 1p.

1763. **Maxwell,** William. Schenectady. To Commissary
Aug. 20. Officers. Orders to pass provision batteaux
for various posts. A. D. S. 2pp.

1763. **Amherst,** Sir Jeffrey. New York. Letter to [John]
Aug. 28. Bradstreet. Acknowledges letter of Aug. 21
with enclosures regarding the Dutch church at
Albany; reports victory of Col. [Henry] Bouquet
at Bushy Run [near Fort Pitt] over a large body
of Indians; summary of losses on both sides;
has ordered officers communicating with Fort
Pitt to furnish no supplies to Indians and to
allow no trader to go among them; has written
[Maj.] Genl. [Thomas] Gage to prevent traders
going up the St. Lawrence and Bradstreet is to
allow none to go out from Albany until further
orders. L. S. 2pp.

See: Bradstreet to Thomas Gage. Oct. 14, 1765.

1763. [**Bradstreet,** John.] Albany. Letter to [Sir Jeffrey
Aug. 29. Amherst.] In obedience to letter of Aug. 20,
will look out for proper persons to take charge
of small posts; movements of Lts. [James] Gamble
and [Arthur] St. Clair; demand of Maj. [John]
Wilkins for bedding at Niagara; needs at Detroit.
Auto. Draft. 2pp.

1763. **Mortier,** Abraham. New York. Letter to [John] Bradstreet.
Sept. 19. Has paid and charged to his account a bill
for £200 drawn on him by Mrs. Bradstreet and presented
by [William] Bayard; latter received it from
[Nathaniel] Wheelwright of Boston. A. L. S. 1p.

1763. **Detroit,** Inhabitants of. [Detroit.]
[Sept.?] Abstract of the losses of the inhabitants of
Detroit by fire etc. during the summer of 1763;
names of 20 persons given including one Englishman
and one interpreter, with amount of loss
of each. Cont. Ms. 1p.

1763.   **Mortier,** Abraham. New York. Letter to [John]
Dec. 4.   Bradstreet. Acknowledges letters of Nov. 22,
25 and Dec. 2; warrant of [Lt. Genl.] Sir Jeffrey
Amherst in his favor for £7000 shall be cashed
and forwarded to him at Albany; can send £5000
in a few days and the remainder soon if there
is pressing need; is much surprised that he has
received no forage money for past three years;
similar grants have been made to Col. [James]
Robertson. A. L. S. 2pp.

1763.   **Mortier,** A[braham.] New York. Letter to [John]
Dec. 12.   Bradstreet. Is informed by [William] Bayard
in behalf of [Charles Ward] Apthorp that the
whole of the warrant for £7000 shall be paid
Bradstreet at Albany by [Abraham] Douw;
states condition of Bradstreet's account with
him. A. L. S. 2pp.

1763.   **Mortier,** Abraham. New York. Letter to John
Dec. 19.   Bradstreet. Has supplied him with a credit
for £1000 at Nathaniel Wheelwright's, Boston,
in accordance with order of [Maj.] Genl. [Thomas]
Gage, dated Dec. 17; acknowledges receipts for
warrant of [Lt.] Genl. [Sir Jeffrey] Amherst in his
favor for £7000; notes certain details relating
to accounts and warrants, and bill of £50 to
Mrs. Bradstreet. A. L. S. 1p.

1763.   [**Bradstreet,** John.] Albany. Letter to [Sir Jeffrey
Dec. 20.   Amherst]. Report received from Capt. [Joshua
Loring as to transportation of provisions by
boat to Niagara; others should be sent by land;
need of ship carpenters, ironworkers and sup-
plies at Oswego during the winter; Lt. Col.
[William] Browning will furnish protection.
Auto. Draft. 2pp.

1764.   **Mortier,** Abraham. New York. Letter to [John]
Jan. 2.   Bradstreet. Acknowledges letter by Capt. [Josh-

The Col. John Bradstreet Manuscripts. 73

ua] Loring; regrets that Bradstreet was disaappointed in receiving no money by messenger; former should draw an order on some person in New York or send messenger of his own; in either case Mortier will pay money on demand. A. L. S. 1p.

1764. Jan. 27. **McKeen,** Robert. Cherry Valley. To [John Bradstreet]. Certificate that Adam Brown has brought baggage for McKeen's company. A. D. S. 1p.

[1764.] [Jan.] **Macvicar,** Duncan. [Albany.] Letter to John Bradstreet. Reports the mustering in of company of Capt. [Nathaniel] Tyce; poor quality of the company. L. S. 1p.

1764. Feb. 6. **Mortier,** A[braham.] New York. Letter to [John] Bradstreet. Sends him by [John] Kendrick £3000 in good paper money; has paid B[everly] Robinson £500 on account; requests acknowledgment on receipt of money sent. A. L. S. 1p.

1764. Mar. 19. **Lamb,** Anthony. [New York.] To John Bradstreet. Account for surveying implements furnished, £57, 15s. 6d. with receipt dated Jul 20. A. D. S. 1p.

1764. Mar. 28. **Browning,** William. Niagara. To [John Bradstreet.] Certificate of service performed by John Stedman with two horses, with receipt of Stedman, dated Mar. 20, 1766. D. S. 2pp.

1764. Apr. 9. **Mortier,** Abraham. New York. Letter to [John] Bradstreet. Acknowledges letters of Apr. 1 and 4; proceeds to make clear the accuracy of his account with Bradstreet, enclosing copy of letter of Mar. 21, 1763 in further explanation; thanks Bradstreet for lumber sent. A. L. S. 3pp.

1764. Roberts, B[enjamin.] Niagara. To [John Brad-
Apr. 11. street]. Certificate of services performed by
John Stedman with his horses, with receipt of
Stedman dated Mar. 20, 1766. D. S. 2pp.

1764. [Bradstreet, John.] Albany. Letter to [Thomas Gage].
Apr. 30. Acknowledges letters of Apr. 22 and 23; describes
movements undertaken in preparation for the
campaign against Detroit. Auto. Draft. 2pp.

1764. [Bradstreet, John.] Albany. Letter to [Sir Wil-
May 5. liam Johnson]. Garrisons to be left in various
New York posts; requests Johnson to await him
at Oswego. Auto. Draft. 2pp.

In Sir William Johnson Manuscripts ante p. 16.

[1764.] Bradstreet, John. Albany. Letter to [Thomas]
May 7. Gage. Provincial troops for the expedition
against Detroit; requests commissions for two
Majors to avoid difficulties in rank; understands
that Sir William Johnson will bring Indian
recruits. A. L. S. 1p.

1764. Glen, John. Schenectady. To Commissary
May 7. Officers. Bearers of letter not to be stopped
or hindered as they have provisions in their
boats for [Lt.] Col. [John] Campbell and 17th
regt; boats in charge of John Miller. A. D. S. 1p.

1764. [Bradstreet, John.] Fort Ontario. Deserters from
May troops commanded by. Descriptive list of men
who deserted from the New York provincial
troops after leaving Schenectady; six men are
named from the company of Capt. [Richard]
Rea, five from that of Capt. [John] Degarius,
four from that of Capt. [John] Grant, two from
that of Capt. [Henry] Dawson, two from that of
Capt. [Alexander] Whyte. In ms. of a clerk. 2pp.

1764. [Bradstreet, John.] Albany. Letter to [Thomas
May 23. Gage]. Troops at Detroit lodged in houses of

people; suggests that carpenters be sent from Albany to erect barracks; encloses return of 80th regiment and of the garrison at Niagara; many companies are short of their complements. Auto. Draft. 1p.

1764. Duncan, Alexander. Albany. To [John Bradstreet]. Certificate of names and companies of 15 men employed as axe men, preparing timber for the Niagara carrying place, Mar. 26-Apr. 10, 1764, with wages due each. D. S. 1p.
May 25.

1764. Bradstreet, John. Orderly Book.
Jun. 27- Orderly Book of regiment commanded by Col.
Nov. 29. Bradstreet at Forts Ontario, Niagara and Erie, as also at Detroit and Albany. 1 vol. 128pp.

1764. [Bradstreet, John.] Niagara. Letter to [Thomas] Gage. Delay in campaign due to distrust of Indian troops; Sir William Johnson considers it unsafe to proceed at once; hopes the enemy will give an opportunity for battle; expects to make a fuller report soon. Auto. Draft. 3pp.
Jul. 12.

1764. Bradstreet, John. Niagara. To Indian Traders at Niagara. Proclamation granting liberty to trade with distant Indian Nations at Niagara and prescribing regulations under which such trade should be conducted. D. S. 1p.
Jul. 19.
This proclamation is reproduced in facsimile facing p. 57.

[1764.] Luke, John. [Niagara.]
[July] Plan of Fort Niagara. Auto. Ms. 1p.

1764. McDougall, George. Detroit. To [John Bradstreet]. Return of the detachment of 118 men from 60th regiment under his command. A. D. S. 1p.
Aug. 31.

1764. Abbott, Edward. Detroit. To [John Bradstreet]. Receipt for stores with detailed list of same. A. D. S. 3pp.
Sept. 6.

1764. **Abbott,** Edward. Detroit. To [John Bradstreet].
Sept. 10.   Return of ordnance, ammunition and stores left for a supply to the garrison of Detroit. A. D. S. 5pp.

1764. [**Bradstreet,** John.] Detroit. Letter to [John
Sept. [10?] Campbell]. Places town and colony of Detroit in his hands; directions for protections of Indians in their rights but for careful watch over them as well; method of government to be modelled after that of Montreal; instructions for Capt. [William] Howard and Lt. [John] Sinclair left with him; any instructions from [Maj.] Genl. [Thomas] Gage to be followed at once. Auto. Draft. 4pp.

1764. [**Bradstreet,** John.] Detroit. Letter to [Thomas]
Sept. 12.   Gage. Gives an account of his negotiations at Detroit with various papers showing same in detail. Auto. Draft. 2pp.

See: Proclamation of Bradstreet, Jul. 19, 1764.

1764. [**Bradstreet,** John.] Detroit. Letter to [Thomas]
Sept. 12.   Gage. Outlines plans for maintenance of position at Detroit and the control of the surrounding Indians; will inform [Col. Henry] Bouquet and [Lt.] Gov. [John] Penn if events go wrong and Indian outbreak is renewed. Auto. Draft. 1p.

[1764.] [**Bradstreet,** John.] Notes for expedition against
[Sept.]   Detroit. This volume contains many notes and records of use to an army moving against Detroit and the West. Among them are manuscript maps of the great lakes, the names and locations of various Indian tribes, notes as to camping places, etc. Some notes appear to have been made before the setting out of the expedition and others to have been added during its course. 1 vol. 27pp.

The Col. John Bradstreet Manuscripts. 77

1764. **Martin,** S[amue]l. Detroit. To [John Bradstreet].
Oct 3. Receipt for £400 New York currency in payment for books and merchandise for the Indians. A. D. S. In French. 1p.

1764. [**Bradstreet,** John.] Sandusky. Letter to [Thomas
Oct. 5. Gage]. Is aroused over breaking of peace by Indians; Oneidas and Senecas the leaders; has sent to every tribe demanding satisfaction; other details. Auto. Draft. 2pp.

1764. **Jones,** John. [Fort Edward.] To [John Brad-
Oct. 8. street]. Return of stores delivered at Fort George and Fort Edward. A. D. S. 1p.

1764. **Glen,** John. Schenectady. To Commissary Offi-
Oct. 12. cers. Pass for bearers with bill of lading of supplies for Fort Ontario. A. D. S. 1p.

1764. **LeHunte,** George, [Sandusky.] To [John Brad-
Oct. 14. street]. Weekly return of light infantry commanded by Maj. Le Hunte. A. D. S. 1p.

1764. **McDonald,** William. [Sandusky.] To [John Brad-
Oct. 14. street]. Weekly return of the New Jersey battalion. D. S. 1p.

1764. **Walton,** Joseph. [Sandusky.] To [John Bradstreet].
Oct. 14. Weekly return of detachment of royal artillery under his command. A. D. S. 1p.

1764. [**Bradstreet,** John.] Niagara. Letter to [Thomas
Nov. 4. Gage]. Encloses copies of nine letters giving summary of each in an attempt to justify his conduct during the Detroit expedition and return to Niagara. Auto. Draft. 4pp.

1764. **Walton,** Joseph. [Albany] To [Francis Colly-
Nov. 19. son]. Certificate of use of three horses for fourteen miles, with receipt by Collyson to

Bradstreet dated Jan. 9, 1767 for payment in full of above account. D. S. 2pp.

1764.
Nov. 20.
[**Bradstreet,** John.] Albany. Letter to [Thomas Gage]. Acknowledges letter of Oct. 26; attempts to explain parts played by various Indian tribes during and after the peace of Detroit. Auto. Draft. 3pp.

1764.
Nov. 21.
[**Bradstreet,** John.] Albany. Letter to [Thomas] Gage. Transmits record of Court of Inquiry on claims of men drafted from the 80th to the 46th regiment; other matters. Auto. Draft. 1p.

1764.
Nov. 25.
[**Bradstreet,** John.] Albany. Letter to [Thomas] Gage. Acknowledges dispatches received on the 24th; Maj. [Richard?] Daly takes down men of 65th regiment and will deliver this letter; proposed distribution of forces; Provincials and Canadians at Oswego. Auto. Draft. 1p.

1764.
Nov. 29.
[Nov. 14?]
[**Bradstreet,** John.] Albany. Letter to [Thomas] Gage. Trouble over payment of men engaged by order of Gage; pay-master of New York battalion refused to pay men; hopes Gage will set matters to rights. Auto. Draft. 1p.
See: letters of Feb. 2 and Feb. 25, 1765.

1764.
Dec. 17.
Robinson, Beverly. New York. To John Bradstreet. Account of monies paid by Col. Bradstreet for pitch, tar, etc. sent to Albany for service of the Crown from Mar. 26 to Oct. 13, 1764. D. S. 3pp.

1764.
Dec. 23.
Hill, Launcelot. Albany. To John Bradstreet. Account of monies paid to 19 men of 55th regiment employed in carpentry or batteau service. Account is from Sept. 19 to Oct. 3, 1764, and is receipted by Hill. D. S. 1p.

1764. [Bradstreet, John.] Albany. Letter to [Thomas
Dec. 24. Gage]. Acknowledges letter of Dec. 15; supposes
he is free to tell officers that Gage will not forward
their petition as to land at Detroit; encloses
return from Capt. [Hugh] Arnot of 46th regiment
commanding at Oswego; would have sent highlanders to Fort George but Gage's orders forbade
it; Capt. [William] Winepress will march away
as soon as road is passable. Auto. Draft. 1p.

[1764.] [Bradstreet, John. Albany]. Letter to [Thomas
[Dec?] Gage]. Plan for conciliation of Indians in
Northern districts of North America; recommends distribution of agricultural implements,
horses, etc. among them and the settlement
of missionaries as was done by the French;
estimates the expense and suggests that the
whole affair be conducted by the Crown and
not by the colonies; considers the Oneidas and
Hurons as best tribes on which the experiment
should be first tried. Auto. Draft. 4pp.

[1764?] [Bradstreet, John. Albany]. Letter to [Thomas
Gage]. Encloses accounts of Baxter and Humphrey with original receipts of individual wagon-
ers employed by that firm in the public service;
vouches for the accounts; believes that even
[James] Livingston can find nothing to find
fault with in them. Auto. Draft. 1p.

1765. Christie, John. Fort George. To [John Bradstreet].
Jan. 2. Certificate of service performed by Peter Fonda
in transporting troops in British service, with
receipt by Fonda dated Oct. 8, 1766. D. S. 2pp.

1765. Degrov, [Michel.] Albany. To [John] Bradstreet.
Jan. 23. Two receipts for £7 and £27, payment for
services as interpreter to Indians on campaign
[of 1764]. D. S. 2pp.

1765.   [**Bradstreet**, John.] Albany. Letter to [Thomas]
Feb. 2.   Gage. Encloses monthly return of 46th regiment and state of garrison at Niagara received from Lt. Col. [John] Vaughan; condition of New York volunteers enlisted by Bradstreet at Gage's order; £3250 currency due these troops and they threaten to sue writer for that amount; having law and justice on their side, Bradstreet suggests that these men be paid and the colony trusted to reimburse the money. Auto. Draft. 1p.

See following entry and references.

1765.   [**Bradstreet**, John.] Albany. Letter to [Thomas
Feb. 25.   Gage]. Acknowledges letter [of Feb?] with warrant; regrets that Gage will not provide money for payment of New York volunteers; details circumstances under which he recruited them and awkward place in which he finds himself, as both British and Colonial authorities refuse to reimburse him; case the same regarding money spent necessarily on the Indians; gives testimony of Maj. [William] Hogan that men served in British army; money due for batteau service also; poor condition of wagons and of cattle at Albany. Auto. Draft. 3pp.

See: same to same, Nov. 29, 1764, and Feb. 2, 1765; also Bradstreet to Shelburne, Nov. 2, 1766.

[1765?]   [**Gage**, Thomas. New York.] Letter to [John
[Feb.?]   Bradstreet]. Articles in "A Brief State of the Circumstances relating to Colonel •Bradstreet's enlisting 107 men for the New York Battalion in 1764 which the General objects to." In ms. of Gabriel Maturin, Secy. to Maj. Genl. Gage, 2pp. A copy of this manuscript was enclosed by Bradstreet in letter to Lord Shelburne, Nov. 2, 1766.

See preceding entry and Bradstreet, John, Account of Enlistments, Nov. 2, 1766.

The Col. John Bradstreet Manuscripts. 81

1765. Maitland, Richard. New York. To [John]
Mar. 14. Bradstreet. Directions for sending cargoes of stores or provisions from any of the King's magazines. A. D. S. 2pp.

1765. [Bradstreet, John.] Albany. Letter to [Thomas]
Mar. 22. Gage. Winter allowances to men cutting boat timber or gathering hay; carriage of provisions; report from Capt.-Lt. [Patrick] Balneaves of conditions at Fort Edward. Auto. Draft. 1p.

1765. Fonda, Jellis & Co. [Albany.] To [John Brad-
Mar. 23. street]. Accounts against the Crown for provisions and transportation during 1764, with receipts by Fonda to Bradstreet for payment in full. A. D. S. 2pp.

[1765.] Glen, Cornelius. [Schenectady.] To [Commissary
[Apr. 19.] Officers and whom it may concern]. Orders to pass bearers, William Sinewood and five others in two batteaux loaded with naval stores for Fort Ontario. A. D. S. 2pp.

Attached are notes of journey of batteaux.

1765. [Bradstreet, John.] Albany. Letter to [Thomas]
Apr. 25. Gage. Explains distribution of liquor and other presents among the Indians and requests reimbursement for money thus expended. Auto. Draft. 1p.

In Sir William Johnson Manuscripts.

1765. Arnot, Hugh. [Niagara.] To [John Bradstreet].
Apr. 30. Certificate of service of non-commissioned officers and privates of the 46th regt. employed Nov. 1, 1764 to date in Quarter Master General's dept. Account for each of seven companies is signed by officer of company and the whole account, £176, 18s. 6d. is countersigned by Arnot. The account bears receipt of Cornelius Cuyler dated Mar. 6, 1766. A. D. S. 2pp.

1765.
April.
Albany, Dutch Church. [Albany.] To John Bradstreet. Church account against Bradstreet for £12, 11s. 2d. payable to Whitehead Hicks in behalf of the church. The account is made out in the name of the minister, elders and deacons of the church and accompanying it is a receipt for the payment of the account, dated Nov. 12, 1766, signed by E[ilardus] Westerlo jr. D[eputy] W[arden]. D. S. 2pp.

[1765.]
[April?]
[**Bradstreet,** John.] Albany. Letter to [Thomas Gage]. Forwards letters by express; is about to send provisions to Fort Stanwix in large quantity unless this be considered unwise and order countermanded [by Gage]; considers the French "at the bottom of this Indian affair and the Five Nations as ripe for putting their grand scheme into execution as any" [other Indians]. Auto. Draft. 1p.

1765.
May 2.
Grant, A[llan?] Schenectady. To [John Bradstreet]. Certificate of services of Samuel Staats in transporting naval stores. A. D. S. 1p.

1765.
May 3.
Glen, John. Sch[enecta]dy. To the Commissary Officers [and whom it may concern]. Order to pass bearers with provision batteaux; if goods are delivered receipt to be given and any deficiency to be noted on order. A. D. S. 1p.

<small>Above is followed by bill of lading of batteaux in charge of Evert Van Gis; six batteaux loaded by Van Gis and eighteen others, all to be delivered at Oswego.</small>

1765.
May 8.
Glen, John. Schenectady. To "John" [Jellis] Fonda. Certificate that Fonda is in charge of engineer stores to be delivered at Fort Ontario, with directions that he be not delayed on any account and that receipt for delivery be made out by officer receiving stores. Attached are receipts of David Buffington dated May 20

for goods, and of Fonda, dated Jul. 23, 1766, for money in payment of services. A. D. S. 1p.

1765.
May 22. Demler, George. Fort Stanwix. To John Glen. Certificate of services in transporting stores, performed by William Quin, with receipt of John Monier, dated Nov. 1, 1766, in payment of above services. A. D. S. 2pp.

1765.
May 23. Etherington, George. Fort George. To John Bradstreet. Certificate of services in transporting baggage, performed by Charles McKay and duplicate in favor of Samuel Dox. Attached are receipts by Guert Van Schoonhoven, dated Jul. 19. A. Ds. S. 2pp. each.

1765.
May 24. Cooke, John. Fort George. To Henry Dowlar and two others. Certificate to Henry Dowlar, Andrew [Andris] Johnson and William Peters for provisions from Halfmoon with receipt by Johnson, dated Aug. 13, 1766, in full of account. A. D. S. 1p.

1765.
May 24. Vaughan, John. Niagara. To John Bradstreet. Encloses bill of John Stedman against Bradstreet for services as wagon master at Niagara, 1764-1765; certifies as to employment as stated and that bill should be paid by Bradstreet. On verso is receipt of Stedman [Feb.] 2, 1766 for payment of above account. D. S. 1p.

1765.
May 25. Glen, John. Schenectady. To Commissary Officers [and whom it may concern]. Directions for passing bearers of letter with provision batteaux; deficiencies to be noted; goods to be delivered to Douw Fonda by James Cary and five men and are for use of Indians. Attached are receipts of Fonda of May 26 and of Cornelius Cuyler of Nov. 6, in payment of services rendered. A. D. S. 1p.

1765.   **Glen,** John.   Schenectady.   To Commissary Offi-
Jun. 11.   cers [and whom it may concern].   Orders to
pass bearers with provision batteaux; when
goods are delivered, receipt is to be given and
any deficiency noted on orders.   Attached are
bills of lading for six batteaux and receipt
signed by Edward Smyth at Fort Stanwix
Jun. 16 for goods listed.   A. D. S.   1p.

1765.   **McIntosh,** George.   Fort Edward.   To [John]
Jun. 14.   Bradstreet.   Certificate of services of John
Fluree [Flower?] employed four and one-half
days in repairing boat used as ferry near Fort
Edward.   A. D. S.   1p.

   During July, similar certificates of services performed
were given Bradstreet regarding Martin Van Alstyn, John
Feather, Solomon Pitcher and Daniel Dunham.

1765.   **Duncan,** John.   [Schenectady.]   To [John Bradstreet].
Jul. 17.   Sworn statement before John Glen jr., as to
character and price of lumber furnished. D. S.   1p.

1765.   [**Bradstreet,** John.]   Albany.   Letter to [Thomas
Aug. 4.   Gage].   Acknowledges letter of Jul. 29, enclosing
petition of [Mathew] Trotter; petitioner was
offered as much pay as he had earned but refused
it; charges were too high; asks instructions as
to enlistment of deserters and interpretation
of act of Parliament for quartering troops etc.
upon the people.   Auto. Draft.   1p.

   This measure for quartering soldiers upon Americans
was passed in Apr. 1765, being an extension of the Mutiny
Act to America.   It was known as the Quartering or
Billeting Act in the Colonies.

[1765.]   **Glen,** John.   [Schenectady.]   To [Commissary
[Aug. 7?]   Officers and whom it may concern].   Orders
[to pass Abraham Van Eps and eight men] with
provision batteaux en route to Oswego.   Four
notes regarding the trip to Sept. 1 are attached.
A. D. S.   2pp.

1765. **Glen,** John. Schenectady. To [John] Bradstreet.
Aug. 10. Certificate of batteaux for royal service delivered by Eleazer Cawey with receipt of Henry Glen in behalf of Cawey dated Jul. 23, 1766 for payment in full of account. A. D. S. 1p.

1765. **Glen,** John. Schenectady. To Commissary Officers [and whom it may concern]. Orders to pass bearers with provision batteaux; on delivery of goods receipt to be given and any deficiency to be noted on orders; Andrew Wimple in charge of batteaux and provisions are to be delivered to Douw Fonda for use of Indians at Caughnawa. Attached are receipts of Fonda dated Aug. 14 for goods and of Peter Comyn dated Nov. 6 for services performed. A. D. S. 1p.

1765. **Glen,** John. [Schenectady.] To Commissary Officers [and whom it may concern]. Orders to pass bearers with provision batteaux for Fort Stanwix; when goods are delivered receipt to be given and deficiencies noted on orders. Attached are three notes regarding passage of boats. A. D. S. 2pp.

1765. **[Bradstreet,** John.] Albany. Letter to [Thomas] Gage. Acknowledges letter of Aug. 12; allowance of wagons to a regiment made by Sir Jeffrey Amherst; difference of conditions between taking the field and marching to port; is forwarding tobacco in accordance with orders. Auto. Draft. 1p.

1765. **Grant,** Allan. Fort George. To [John] Bradstreet.
Sep. 1. Certificate of services of Vincent Benneway [or Benoit] in movement from Albany to Fort George with receipt of Benneway dated May 25, 1766 for payment of account. A. D. S. 1p.

Similar certificates were given Bradstreet during September and October regarding Jacob Van Vordt, Jykeris

Van der Bogart, Cornelius Cuyler, and notes as to services of John Heimstrart, Lawrence Clew and Henry and Isaac Lawnson. Many of these manuscripts have receipts for payments for services attached.

1765.
Oct. 14. [Bradstreet, John.] Albany. To [Thomas] Gage. States charge made against himself by the Atty. Genl. of New York in dispute with "Dutch Church"; is charged with using and injuring lands of church 1759-1762 to extent of £1000; despite lack of proof that land belonged to church or that any trespass was made by his order and refusal of Commander in Chief [Sir Jeffrey Amherst] to support claim, arbiters decide that he must pay £210; advises Gage to submit proceedings to the king's ministers together with copy of charter of city under which land is claimed; charter is not good in law and people should be informed that there is no basis for claim. Auto. Draft. 2pp.

See: Bradstreet to Sir Jeffrey Amherst, May 23, and Amherst to Bradstreet, Aug. 28, 1763, ante pp. 70, 71.

1765.
Oct. 31. Arnot, Hugh. [Niagara.] To [John Bradstreet]. Certificate of service of non-commissioned officers and privates of the 46th regiment employed May 1 in Quarter Master General's department. Account for each of eight companies is signed by officer of company and the whole account, £68. 18s. is countersigned by Arnot. On verso is receipt by Cornelius Cuyler to Bradstreet dated Mar. 6, 1766. A. D. S. 2pp.

1765.
Nov. 9. Glen, John. Schenectady. To [John] Bradstreet. Statement of account of Teunis Van Vleck against the Crown for carriage of baggage fourteen days, with receipt of Van Vleck dated Jul. 15, 1766 in full of above charge. A. D. S. 1p.

1765.
Nov. 10. Glen, John. Schenectady. To [John] Bradstreet. Certificate of service of Adam Smith in impressment of carriages for King's use with receipt

The Col. John Bradstreet Manuscripts. 87

of Smith dated Apr. 7, 1766, in full of above charge. A. D. S. 2pp.

1765. [**Bradstreet**, John.] Albany. Letter to [Thomas]
Nov. 17. Gage]. Sickness of barrack master at Fort Edward; difficulties in procuring wood for the winter; supplies which need renewing; poor condition of roads. Auto. Draft. 1p.

1765. [**Bradstreet**, John.] Albany. Letter to [Thomas
Nov. 23. Gage. Acknowledges letter of Nov. 17; to prevent the corporation of Albany destroying the new barracks before arrival of additional troops has moved a portion of the garrison thither; encloses copies of correspondence with the Mayor on the matter, also return of additional troops; bearer of letter has petition of Assembly regarding men raised for the New York battalion in 1764. Auto. Draft. 1p.

1766. **Byerly**, Frederick. Fort Edward. To Gerrit
Feb. 17. Knoet [Abert?]. Receipt for 12 bbls. of flour brought to post by Gerrit Knoet, Jacob Knoet and Nicholas Van Vrank. Attached is receipt of Apr. 13, for payment for flour. A. D. S. 2pp.

1766. **Maitland**, Richard. New York. To [John Brad-
Feb. 28. street]. General orders respecting marching of troops and all contingent charges; method of arranging accounts; allowances for detachments; payment of incidental expenses, etc. D. S. 3pp.

1766. **Vaughan**, John. New York. To John Bradstreet.
Mar. 10. Account of money due Quartermaster George Butrick of the 46th regiment in payment of wages of four men for 36 days' service making hay at Niagara, £7. 4s. N. Y. currency. Attached is receipt of Butrick dated Mar. 16 for above account. D. S. 1p.

1766. **Bayley,** William. Schenectady. To [John Brad-
Mar. 24. street]. Certificate of services of John Vedder and
of Jean Baptiste Van Eps in transporting provisions from Albany. Attached is receipt of Jacob
W. Schermerhorn dated Aug. 14 for payment
in full for Vedder's services. A. D. S. 3pp.

1766. **Maitland,** Richard. New York. To [John] Brad-
Jun. 14. street. Orders for march of six companies
1st battalion, Royal American regiment to
Quebec. D. S. 1p.

1766. **Bleecker,** Henry, jr. Albany. To John Bradstreet.
Jun. 30. Receipt of £7. 4s. "which with £80 from * * *
Abraham Dow" is for the pay of the late Anthony
Bleecker, Interpreter May 1-Dec. 4, 1764 in the
[Indian] expedition of that year. D. S. 1p.

1766. **Gage,** Thomas. New York. To [John] Bradstreet
Jun. 30. or Officer in command at Albany. Directs
examination of evidence against John Dubell
and Garret Van Slyke of Albany for aiding
deserters; information may be obtained from
Capt. [Philip] Schuyler; four deserters named.
L. S. 2pp.

1766. **Glen,** John. Schenectady. To [John] Bradstreet.
Jul. 1. Certificate of batteaux for royal service delivered
by John Johnson and Adam Fonda. Attached is
receipt of Jellis Fonda dated Jul. 23 for payment
in full of above account. A. D. S. 1p.

 During July similar certificates of service performed
or of material furnished were given Bradstreet regarding
Jan Vrooman, Jacob Hemstreack, Gerrit Knoet [Abert?]
and John Van Vrank all of which have receipts attached
for payment of services rendered.

1766. **Carye,** L[ucius] F[erdinan]d. Fort Edward. To
Jul. 4. Philip Schuyler. Has been charged ferriage
for 224 men and 17 wagons but finds no precedent for payment of such charges for king's

troops; if charge is just requests Schuyler to pay it and repayment will be made upon his return to Albany. A. L. S. 1p.

1766. [Jul.] 21. [**Bradstreet**, John.] Albany. Letter to [Thomas Gage]. Has applied to the Mayor [of Albany] as to completion and furnishing of barracks for soldiers; present conditions; existing scarcity of boats due to demands of Sir William Johnson. Auto. Draft. 1p.
    See: Bradstreet to Gage. Nov. 23, 1765.

1766. Sept. 15. [**Bradstreet**, John.] Albany. Letter to [Thomas] Gage. Acknowledges letter of Sept. 1; will follow instructions respecting 17th regiment upon their receipt; explains delay in forwarding public accounts for previous year; [Philip] Schuyler not able to sell bills upon satisfactory footing; asks if any word has been received from England as to payment of men raised for the [New] York battalion [of the 55th regiment]. Auto. Draft. 1p.

1766. Oct. 25. [**Bradstreet**, John.] Albany. Letter to [Thomas] Gage. Acknowledges letter of Oct. 20; as he was so pressing for settlement of last year's accounts writer advanced money to do so not waiting for sale of [Gage's] bills; has been informed by [Philip] Schuyler that bills have since been sold; has referred the portion of letter relating to Schuyler to that person; considers [John] Glen a very capable assistant and prefers to make up from his own pocket any reduction in Glen's salary rather than to lose that official; will send last year's account to him by Schuyler. Auto. Draft. 2pp.

[1766.] [Oct?] **Comyn**, Peter. [Albany.] To [John] Bradstreet. Statement of account showing cash received from [Maj.] Genl. [Thomas] Gage and succeeding items furnished. In Ms. of clerk. 1p.

1766. [**Bradstreet**, John.] Albany. To [William Petty,
Nov. 2. Earl Shelburne?] Explains circumstances connected with his enlistment of men for the New York battalion [of the 55th regt.] by order of Maj. Genl. [Thomas] Gage Apr. 2, 1764 to date; refusal of province and of Gage to pay men; has been sued for wages of soldiers amounting to nearly £2000 and is told by lawyers that he must pay; asks whether he better enter suit against Gage for amount; has forwarded a memorial of the matter to the Treasury through Gage but has heard nothing of it; requests Shelburne's influence; will write the king or his Secretary at War if advised to do so. Auto. Draft. 2pp.

See: Bradstreet to Gage, Feb. 2 and Feb. 25, 1765; Jan. 15, 1767; and the following account.

[1766?] [**Bradstreet**, John. Albany.] Account of enlist-
[Nov. 2?] ments in New York 1764. Account is in reply to [Maj. Genl. Thomas Gage]: "A Brief state of the circumstance relating to Colonel Bradstreet's enlisting 107 men for the New York Battalion in 1764". The reasons for the enlistment are given and the position in which Bradstreet as well as the troops enlisted are left because of the neglect of province and of Commander in Chief is set forth. Auto. Draft. 4pp.

Enclosed in preceding manuscript.
See: Gage to Bradstreet, Feb. 1765.

1766. [**Albany**, Dutch Church.] Albany. To John Brad-
Nov. 12. street. Receipt by E[ilardus] Westerlo, jr.

See: Account of the Church against Bradstreet Apr. 1765.

1766. **Maturin**, G[abriel.] New York. Letter to [John]
Nov. 29. Bradstreet. Explanations [of accounts presented] are satisfactory; returns vouchers with abstract of what has been paid and what remains due on contingent account; clerk will pay balance

whenever desired; Board of Treasury hold [Maj.] Genl. [Thomas Gage] accountable for all disbursements in North America; latter desired heads of departments to have account with Treasury as before subject only to his approval. A. L. S. 2pp.

Maturin was Gage's Secretary at headquarters, New York.

1766. **Maturin,** G[abriel.] Head Quarters. [New York.]
Dec. 4. Letter to [John] Bradstreet. Has examined charge for soldiers annexed to Bradstreet's memorial; requests list of such bills as Bradstreet can most conveniently use to the total of above charge; temporary receipt to be given [Maj.] Genl. [Thomas Gage] until permanent policy of Board of Treasury is known and answer to memorial received; has forwarded balance of account for 1765 and £1000 currency toward expense of current year. A. L. S. 2pp.

1766. **Crippen,** Joseph. Sharon, [Conn.] To John Bradstreet.
Dec. 26. Assignment to Solomon Strong of power to collect wages when serving in company of Capt. Isaac Van Valkenburgh in 1764. The manuscript is in the hand of John Williams, is witnessed by John and William Williams, and sworn to before John Williams, Justice of the Peace. D. S. 1p.

1767. [**Bradstreet,** John.] Albany. Letter to [Thomas]
Jan. 15. Gage. Acknowledges letter of Jan. 6; had no intention of asking for a gratuity when seeking reimbursement for expenses in connection with raising troops for campaign of 1764; case of Col. [Henry] Bouquet not like his nor are the cases in European service; if his "expenses for the good of the service" can not be repaid in whole requests a part, thanks Gage for services thus far rendered. Auto. Draft. 1p.

1767. [Bradstreet, John.] Albany: Letter to [Thomas]
Jan. 22.   Gage. Troops have interfered to prevent townspeople tearing down government store house; "some gentlemen of the law at New York" claim the building could be torn down as a public nuisance but troops acted in accordance with Gage's orders; fears the courts will uphold the view of the lawyers. Auto. Draft. 1p.

1767. Wood, Draper S. Albany. Letter to John Brad-
Feb. 3.   street. Sleds wanted for Sir William Johnson's Indians. A. L. S. 1p.

In Sir William Johnson Manuscripts ante p. 25.

1767. Stephens, James. Fort Stanwix. To John "Glyn"
Jun. 26.   [Glen]. Certificate of services of Robart Strange in transporting ordnance to Schenectady; six days delay at Fort Stanwix. Attached are receipts of James Nash dated Jul. 4 for ordnance received and of Abraham Oothout dated Jan. 23, 1768 for money in payment of services rendered. D. S. 2pp.

1767. [Bradstreet, John.] Albany. Letter to [Thomas
Nov. 14.   Gage]. Understands that Assembly meets Nov. 17 and that Gov. Henry Moore is to urge payment for men enlisted by Bradstreet [in 1764]; gives account of the circumstances that Gage may submit the matter to the legislature in his own name; Col. [Philip] Schuyler will render any assistance desired in the matter; letters given to Schuyler to be placed before Assembly if Gage consents. Auto. Draft. 1p. incomplete.

1767. [Bradstreet, John.] Albany. Letter to [Thomas Gage].
Nov. 22.   Encloses account for 1766 and will forward return of outstanding debts as soon as possible; guns taken from French at Oswego by desire of Sir William Johnson; wishes the number

received by [John] Butler for use of Indians; refers to Capt. [Gabriel] Maturin for information; sends two accounts of what is due him [Bradstreet] for campaign of 1764; one includes expenditure for secret service; by precedent of 1756 this service is allowed; if not approved, will try to have it paid "at home." Auto. Draft. 2pp.

1768. **Schuyler**, Abraham. Albany. To Jellis Fonda.
Jul. 25. Receipt for five bear skins from Petrus Van Driessen. A. D. S. 1p.

1768. **Glen**, John. Schenectady. To Commissary Offi-
Aug. 2. cers [and whom it may concern]. Orders to pass bearers with provision batteaux under charge of "Wouter Dance"; on receipt of goods acknowledgment to be made and deficiencies to be noted on orders. A. D. S. (2) 2pp.

On verso are Glen's instructions to Wouter Dance and receipt from Lt. [John] Galland to Dance, each an A. N. S.

1768. **Glen**, John. Schenectady. To John Bradstreet.
Nov. 4. Certificate that Cornelius Glen has furnished one batteau for royal service with receipt by Abraham Cuyler dated Jan. 10, 1771 for payment of account. A. D. S. 2pp.

1768. **Glen**, John. [Schenectady.] To [John Bradstreet].
Dec. 20. Certificate of services of Albert Vidder [Vedder?] in repairing 13 batteaux. A. D. S. 1p.

1769. [**Bradstreet**, John.] Albany. Letter to [Thomas
Jan. 15. Gage]. Trouble over the payment of debts outstanding from 1767, a list of which was forwarded in Oct. [Dec.] of that year; people are sueing [John] Glen and latter, being only an agent, falls back on Bradstreet; hopes he will not be compelled to pay just debts of the army;

encloses accounts for 1768 "chiefly for Sir William Johnson's Department" and unpaid debts of 1767; disputes between late Capt. [John] Stevens and batteau men; troubles with Capt. [Joshua] Loring and testimony of Col. [Delancey] Robinson in this matter; if money is allowed as desired, writer will draw on [Abraham] Mortier for it. Auto. Draft. 2pp.

1769. [Bradstreet, John]. Albany. Letter to [Thomas
Feb. 18. Gage]. Encloses account of contingent expenses and outstanding debts for previous year; precautions taken to prevent fraud; encloses copy of instructions from Sir Jeffrey Amherst for discharge of outstanding debts contracted during [William] Shirley's administration; trouble anticipated for [John] Glen; position of Capt. [Robert] Rogers in the past. Auto. Draft. 2pp.

[1770?] Bradstreet, John. [Albany. To Gov. John Murray,
[May] Earl Dunmore, and the Council of New York.] Petition and argument setting forth the invalidity of the Hardenbergh patent in New York and petitioner's right to 300,000 acres of lands purchased from the Indians in 1769; purchase was by consent of Sir William Johnson and in the presence of Sir Henry Moore; requests that claim be confirmed by royal grant. The argument, framed by Bradstreet's attorney and strengthened by additions, was forwarded [by Dunmore?] to the Lords of Trade and Plantation March, 1771. Draft. 72pp.

See Docts. relating to Col. Hist. of New York, VIII, 267, 268, 271, 287, 289, 294, 347, 378, and following entry. This manuscript is printed in full on page 147 of this volume.

1771. [Johnson, Sir William.] Johnson Hall. Letter to
Jan. 22. Col. [John] Bradstreet. Acknowledges letter of Dec., 1770; considers it but just to state that Six Nations declared that they and they only had the

right to sell lands west of Popaghtonk branch; although lands were claimed under Hardenbergh patent, Indians granted land to Bradstreet in presence of Sir Henry Moore; could be more circumstantial but thinks above statement sufficient for Bradstreet's purpose. Copy. 1p.

<small>Draft of above is in Sir William Johnson Papers in New York State Library.</small>

1771. Coventry, George. Fairhill near Hamilton, [Ber-
Jun. 25. muda?] Letter to John Bradstreet. Difficulties regarding his brother and his work in New York; career of latter and of his nephew; asks advice as to return to America; acknowledges letters of Dec. 9 [1770] from Bradstreet and Sept. 12 from Capt. [Philip] Schuyler. A. L. S. 2pp.

1771. Coventry, George. Hamilton. [Bermuda?]. Let-
Aug. 20. ter to John Bradstreet or Capt. Philip Schuyler. Acknowledges letters of Sept. 12 and Dec. 9, 1770 from Schuyler and Bradstreet respectively; gives directions regarding management of farms; Stevenson farm at Claverack to be taken from his brother and put in charge of his nephew Alexander Patterson; other personal matters. A. L. S. 1p.

<small>On verso in auto. of Bradstreet is list of provisions placed on board two sloops.</small>

1772. Monier, John. Albany. To [John] Bradstreet.
Oct. 19. Account of Post Officer at Albany against Bradstreet from Jul. 5, 1771 to Sept. 26, 1772, with receipt for payment of account in full. D. S. 1p.

1773. [Bradstreet, John. Albany.] Letter to [William
May 10. Petty, Earl Shelburne?]. Recounts his services in behalf of the Crown from 1745 to date and declares himself to have been hardly used;

several inferior officers promoted over his head; is the only general officer in the service without a regiment; hopes for this recognition of his services although he has "not gone to England to importune for what he had a right to expect." Auto. Draft. 2pp.

 Bradstreet had been promoted to a Major Generalship May 25, 1772.

1773. **Glen**, John. Sche[nectad]y. To [John] Bradstreet.
Aug. 20. Returns Book of [Land] Patents; finds that he has just claim to large estate in Schenectady; movements of Gov. [William] Tyron. A. L. S. 1p.

1773. **Bradstreet**, John. Albany. Letter to William
Sept. 29. Tryon. Petitions that [George] McIntosh and others from New England be put off certain lands purchased by Bradstreet from the Indians under leave of Sir Henry Moore; location of lands on main branch of Delaware river; considers Hardenbergh Patent [1706] not inclusive of his lands but rather invalid and of no force. A. D. S. 4pp.

 See: Bradstreet, John. Petition May, 1770, and Docts. relating to Col. Hist. of New York VIII, 272.

1773. **Coventry**, George. Fairhill, [Bermuda?] Letter to
Oct. 11. John Bradstreet. Has purchased land in Island of St. Johns; will sell home place as soon as possible for he wishes much to go to his new purchase; intends sending Alexander Patterson to begin a settlement there; asks regarding his brother; in case latter leaves farm which he is working, desires Bradstreet to put William Martin in charge; offer to his brother in case he will leave; respects to [Philip] Schuyler. A. L. S. 1p.

1773. **Glen**, John. Schenectady. To [John] Bradstreet.
Dec. 30. Explanations regarding stores for the Indians; acknowledges note by Adam Condie. A. L. S. 1p.

[1773.] **Bradstreet**, John. [Albany.] State of Account with Phyn & Ellice. Existing relation between the two parties; claims against Bradstreet with reply of latter to these claims. Auto Draft. 6pp.

1777[?] **Wain**, Anthony. [Albany.] To [Estate of] John
Sept. 11. Bradstreet. Account against Bradstreet for meats, with receipt in full dated Oct. 16. A. D. S. 1p.

Endorsed: Anthony Wayne.

THE CLAIMS OF
COL. JOHN BRADSTREET
TO
LANDS IN AMERICA.

NOTE.

Few Colonial land titles in America have been contested with more vigor than that of Col. John Bradstreet to certain Indian lands within the limits of the present state of New York. Interfering as it did with claims under the Hardenbergh patent of 1706, Bradstreet's title was as aggressively opposed as it was ardently maintained, both in the colony of New York and at the Court of Great Britain. A summary of the action taken upon the Bradstreet claim will not be amiss as an introduction to the argument by which it was supported.

So far as the native title was concerned, Bradstreet's claim originated in an Indian deed of October 29, 1768, and was completed by the acceptance of the deed and the payment of the purchase money in the following year. On presenting a petition for a patent from the Government in May, 1770, Bradstreet was at once opposed by the Hardenbergh proprietors, following which the Council of New York on May 30, 1770, directed Bradstreet to serve a copy of his petition and the order taken thereon upon the Hardenbergh proprietors with a summons to them for July 4, to show cause why his prayer should not be granted. After some delay, Dec. 10 was assigned for the argument of counsel for the Bradstreet claim and on that date the major portion of this argument, printed upon the following pages, was presented. In opposition to Bradstreet's claim which held the earlier patent invalid and its construction strained, counsel for the Hardenbergh proprietors presented their case on Feb. 5, 1771, following which the Bradstreet argument was concluded. Further evidence was given on March 11 and 18, and on the 20th of the same month a grant of 20,000 acres was made by the Council to Bradstreet.

Upon reference of both petition and grant to the British authorities for their formal approval this action was on June 5,

1771, declared illegal, the home government holding that the New York Provincial Council lacked power to decide upon the petition. The letter of Lord Hillsborough giving this decision aroused the Council and on August 14 that body made a report at length in answer to Hillsborough maintaining the powers of the province.

As a result of this additional contest the validity of the Bradstreet claim remained unsettled for two years. The discussion was transferred to England and not until August 31, 1773, was the petition granted once more by the Council of New York. The death of Bradstreet in the following year left the claim to his heirs for final settlement with the later state of New York.

The manuscript as printed on the following pages gives in full the argument of Bradstreet's counsel, those portions being noted which were added before presentation in England. So far as known, no other copy of Bradstreet's argument exists in this country, and the commissioners from New York appear to have found nothing of the character when transcribing in England the manuscripts there filed relating to the Colonial history of New York. It is here printed as a good illustration of the vagueness with which land grants were described and the character of the arguments by which they were maintained during the Colonial period of American history.

THE ARGUMENT.

May it please your Lordship & the Honorable Board:—
 There is perhaps no Tribunal at which Declamation will less succeed than at this Honorable Board. When Judges are of a Rank superior to those Emotions which in vulgar Minds usurp the place of Reason the Orator cannot expect to bear his blushing Honors thick upon him. The Weight of Evidence the Energy of Argument will command Attention & the plain Road of Common Sense will lead to conviction while the flowery Path of Rhetoric remains neglected and untrodden. Had those Sentiments been adopted by the Gentlemen who spoke agt us much Time unnecessarily spent might have been Excused and were it not that the Matter in Controversy is of very great importance to the Crown & my Claim I should have saved your Lordship & this Board the Trouble of attending to this Reply. The Gentlemen who oppose us have endeavoured to support such an Extension of the Patent to Joh[1][annes Hardenbergh as is opposed to] the Right of the Crown and Deprives my Client & his Associates of the Benefit of an Indian pact Regularly obtained and of the [advantage] of his Majesty's Letters patent for the Lands in Controversy. And as at the opening of this [Controversy] it was made a Question whether Col. Bradstreet is entitled to the Grace of the Crown even were the Lands vacant. I shall in the Course of this Reply—
 First shew that he is in a Situation [which] entitles him to ask that Grace and Secondly, that there is room for contending if the Patent to Hardenbergh and others be justified [it should be restricted] within proper bounds. And as to the first point my Lord[2]—
 According to the Regulation that has for some Years existed

First Set of Proofs. no purchase can be made of the Indians but by the Govr. or Commander in Chief for his Majesty's use at some public meeting with the Indian Tribe to whom the

---

[1] The words within the brackets are supplied by the Editor when the original manuscript is torn or illegible.
[2] These two introductory paragraphs appear to have been added when the argument was taken from the New York authorities and presented to the British Court. Other changes of wording will be noticed as the argument proceeds.

Lands belong—That the Lands in Controversy were thus
Indian Deed No. 1. purchased will be rendered evident from an
Read it. Indian deed procured in conformance to the
above mentioned Regulation at the Expense of Col. Bradstreet
and his Associates.

From this deed it appears that Col. Bradstreet and his
Associates paid the Indians a large Consideration, that the
Govr. obtained the Conveyance to his Majesty's Use at a General
Treaty and that it was made by the Indians expressly with
the Intent that Col. Bradstreet and his Associates should have
the preference to all others in obtaining his Majesty's Letters
patent for the Lands thereby conveyed.

But besides this Conformity to the Regulation prescribed
by the royal Proclamation the purchase was made with the
privity of Sir W^m. Johnson Superin(ten)dent for Indian Affairs
in the Northern District.
No. 2 Sir W^m.
Johnson's Letter. This appears by his Letter[3] to Col. Bradstreet
Read it. on the subject—

This Letter my Lord will serve not only to shew Sir William's
Privity to the purchase and that it was publickly transacted
as appears from these Words in it "If I was sufficiently
recovered to have recourse to the several proceedings at that
Time I might possibly be more circumstantial but I fancy
this will prove satisfactory as to the Idea the Indians enter-
tained and their Intentions in making the Grant to You" [but]
it will also be of use under the Second General Head and
shew in Addition to what has been offered in proof from the
Acts & Declaration of the Esopus Indians (under whom the
Proprietors of Hardenbergh's patent Claim their Indian Title)
that both those Indians & the Six Nations agreed that the
property of the Lands in Controversy were in the latter as the
native original prop^{rs} thereof.

True it is that the Lands in Controversy are within the Line
established at the above mentioned Treaty as the boundary
of the Lands ceded by the Indians to the Crown; but as that
No. 3 Extract of Cession was posterior to our purchase and as
Indian Treaty. by the Terms of the Treaty (of which we are
Read it. informed the Gov^t. is possessed) it will appear that
the Indians made a Saving in favor of those of his Majesty's Subjects to whom they had sold Land, the Cession must operate as a
Confirmation of our Indian Title. And that We reason justly,
my Lord, will appear from an Extract of the Treaty which I
beg leave to read.
No. 3 Col. Cro- The Fairness of this Transaction will further
ghan's Certificate. appear from a Certificate of Col. Croghan who
Read it. was present at the Execution of our Deed & at the

---

[3] See summary of letter in Calendar under date Jan 22, 1771.

Indian Treaty at which it was executed. But this fact is further
<small>No. 4 Adems Certificate. Read it.</small> Confirmed by the Certificate of Robert Adems one of the Witnesses sworn to by John Butler interpreter and the other Witnesses to the Indian Deed.

From those several pieces of Evidence my Lord we humbly conceive that it appears to a demonstration evident that the Lands in Controversy were purchased by Sir Henry Moore at our Expense at a public Meeting or Treaty with the Native Indian prop^{rs}., and tho' to his Majesty's use, yet in fact for our Benefit, and with a declared intent to entitle us to his Majesty's Letters patent for the same, that the Consideration was actually paid & the deed executed in the presence of Sir Henry Moore, that the purchase was confirmed by the Af^d. Treaty of Cession and we presume there is not the least Reason to doubt we should long since have experienced the Grace of the Crown in Common with several others of his Majesty's Subjects whose purchases were in the same predicament with ours, by the Grant of his Majesty's Letters patent, had it not been for that Groundless opposition of the proprietors of Hardenbergh's patent, which has hitherto obstructed all our Attempts made at a Great Expense to avail ourselves of his Majesty's Royal favor. But, my Lord, to shew that this Opposition is groundless, We shall proceed under the Second General Head.

1st. To recapitulate the arguments & proofs which we offered at the first Hearing against the Claim of our Opponents, etc.

2^d. To obviate such Objections as at the last hearing they attempted to avail themselves of—In the Execution of this part of our Task I shall aim at all possible Brevity; and flatter myself that every Obstacle which has hitherto prevented us from reaping the fruits of his Majesty's Royal Munificence will be effectually removed.

To do justice however to a Cause of so much importance, as we barely opened the points & read the Evidence we had to produce in support of them, without scarcely enforcing them with a single Reflection, I must beg the favor of your Lordship & the Honorable Board, that I may be a little more copious in this Reply.[4]

In the opening Argument, I broke two points. (1.) The suspicious Circumstances that attended the issuing of Hardenbergh's patent & from those concluded that the greatest favor the prop^{rs}. of that patent could expect was a rigid construction of their Boundaries—especially as it is a Crown Grant; (2.) That from a variety of Evidence it was extremely apparent that neither the Indians of whom they purchased nor the

---

[4] The reference is to the opening argument and petition presented in May 1770. See summary of proceedings in prefatory note.

proprietors themselves ever till of late years esteemed the boundaries of that patent to extend beyond the Popaghtonk or East Branch of the Fish Kill or Northernmost Branch of Delaware River.

Under the first point my Lord I observed that as by the Policy of Law all Letters patent in England must pass thru' certain different Offices, which serve as a Check each upon the other to prevent undue alienations of the Crown Lands so in this Country there is and at least ever since the Gov.^{t} came into the Hands of the Crown, has been a fixed and established Channel thru' which every Grant of the Crown Lands must pass in order to be good and valid in the Law.

That his Majesty & his Royal predecessors have tho't fit to make the participation of his Council as well as that of his Govr. or Commander in Chief absolutely necessary in the Grant of Crown Lands—

That therefore every grant as to situation & Quantity which has not been fully & apparently assented to by the Council for the Time being must be null & void as issued without authority.

I then proceeded my Lord to shew that the Grant to Hardenbergh & Company was in that predicament. To evince this I adduced the following proofs.

Second Set of Proofs.

(1.) Johannes Hardenbergh in behalf of himself & Company on the 18th July 1706 presented his petition to [Edward Hyde,] Lord Cornbury then Govr. of this province setting forth a discovery of a *Small* Tract of vacant & unappropriated Land in the County of *Ulster* & desiring to settle & improve it, he prays a License to purchase it of the Indians.

A. Petition of Johannes Hardenbergh for a License to purchase a Small Tract in Ulster.

This my Lord was the first Step taken towards obtaining the patent in Question.

The petition is for a *Small* Tract of Land in the County of *Ulster only*—and yet scanty as the limits were which the petitioner assigned to himself, this petition was the first step towards a Grant containing, exclusive of the present & all other Controversies, upwards of 1100 M. [1100 000] Acres & extending into the County of Albany as well as that of Ulster.

(2.) The Govr. probably deceived with the pretence of the Smallness of the Tract without strictly enquiring into the Bounds or extent of Country the petitioner had in view did by an Order in Council the same day give the Petitioner a License to purchase a small Tract of Land in the County of Ulster

No. 1 B License to purchase a small Tract in Ulster.

(3.) What Use the petitioner & his Associates made of this License for the purchase of a small Tract is not uncertain—For tho' the first petition & the License grounded on it were

The Col. John Bradstreet Manuscripts. 107

No. 2 Second petition of Hardenbergh. for a small Tract of Land yet the petitioner & his Associates as appears by their Second petition dated the 17th March 1706/7 had so enlarged their plan that instead of purchasing of the Indians a small Tract they had procured from them a Conveyance of "All That Tract of Land lying and being in the County of Ulster stretching from the Northwest Bounds of the Township of Marbletown northwesterly ten Miles beyond the Hills that lye on the southeast Side of the Low Lands or Meadow Land that lies on the Fish Kill or River and runs northeasterly with said Breadth till You come opposite to a Creek called by the Indians Anquothkon Kill where William Leggs Saw Mill stood, and further still running Northeasterly with the Breadth of Ten Miles from said Kill northwesterly, to the County of Albany & running Southwardly along the Northwest Bounds of the Town of Marbletown and Rochester with the full Breadth first above ment^d. till so far as to run with a due South East Line to a certain fall in the Rundour [Rondout] Creek called by the Indians Hoanekt^r. which is the northerly bounds of the Land called Nepenack [Napanock] belonging to Jacob Rutsen & Jan James Bleeker [Bleecker?]". This Extravagant purchase founded on a License for buying a small Tract appears from this petition to have given great Umbrage to their Neighbours. For this second petition declares that a Caveat had been entered ag^t. their obtaining a patent for the above described Tract which probably interfered with their Neighbours They therefore pray a day may be assigned for hearing the parties—

What became of this Contest we are not, perhaps for want of a proper search in the Secretary's office, able to determine. We will suppose however my Lord that for the present it was dropped. But

(4.) On the 19th June 1707 Hardenbergh & Company renewed their Application to Gov^t. by a third petition & prayed a Grant for the Lands they had purchased of the Indians—which was read in Council. On that very day a petition of the Inhabitants & Freeholders of the Town of Hurley praying a Grant of a parcel of Land between Marbletown & Kingston & of another parcel between Kingston & the Blue Hills was also read in Council & both petitions were ordered to lie on the Table.

No. 3 A. Third petition of Hardenbergh.

No. 3 B. Order of Council on petitions of Hardenbergh & Hurley.

(5.) On the 4th of Feby 1707 Hardenbergh & Co. presented their petition to my Lord Cornbury by which they enlarged their Request even beyond the Bounds of their Indian purchase & beyond the Bounds of Ulster & extended it into the County of Albany; and by this petition they assert what is a downright Falsehood to wit that by his Excellency's favor & License they had purchased some certain *vacant Lands* in the Counties of Ulster & *Albany* and then under a pretence that they were put off meerly from an Apprehension that the Lands they had purchased might interfere with some former Grant, they, artfully pretending to avoid all Contest, pray for a Grant exactly in the Words of their present patent which include Lands in the County of Albany.

No. 4 B. Order that the petition lie on the Table. (6.) On the day following, 5th Feby. 1707, the last mentioned petition was read and so Cautious still were the Govr. & Council that they ordered that the petition should lie on the Table till the first Thursday in March then next and it was ordered that on that day the petitioners & the Inhabts of Hurley who had petitioned for a Tract of Land in the said County (Meaning the County of Ulster) should appear & be heard on their respective petitions on the first Tuesday in March then next.

No. 5 B. (7.) The Inhabts. of Hurley however did not appear at the day appointed & therefore on the 4th of March 1707/8 probably the day appointed for the purpose we find an Order of the Govr. & Council that the Inhabts. of Hurley do preemptorily appear that day Month to make out the Allegations of their former petition.

No. 6 B. (8.) On the 18th March 1707/8 but 14 days after the last Order there is an Entry in the Council Books of a petition of Cornelius Cook and Adrian Gerritse in behalf of themselves & the other Inhabitants of the County of Ulster withdrawing their Caveat & praying a Grant of the Lands mentioned in their former petition which are not included within the petition of Hardenbergh;

In consequence of which it was ordered by the Govr. & Council that a Warrant be prepared for the Atty General to prepare a Draft of Letters patent for the Lands petitioned for by Johannes Hardenbergh & Company in the County of *Ulster* and

No. 7 B. (9.) By an Entry in the Minutes of Council it appears that a Warrant to the Atty General to prepare a patent for Johannes Hardenbergh and Company was signed—The Quit rent three pounds—

Upon those pieces of Evidence we insisted that the Crown had been deceived in the Grant in Question for that the patentees had originally petitioned for a License to purchase a small Tract of Land in the County of Ulster & had abused that License by purchasing of the Indians a Tract of ten miles in Breadth & of a much more considerable Length, that they persisted in this Abuse, by petitioning for a patent for it; That after the Obstructions to their obtaining the patent for the Lands they had actually purchased beyond all reasonable Construction of their License were removed, they then rose in their Demands yet they did it with great Artifice in their last petition by setting forth that to avoid Contests with their Neighbours they only prayed for the Tract of vacant Land as since described in their patent & lying within the Counties of Ulster & *Albany* & therefore extending beyond either of their former petitions and their licensed Indian purchase, that nevertheless the Order of Council on their last petition expressly restricted them to the County of *Ulster* notwithstanding which, Contrary to the established Rules for the Grant of Letters patent which require the participation & Consent of the Council as well as that of the Governour the patent issued in its present form and gave the Patentees Lands in the County of Albany contrary to the express Intention of the Council.[5] That the Govr. & Council are in effect commissioners for granting the Crown Lands & must act jointly—That neither of them could execute this Trust alone, That the Govr. had not the Advice of Council to grant Lands in the County of Albany, but on the contrary acted ag^t. such advice in granting the patent in Question—That to suppose the declaration in the patent that it passed with the Advice of Council should be evidence of the fact, would be to contradict the last Entry in the Council Books which restricts the patent intended to be granted to the County of *Ulster*—That to give such efficacy to that declaration would be in effect to deprive the Council of their Right to participate with the Govr. in the Grant of Lands, by leaving it in his power in defiance of that Right to divest the Crown of its property even without the Knowledge of the Council & that by a single Assertion which in fact would be false—That tho' the Grant of the Crown is a Matter of Record yet any grant under the Great Seal of this province which notwithstanding any thing asserted in it, could be shewn not to have passed thro' the ordinary Channel would be as null & void as a patent under the Great Seal of Great Britain reciting all the prerequisites yet in fact & Truth supported by none of them would be. From all which it was concluded that the patent in Question issued upon false suggestion & deceit of the Crown & that therefore according to the clearest Rules of Law it is absolutely null & void & leaves full room for the Application of Col. Bradstreet's Indian purchase & petition, a Grant in Consequence of which cannot possibly interfere with any one's Right.

But to all this it was answered by the Counsel for Hardenberghs patent, that however clear it may be that the Council Board might have originally intended to confine the patent

---

[5] Six lines are erased in the original manuscript at this point and as the following six lines give the argument in a form preferred by the Attorney they are omitted from this text.

to the County of Ulster yet there is evidence that they afterwards consented to an Enlargement of the Bounds of the Grant—
No. 8 [B.] To support this Assertion the Warr^t. to the Attorney General to prepare the Draft of the Letters patent dated the 15th April 1708 was produced; the Bounds of which run exactly in the same words with those of the patent itself. And to justify this Warrant Reference
No. 7[6] was had to the Entry in the Council Books of that day by which it appears that the Warr^t. for the patent was signed. From whence it was concluded that the Council were privy to the Terms of the Warrant & consequently to the Boundaries contained in the patent.

When I first opened this Matter, my Lord, I was utterly ignorant that such a Warrant existed—Col. Bradstreet informed me that he could find no warrant in the Office. whence I naturally concluded that the Warr^t. referred to in the last mentioned Entry in the Council Books, if any ever issued, must have been grounded on the Order of the 18th March preceeding which expressly directs that the Warr^t. to the Atty General to prepare a patent should be confined to the Lands petitioned for in the County of Ulster.

Nor my Lord can I still help thinking that this warrant was run either upon the Governour or the Council or both without due Knowledge of its contents.[7] For neither the Warrant nor the Entry which in date corresponds with it appears to have been read in Council, nor is there the least Entry in the Council Books to show that the Govr. and Council had reconsidered the last petition of Hardenbergh the formal Order of Determination on which was that he should have a patent for the Lands petitioned for in the County of Ulster. It is easy therefore to conceive that as the Warrant was merely signed in Council its Variance from that formal Order passed unobserved; and ought to have no more Credit from the Circumstance of its being signed there & the Entry of the Secretary that it was so signed than if it had been signed in the absence of the Council. Had it corresponded with the Order it had been immaterial where or in whose presence or with whose privity it was signed. But I humbly conceive as the Council are as necessary Agents as the Govr. in the Grant of the Crown Lands, and as it appears that they had in Conjunction with the Governor by a solemn Determination restricted the petitioners to the County of Ulster, nothing less will do to remove all suspicion of Fraud than clear proof of a Revision & Renewal of that determination which our Opponents have not produced.

---

[6] See No. 7 B. Ante p. 158.

[7] Six lines are erased in the original manuscript at this point the argument being developed in the following text.

The Col. John Bradstreet Manuscripts. 111

There is perhaps my Lord, further reason to suspect unfair Dealing towards the Crown in this Instance. My Lord[8] Cornbury was well known both in Britain & America as a Gentleman remarkably unattentive to Business and therefore very liable to be deceived. Hardenbergh was the only man whose name appeared as a petitioner. But there were persons of more weight behind the Curtain who were to be benefited by the Grant. When the Warrant had issued Mr. [May] Bickley the Attorney General appeared as a patentee, and Mr. [Thomas] Wenham was more occultly personated by Mr. Robert Lurting who tho' inserted as a patentee lent his name to Mr. Wenham, for it appears from the Records of the Secretary's Office that the deed was executed by him to Mr. Wenham for 1/7th of the Tract, it bears the date 12th January 1708, is for Call for the Record a trifling Consideration and shews that the and read it. Grant was a Trust for Mr. Wenham. Nor is it If opposed observe it is for the Benefit I humbly conceive my Lord unworthy of Re- of the Crown. mark that Mr. Wenham was so attentive to his Object that he was not absent one Council day in which this important Business came on the Tapis, and that particularly on the day in which the Warrt. was signed in Council he was one of four of the Council present As therefore my Lord this Honorable Board when employed on the Subject of granting away the Crown Lands is always considered as a Court of Requests, as Mr. Wenham appears upon our opponents use of the signing of the Warrant of Council to have sat as one of the Judges of this Court of Requests in his own Cause, which is contrary to all Reason & Law & extreamly dangerous to his Majesty's Right (for otherwise it cannot be when one of the Guardians of his Majesty's Land stock becomes a Suitor before himself for a part of that stock) I say my Lord as all those things appear I humbly conceive that the Warrant in Question cannot cure the radical Defects of the patent. And I would further beg leave to suggest it as a Subject of Enquiry to your Lord & the Honorable Board whether five members besides the Govr. have not always been as they now are necessary to form a Quorum for Business, and if so as it appears that as well at the Meeting in which the Warrant was ordered for the Lands in the County of Ulster only as at that in which the Warrant was signed on which our Opponents so much rely one of the Here offer the proof [shown in Record Jan. 12, 1708.] four Councillors present was a party the whole Basis of the patent does not fail, and if so we must submit it to your Lordship & this Board to determine what becomes of the patent itself.

Having thus shewn my Lord that the patent is void there can be no controversy between us but if your Lordship & the

---

[8] Edward Hyde, Lord Cornbury, Governor of New York 1702–1708.

Honorable Board should be of a different Opinion which we flatter ourselves cannot be the Case, yet from the very suspicious circumstances which attended the issuing of Hardenbergh's patent I conclude that the greatest favor the proprietors of that patent can expect in this Controversy is a rigid Construction of its Bounds—I proceeded—

Under this Head to observe that your Lordship and the Honorable Board were Trustees of the Crown's Land Stock and the revenues either actual or contingent thence to arise and that in this View I made not the least doubt that to every Grant the Bounds of which come into Question here the Rules of Law would be applied as the proper Test; That the Law clearly is, that Grants of the Crown obtained on a suggestion of the party shall be construed strictly ag[t]. the Grantee & most favorably for the Crown; That in this Case the Rule is the Reverse to that which prevails in the Construction of Grants between Subject & Subject—for in the Latter recitals may operate ag[t]. but never can make for the Grantor because they are his own Words, But that in Grants of the Crown suggestions of the Grantee tho' adopted by the Crown in its Grant, can never make ag[t]. the Crown but may & if the Matter of them is ag[t]. the Grantee will operate ag[t]. him; That whenever the Grant of the Crown issues on the suggestion & petition of the party, he is held to suggest at his peril because the Attention of the Crown being ingaged on the *Arduis Regni*[9] the Law has not only discharged the Crown from any Guards ag[t]. false suggestions in fact but has made it a Rule that wherever a Grant is made on petition & suggestion of the party it shall be construed strictly in favor of the Crown; That therefore in every such Grant where the Construction is doubtful or in other Words where two constructions may be put that which is most in favor of the Crown shall be received; that tho' it is a general Rule that Grants which express themselves as issuing of the special Grace certain Knowledge and meer Motion of the Crown shall for the King's Honor be construed most liberally in favor of the Grantee, yet those words become a dead Letter when the Grant is founded on the prayer and suggestion of the party and that for this most evident Reason that those Words being expressive of the King's spontaneous & selfmoved Exuberance of favor are expressly contradicted & their Operation utterly annihilated by the Express Suit and Suggestion of the party as the moving Cause of the Grant which Observations were, it was urged, so clearly & indubitably supported by Law, that it would have been an impassable Affront to offer to your Lordship & this Hono[ble]. Board, under whose imme-

---

[9] Concerns of government

diate Care & direction the royal Land Stock is placed, a single Authority in their Support.

This patent my Lord usually called by the Name of the Great Patent pays but £3 annual Quit rent. Supposing therefore that it were not void yet the Attempts of the propr^{rs}. to extend it beyond its real Bounds is a most manifest Attack upon his Majesty's Revenue—For if it should be construed rigidly yet by its Terms it is made to contain so much more Land than was really intended to be granted them in consequence of their 2^d. petition that the Crown has lost an immense part of its Revenue, which had not been the Case had those Lands been patented at the rate of Quit Rents established a few Years after, which might probably have long since been the Case had those Lands been vacant. This Loss added to the Loss [to] the public arising from the hitherto unpeopled State of [so] large a Tract as the whole patent, ought as we humbly Conceive to induce the Gov^t. to look with a Jealousy [sic] eye on the late Attempt to give it an amazing Extent beyond what the Words of the patent can properly warrant.

[Proper Construction of the Hardenbergh patent.] Having thus my Lord cleared the way for a proper Construction of the Bounds of the patent we proceeded to shew how many Constructions this Grant was capable of from its own Words independent of any Evidence from without. We shewed that it was capable of four different Constructions, ground[ed] on these words of the Bound-

Here lay open the Maps. No. 1 B. aries to wit "So running along that Line that is the Line of witness's patent Northwestly as the said Line Runs to the Fish Kill or River and so to the head thereof including the same, thence on a direct Line to the Head of a small River commonly known by the name of Cartwright's Kill" That upon these Words it appears that the Fish Kill or River is the Stream the head of which is the Boundary according to the Words of the patent. The Question is—

(1.) Shall that be Esteemed the Head of the Fish Kill or River where the Stream loses that Name, that is at the point of Conflux of the East or Popaghtonk Branch & West or Cookhouse or Mohawk Branch which Construction would be most in favor of the Crown or

(2.) As the Popaghtonk or East Branch divides itself into two Branches shall the Head of the Southermost of those two Branches which would furnish the next best Construction in favor of the Crown be the Boundary or

(3.) Shall the Head of the Northermost of those two Branches which would be more ag^t. the Crown be the Boundary,

Either of which three constructions will Leave the Lands in controversy vacant or

(4.) Shall the Head of the Mohawk or Cook-house Branch, which will furnish the Construction the most ag^t. the Crown of any that can possibly be & include the Lands in Controversy be the Boundary?

I insisted my Lord that as this Grant is to be construed most strictly ag^t. the grantees & most in favor of the Crown, the first of the above four Constructions ought to take place because it would take least from the Crown. To shew that this Construction was not only possible but natural I observed that in the Grant the Fish Kill which is the Stream Below the forks of Shewakin or the place of Union of the Mohawk & Popaghtonk Branches, is the River the head of which is in the Grant declared to be the Boundary by the Words "*and so to the head thereof.*" That therefore the Question arises to wit which is the Head of the Fish Kill or River, the answer to which I conceived was that the forks of Shewakin or the place of Union of the Mohawk & Popaghtonk was the head of the Fish Kill or River. My Reasons my Lord were these

(1.) That there the Fish Kill or river Ends because it there loses its Name.

(2.) That if the Sources of Branches or smaller streams may be called Heads of the River because they empty themselves into it, the Fish Kill has a variety of other Heads as the Source of the Lochawapin & many others on the West Side, & those of the Massacomeck [?] & many others on the East Side; That both the East & West Branches have their respective peculiar & appropriate names and that in Geographical Descriptions a River is never made to extend farther than it carries its name; That there is as manifest a Distinction between a River and its Branches as there is between a Tree & its Branches, and that as the head of the Tree is properly the head of the Trunk or place where the Branches insert themselves so is the Head of the River the place where the Branches insert themselves and that the Mohawk & Popaghtonk are confessedly and evidently Branches only and the Fish Kill or River with respect to them is the main Body or Trunk.

(3.) That this Construction will not only give least Land to the Grantees but will also be attended with less doubt; for that if by the words *Head of the River* should be understood its source or that fountain by which its Stream is fed through a Branch flowing into it there are a variety of such heads. In this sense the source, spring or fountain of all the smaller streams having their proper Names & feeding the main Stream are equally heads of Fish Kill or River; That more especially as the Fish Kill or River divides itself into two Branches at the forks of Shewakin to wit the Mohawk or Cook-house & the

The Col. John Bradstreet Manuscripts

Popaghtonk, the Sources of the two Streams are equally the Heads of the River; that the Popaghtonk is known to Divide itself into three Branches two main Streams & a smaller one [and] therefore in the Sense of our Opponents has three heads which according to their Reasoning are all heads of the Fish Kill or River; that the Cookhouse or Mohawk Branch may have as many or more the Country having not been sufficiently explored to determine that fact; That should the Case be otherwise our Opponents have furnished us with at least three heads of the River, which makes it necessary to confine the Boundary to the Forks of Shewakin to remove Doubts & prevent the Grant from being void. For as on the one hand if the doubt can be removed it must be construed as I have shewn most in favor of the Crown, so on the other if the doubt remains unsoluble the Grant must be null & void.

But if the Construction which would confine them to the forks at Shewakin be rejected I insisted that nothing could justify their extending up to the Head of the Mohawk Branch—It is more than probable that in that early day when the patent was granted it was uncertain where the Head of the Fish Kill was in their Sense of the Word. The Grant therefore must have intended according to their Construction to give the Head of the Fish Kill wherever it might be as the Boundary. But in their sense of the Word the Fish Kill has several Heads and which to Chuse is the difficulty. That which gives most land I have clearly shown ought not to be adopted because it would be contrary to the clearest & most uncontrovertible Rules of Law, but on the contrary that and only that which gives Least to the Grantees must be received or all the Laws relating to Crown Grants must be rejected, and therefore if they should be permitted to extend Beyond the forks of Shewakin they must still be confined to that head of the Fish Kill which will give them the least Land, which as I observed before must be the Head of the South Branch of the Popaghtonk. But my Lord if the Several Branches had then been explored to their respective Sources the Question still remains, which was the Head in the Sense of the Crown. The Answer I humbly conceive is, that head which will injure the Crown least and this too seems to be the most natural Construction from a View of the Maps because that head is the nearest to the Head of Cartwrights Kill & is so situated that a line extending from the one to the other nearly coincides with the Main Course of the Popaghtonk.

But I further observed that should your Lordship and the Honorable Board be inclined to relax the Rules of Law in meer indulgence to our Opponents it would not rid them of their difficulties. That this indulgence could not be extended so far as to assign to them the Head of the Mohawk Branch as their Boundary, meerly because that will give them more Lands; That such an Indulgence could not with any Colour of Reason be expected from the Guardians of the Rights of the Crown; That the East Branch followed to its Source formed the Head of the River as much as the West Branch; That it would be absurd to distinguish that which was the most remote as the Head of the Fish Kill because that in their own Sense of the Word every Source of a river is its head be it more or less remote; That the words of the Grant are not to the most remote head but to the Head thereof, & That the East Branch if it be measured in its meanders is at least as long as the West Branch, And finally that should the River be deemed to head either at the forks at Shehawkin [sic] or at the Head of the South Branch of Popaghtonk, or even at the Head of its North Branch the Lands in Controversy will still remain vacant.

I would beg Leave my Lord to add one thought more that has lately occurred to me. Where a Tract of Land is described as adjoining to a River as the Hardenbergh Tract evidently is, I believe even in a Grant from subject to subject it would be thought a very strange & unnatural Construction to extend it across one of its main Branches & yet such is the Construction [Grant to William Penn cited.] set up against us in the present Case. Should Wm. Penn or any of his descendants have put such a Construction on his Grant as to have extended it across the Mohawk & up to the Popaghtonk Branch, it would be thought by all the World to be an absurd Extension, and yet that Grant ought to be construed with the utmost Liberty as it issued not only as it is expressed of the Crowns special Grace, certain Knowledge & meer motion but expressly out of Regard to Memory & Merits of his late Father in divers Services & more particularly in Consideration of his Courage, Conduct & discretion under the Duke of York in that signal Battle & Victory fought & obtained ag^t. the Dutch fleet commanded by the Heer Van Opdam in the Year 1665[10].

In short my Lord if We consider the Words of the Grant [Interests of Crown to be guarded.] without any Aid from without, which I humbly contend must ever be the rule when they are capable of their own Exposition as the Words of the Grant in Question undoubtedly are; if we Consider what Construction of them Reason would naturally dictate & if finally we apply the Rules of Law to them which demand such a Construction as is most for the Interest of the Crown, and cannot as I humbly conceive be dispensed with, all these conspire to prevent the Hardenbergh Tract from including the Lands between the

---

[10] Battle of Lowestoft June 3, 1665.

Popaghtonk & Mohawk branches & consequently leave Room for extending the Bounty of the Crown to Col. Bradstreet.

We might indeed my Lord have relied on the Objections arising from the Manner in which the Grant in Question was obtained & upon the Words of the Grant itself construed in a rational Sense & in Conformity to the known Rules of Law as amply sufficient to insure us a Victory. But in a Case of so much moment it [we?] thought it prudent to supererogate by adding some Collateral proof to fortify our Reasoning on the Subject.

The Gentlemen in Support of The Patent observed that there were no recitals in it but of the petition on which it was grounded —That an Indian purchase is not necessary to make a Title at Law & that it is in no Case admissible as Evidence but to clear up doubts about Boundaries—I agree with the Gentlemen that by the Laws of England the Crown is the fountain of all Titles as well to Estates as to Honors & Offices; but I believe no Man of understanding ever meant to assert that this prerogative of the Crown was ever carried in the Ideas of Government to such a Length as to divest the aborigines of their natural Rights. The Government cannot be ignorant [Indian rights in the premises.] that King Charles the Second issued his royal proclamation whereby he asserted those Rights and forbade the Grant or Occupation of any Lands without an Indian purchase. Nay the very Idea aimed to be established by the Gent^n. who oppose us is that the Six Nations & the Mohicanders or River Indians have rendered themselves subjects to the Crown of Great Britain, which implies their protection in their person & Estate.—And upon a principle of protection has the Gov^t. always acted towards them by making an Indian purchase necessary previous to the Grant of a patent. However true therefore it is that in a Court of Law an Indian purchase is not a necessary Link of Title it is as true that before this Honorable Board it ought to be considered as the first Link and if the Bounds of a patent come into Question here, as our Opponents admit that in a Court of Law an Indian deed will serve to Explain Boundaries surely this Honorable Board will conceive that the apparent disparity between the Bounds of the Indian purchase made by License of Gov^t. & the patent grounded on it furnishes the strongest Reason for construing the patent rigidly.

But my Lord it is not only clear that the Indian purchase on which the proprietors of Hardenberghs patent founded their patent does not include any Lands in the County of Albany nor across the East Branch of the Fish Kill, [but] We shewed from the most irrefragable Testimony that the proprietors of that patent never till of late Years conceived that it included any Lands between the East & West Branches.

For this purpose we produced sundry pieces of Evidence.[11] The first was a Treaty held with the Esopus Indians in whom the property of the Lands now in Controversy are pretended to have been vested. The preliminary measure to this Treaty was as we shewed an Order of certain Justices at Kingston suggesting that Major Hardenbergh had complained that the Indians hindered the Running of the Outlines of the patent & appointing a day for the Treaty. At which day which was the 27th. Augt. 1743 the Treaty was accordingly held & among other Indians Sander their Chief Sachem & Hendrick Hegan were present. This Hendrick several of our Opponents say lived on the West side of the Popaghtonk Branch where he had an orchard. The very Cause of the Treaty appears to have been Hardenberghs Intention to run the out Lines of his patent; The Business was so opened to the Indians by Hardenbergh himself. He shews his Intention to have been to make a Survey of more Lands than he had ever purchased of the Indians, for he expressly informed them that he desired to run the out Lines of his patent to find out the true Owners of the Land and that after it was measured he would not take any Land without first agreeing with & paying the particular owner of each Tract.

Is it possible My Lord for a Man to have been more explicit than Hardenbergh was, or can any Thing be clearer than his design to run out the Boundaries of his patent in the full Extent of his Claim? And what such extent was is as evident from the answer given to him by the Indians. It was that he should have Liberty to Survey round the patent and up the River Papakonk [Popaghtonk?] and also to divide the Land, but not to Claim any Right to the Soil before a purchase of them; Had he then Intended to make the west Branch his Boundary he would have desired Leave to run up that Branch, he would have so expressed himself, And to this there could have been no Objection but the true one, a Want of property in the Esopus Indians, because he expressly disavowed a Claim of property to any of the Lands before a purchase & the Indians as expressly stipulated ag^t. such Claim until a purchase— Thus then my Lord it appears that Hardenbergh in a solemn Transaction extant of Record asserted the Popaghtonk or East Branch as his Boundary.

[Survey of Henry Worster 1743.] This Treaty[12] was in Consequence of a Survey that had been attempted by Henry Worster a few days before [the treaty of Aug. 27, 1743] who from the

---

[11] Fifteen lines of the original text have been erased at this point. The same argument being developed in the following lines the erasures are omitted.

[12] Four lines of original text erased have been omitted at this point the argument being developed in the following lines.

Testimony of Peter P. Low was the person employed for the purpose, and in this Attempt the Indians took away his Chain when he had got up the River as far as within ab^t. 5 Miles of Papakonk [Popaghtonk] Village. Which chain the Witness declared he purchased from the Indians by Worster's directions. From the Testimony of this Witness therefore it appears clearly that in the first Attempt to make a Survey of the patent Worster ran up the East or Popaghtonk Branch. In Consequence of the Ill success of this Attempt the treaty was held at Kingston expressly grounded on a Complaint of Hardenbergh. that the Indians had hindered the Surveyor appointed by the Prop^{rs}. of the patent from running the Outlines of the Tract. Thence it is evident that Hardenbergh esteemed the East Branch to be the outline of the patent, & in effect so asserted in his Complaint on which the Treaty was grounded, and it was accordingly expressly stipulated by that Treaty that the outlines should be run & that the Indians should permit him to run up the Popaghtonk or East Branch. The work was accordingly performed a few days after by Worster; for [as] the same Witness Peter P. Low deposed—Worster informed him that the Indians had been invited to the Treaty at Esopus, That in a few days after Worster returned from Esopus & informed him that they had agreed with the Indians & that there would be no Danger in proceeding with the Survey, hired the Deponent as an Interpreter at 6 / per day & proceeded with him to the Papaconk [Popaghtonk] Village, That Worster left him there & went down the River ab^t 5 Miles to the place where the Indians had stopped him & surveyed the out Line to Papaconck from thence to papataghan [Pakatakan?] & from thence to the head of the River & having there marked 2 or 3 Trees they crossed over to the Head of Catrix Kill where Major Hardenbergh was waiting for them. What clearer proof there can be that the East Branch was then agreed to be the out Line of the patent is difficult my Lord to conceive.

[Other surveys in 1745.] It appears from the Evidence that in the Year 1745 another Survey was made by Ebenezer Worster at which Time they stole the Opportunity of running across from the East to the West Branch but conscious that it was inconsistent with the Right of the patentees & the Sense of all the parties to the Indian Treaty they never attempted to survey down the West Branch & accordingly have not laid down that Branch in the Map which they gave in Evidence. After this Survey in which the Course of the Popaghtonk was run as the out Line of the patent, another Survey was made in 1745 by Order of the prop^{rs}. at which Thos. Nottingham was present. In this Survey which was performed by Ebenezer Worster they exactly followed the

Line of the first Survey along the Popaghtonk Branch and up to its Northermost head passing by the River called the Tweed which ought to have been their True Bounds agreable to the Words of the Indian Treaty, that being naturally the Stream intended, not only on account of its Course directly towards but also its Approximation to the Head of Catrix Kill. On this Survey as Thomas Nottingham deposed they found several Monuments of Stones & marked Trees that had been before made by Henry Worster at the Time of his Survey in 1743 and particularly at the Head of the North Branch of Popaghtonk and that Ebenezer Worster on this Survey did something towards a division of the patent into Lots & for that purpose made stone monuments & marked Trees as he went along. That during this Survey they never attempted to cross the East Branch but at such places where its East Bank was so mountainous & steep as to be impassable & whenever this was not the Case they always kept their Survey on the East Side of the Branch. This scrupulous punctuality was indeed attempted to be accounted for by their fear of the Indians & not as proceeding from a Consciousness that their patent did not extend to the West Branch. But how far this pretence is well founded will appear from the above noticed Complaint of Hardenbergh & the Indian Treaty in Consequence of it on both which occasions he so effectually declared the Popaghtonk to be the out line of his patent. It is indeed rendered still more groundless by the Boundaries of their Indian deed dated the 6th June 1746 near 3 Years after that Treaty. The Words of those Boundaries are as follows: Beginning at Papaconk at the River & running down the said River as far as to the Bounds of the [13]Cashiktonk [Cashietonk?] Indians including half the River & half the Islands as far as aforesaid, then along the Bounds of the Lands of Cashiktonk Indians to the Bounds of Rochester patent, then beginning again at Papakonk af^d. & running up said River including half the River & half the Islands as af^d. to Pakatakan & so up to the head thereof, from thence with a streight Line to the Head of Catrix Kill &ca the Mohawks Claim excepted. This deed evidently pursues the Words of the Indian Treaty with the utmost precision, and was doubtless procured in Consequence of the Stipulation contained in that Treaty that notwithstanding the permission thereby given to Hardenbergh & his fellow proprietors to survey up the Popaghtonk Branch as the Outline of their patent they should not presume to claim any Lands comprehended within it which they had not bought of the Indians.

---

[13] This Indian name occurs in various spellings the one within the brackets being perhaps the most approved. See: post p. 123.

It is further observable my Lord that in this Deed the Mohawks Claim is excepted. What this Claim could possibly be but the Right of the Mohawks extending to the East Bank of the East Branch we cannot conceive because it was never pretended that a Line from the Head of that Branch to the Head of Catrix Kill would include any Land belonging to the Mohawks on any other Supposition, unless it be that which we urged in the Opening Argument that all the Lands possessed by the River Indians belonged to the Mohawks by right of Conquest.

But it is further Remarkable that this East Branch is declared in the Indian deed to be the *River* contrary to the present attempt of our Opponents to make the West Branch pass for the River,—and this remark is strengthened by another Indian deed procured by the patentees only two Months after the one just noticed. It is dated the 2d August 1746, is for a tract lower Down the River or to the Southward of the other Tract. It was obtained of the Kashightonk [Cashietonk?] & Minisink Indians, begins at the Great Yagh House and with a Course W. & by North strikes the Fish Kill or Main Branch of Delaware River & after crossing it four Miles runs parallel with it as far as the Cashightonk or Minisink Indians Right or Claim extended & then runs easterly to the late purchase of the Esopus Indians bearing Date the 6th June 1746 on the said River. But that purchase is evidently bounded on Popaghtonk. Therefore those two Deeds compared together demonstrate that the Popaghtonk was in the Estimation of Major Hardenbergh who was one of the patentees & Mr Livingston who was a purchaser under a patentee and 57 Minisink Cashightonk & Esopus Indians the *Fish Kill or main Branch of Delaware River* and consequently serve in conjunction with Hardenbergh's Complaint, and the Indian Treaty entered into with Hardenbergh in consequence of that Complaint, to demonstrate that the Intention of the Crown & the patentees in the Words by which the Tract is described to run up the Fish Kill or River to the Head thereof was that the Tract was to run to the Head of the Popaghtonk Branch.

Indeed so clear & conclusive is this Evidence arising from the Complaint of Hardenbergh, the Treaty to which that Complaint gave Birth & the two Indian deeds all clearly expressive that the Popaghtonk was the out Line of the patent that no doubt can possibly remain on the Subject.

We shall therefore my Lord for Brevity Sake waive observing either on the other Evidence offered by us to prove that the Lands between the two Branches belonged to the Mohawks or on the two Certificates of Doctor Shucksburgh [Richard Shuckburgh] relative to Govr. [William] Cosby's Mine to prove the Lands between the two Branches were vacant, or on the several patents which have been granted by the Crown all which are incompatible with the Supposition that the West Branch is the Boundary of the patent now under Consideration & proceed to a short Survey of what has been offered by our Opponents in proof of that point.

The first fact they Relied on was that one [Jacob] Rutsen on the 31st July 1706 made a purchase of the Indians of sundry small pieces of Land between the East & West Branches & besides those of a particular Spot on the West Side of the West Branch called Akanunkapunk. Great pains were taken to ascertain the Location of this same Akanunkapunk by the Testimony of Mr. [William] Cockburn & others. But my Lord it was obvious at the Time that Evidence and the Affidavit of Rutsen's Son [John?] to support it were produced that this purchase was made without a License for the purpose, & tho' from the Sons Affidavit it appears the father had declared that he was to have been a patentee & was unjustly deprived of his Right, yet certain it is that nothing can be concluded from any Evidence that has been offered that this purchase was made with an Intent to ground the patent on it. Those who know the Disposition of Indians know also that they may for the most trifling Recompense be prevailed on to sell Lands that do not belong to them, tho' they are extreamly apt to hold their indubitable property at a high price. The Supposition is further exploded by every Step taken towards obtaining the patent in all which this unlicensed purchase is utterly disregarded. And as a proof how much our Opponents are put to their Shifts I shall only remark that Col. Hardenbergh the Gent^n. who produces this Evidence has thought it necessary to prove that his father one of the patentees & thereby Agent in procuring the patent that was known to the Gov^t. was accessory to a manifest Wrong done to Rutsen.

[Claims advanced by opponents. Rutsen Purchase of 1706.]

[Indian Deed 1751.] Another Indian deed dated the 3 June 1751 was produced ag^t. us; but for what valuable purpose I cannot conceive. It was however evidently obtained to facilitate their present Claim & to Extend their Tract to the West Branch & is in Substance a Grant of the Lands between the two Branches. It would appear very extraordinary my Lord if this deed should have any weight in the Controversy, obtained as it was near half a Century after the patent issued and evidently after the proprietors had formed the Scheme of extending their patent beyond its original Bounds contrary to the most solemn, express & repeated Acts to which they were parties. To what an enormous Extent patents will grow if the proprs. are permitted to explain their Bounds by Indian deeds taken near fifty years after their dates, Your Lordship & this Honorable Board will readily conceive. In proportion as Lands rise in Value such Deeds which can always be procured at the Expense of a few Gallons of Spirits will multiply & descendants from the first patentees will by such means be able to reap at the Expense & to the prejudice of the Crown what their forefathers never sowed.

But there is indeed a most cogent Reason why if that Indian deed is to receive any Notice it ought to operate so strongly agt. our Opponents as to give us the full enjoyment of all We expect. Your Lordship & every Member of this Honorable Board must perfectly remember that the Instrument ushered in as the Indian Deed contained Many sheets of paper, that I requested the Whole should be read, that my request was answered by a Declaration from the Mouth of one of the Counsel for our Opponents that I should have the Sight of the Instrument & make what Use of it I thought proper. I accordingly applied for it, my Application was indeed backed with the respectable Weight of Government, But what did all this avail? Neither the Justice of the Request nor the possitive promise of our Opponents nor even the Authority of Gov^t. has been sufficient to command its production. On the contrary a single sheet of paper has been lodged in the Hands of Mr. Deputy Secretary instead of that voluminous Instrum^t. & of which I have not asked a Sight, because it was not the paper given in Evidence. But why permit me to ask it my Lord, why this strange & unprecedented Concealmt? Is it not a maxim that the whole Contents of every written Evidence shall be read if required? Why do our Courts of Justice daily determine that where a Deed is proved by a party to be in the Hands of his Opponent the strongest Argument is furnished ag^t. him by its non production? Is not the Reason evidently this my Lord that he would produce it did not the whole Instrumt. taken together strongly operate agt. him. Concealed Weapons not only beget Jealousy but are productive of Danger, and he who wears them is strongly to be suspected of a Design to make a most improper use of them. I flatter myself therefore as I appeal to the Honor & Dignity of Govt. that this concealed Instrument will not only be taken from our Opponents; I trust that its point will by the Hand of the Govt. be turned agt. them and that were there no other Reason for it, your Lordship & this Honble Board to do us full Justice & discountenance so dangerous a proceeding will favor us with a Grant of the prayer of our petition, which I would only hint my Lord may be done consistent with the strictest Justice as a Grant to Us cannot divest our Opponents of a single Iota of their Right.

But to pass my Lord from a piece of Evidence so disagreably circumstanced with one single reflexion more—I would beg Leave to observe that this piece of Evidence obtained without a License to purchase & to give Colour to the Enlargment of the Bounds of their patent is it seems Urged as an Argument of preference in their favor to our Indian Deed obtained at the Treaty with the Six Nations at which Sir Henry Moore, Sir Wm. Johnson & several other Gentn. of the first Rank were present & obtained too by the immediate Agency of Sir Henry Moore with the Knowledge of Sir Wm. & in exact conformity with the royal proclamation. But how unequal the Competition between this Deed thus regularly obtained & the other procured from vagrant Indians to serve the purposes of Countenancing an undue extension of the bounds of a patent issued near 50 years before, I need not mention.

The next piece of Evidence offered by our Opponents will not I flatter myself weigh a single Grain in the Scale of Evidence. It is composed of Sir Henry Moore's appointmt. of Mr. [Simeon?] Metcalf to run the Line of Cession agreed to by the Six Nations at the above mentioned Treaty and his Oath that he ran the Line agreable to that appointment. And the only fact colligible from this Evidence is that Sir Henry Moore in the Construction of that Cession considered the West Branch as Delaware River—Agreed my Lord.

[Line of Indian Cession as run by Mr. Metcalf.]

But it is obvious that the late Govr. who besides his good Sense had a just Knowledge of the Geography of the province knew that the Fish Kill or Main Branch of Delaware divides itself into two principal Branches the Popaghtonk & the Mohawk Branch. That this River being by the Indian Cession made part of the Boundary of the Lands ceded to the Crown it was fit & right for him to direct that Branch which would give the Cession the most Beneficial Operation for the Crown to be observed as the Boundary and accordingly he directed the Surveyor (without any distinction between the Delaware & its Branches) to begin his Survey where a due East Line from Owego strikes Delaware & to extend it up the River till opposite to where Tienonderah falls into the Susquehannah thereby fixing the West branch for the purpose of that Survey to be Delaware river as intended by the Cession. But surely my Lord When Delaware River & its branches are thus complexly considered, from the preference given by Sir Henry Moore to the West Branch it can never be esteemed that the Govt. near sixty years before & upon another subject, & agt. the most solemn Acts & express Declarations of Our Opponents intended to fix the West Branch as the Bounds of their patent. When a Tree and its Branches are complexly mentioned every

Branch is the Tree but when a Distinction between the Tree & its Branches is taken up the Construction is vastly different. In our Case the Fish Kill was evidently considered as the Main Branch of Delaware River & the Popaghtonk Branch was as evidently a Continuation of that Main Branch in the Sense of our Opponents—

If my Lord we weigh the Testimony of Jacobus Bruyn in the Scale of Evidence it will like Beltshasar tried in a more awful Balance be found wanting. In short it is much of the kind with that administered by Sir Henry Moore's Commission to Mr. Metcalf for it proves no more for our Opponents than that Mr. Bruyn was surveying Lands many years ago, on the West Side of the West Branch & that in pursuing his Survey Downward he struck upon a Branch (doubtless the West Branch) which he concluded to be Delaware River because (& for a very good Reason too) the Fish of passage came a great Way up that stream. But this certainly proves no more than that the West Branch was one of the Waters of Delaware as it unquestionably is, and so as undoubtedly is the East Branch and therefore from this Reason only without mentioning more, may as properly as the other be called the Delaware River. When such a monstrous Fabric is built upon so slender a Basis it may well be said—*Debile fundamentum fallit opus.*

But my Lord we have other Evidence administered by our Opponents still more curious than this—Nothing less in Truth than their own deeds of partition by which it appears that they had divided the Lands between the Two Branches among them—I have often heard that a Mans own Words and Actions were the highest possible evidence agt. him; but it is to me a doctrine entirely new & adjusted to the Latitude of this patent only that a division of Lands between a Number of persons should be evidence of their Right to them, Nay what is more Absurd that such Division should so operate even agt. their own most solemn Acts. I hope this Doctrine will not become fashionable. Should it grow into general Taste there would be an End to all further Grants of the Crown Lands for what Company of Land Jobbers would submit to the Expense of patent fees and the never ending Quit Rent of 2/6 Sterling per hundred Acres, to procure a Title to the Lands of the Crown adjoining to their property when a common Scrivner at the Trifling Expense of five pounds could by the Manoeuvres of the pen vest them in full propriety with all the neighboring Territory. Besides what horrible Confusion of private property would ensue upon this principle; partition agt. partition would confound all the Bounds of Right and be the Source of endless Litigation profitable to be sure to the Men of our profession

[Deeds of Partition among Claimants under Hardenbergh Patent.]

but never to be wished for by those of us who are Friends to justice, order, decency & regularity in civil Life. I cannot therefore my Lord but admire at the Attempt of our Opponents to avail themselves of a piece of Evidence so dangerous in precedent, in itself as light as Air & relied upon agt. their own solemn Acts as a proof of the Extent of their patent to the West Branch of the Fish Kill.

But my Lord my surprise is increased when I find this piece of Evidence attended with an Act of their Surveyor & Servant. It is his Map of the patent which on its face carries the strongest Evidences agt. them. How strangely inconsistent is our Conduct when the Love of property is our principle of Action. Sanguine in our pursuits, everything carries with it demonstration in our favor. Utterly blind to the apparent Inconsistencies of Evidence we fancy a beautiful Harmony, a rational Consistency & Co-operation reigns through all the parts of our proof. These unnaturally blended together by the Heat of passion form to our View an engaging picture while to others less prejudiced the piece appears grotesque indeed and truly verifies the observations of the elegant Roman poet—*Spectatum admissi risum teneatis Amici.*

[Map of 1749.] This Map exhibits to your Lordship the following Matters of fact. On the face of it we see no delineation of the West Branch of the Fish Kill & the Lines of division of the Lands lying to the Eastward of the East Branch tho' continued across it towards the West Branch remain unfinished and are not butted by any Object. This *res infecta* which however proves no more than a design of the parties to appropriate to themselves were it possible the Lands between the two Branches appears to be a compleat Actual Survey & Allotment of the Lands on the East Side of the *East* Branch. This Map is dated Novr. 8th. 1749 41 Years after the date of the patent & before the Settlemt. & improvemt. of any part of it. It speaks of itself as made at the Request of Mr. Robert Livingston & Gulian Verplan [c] k & Company and as being a survey and division of the Tract of Land called Hardenbergh's or the Great patent. It imports that the actual Survey was began on the 7th April 1749 & finished the 8th of Novr. following which is the day of its date. The Surveyor annexed to it a field Book containing a description of the Lands & form of the Mountains & of the Monuments & remarkable places near which they are placed but all this appears to relate only to the Lands on the East Side of the East Branch. What evidence then can this Map furnish for our Opponents but that it is an actual survey of those Lands & [an] unfinished attempt to appropriate by a random allotment the Lands between the two branches, Nay there is not the least syllable inscribed on it to shew that it was intended as an actual Allotment of the Lands between the two Branches. On the contrary the whole description in the field Book relates entirely to the Lands on the East Side of the East Branch, For when the Surveyor after having described his several Courses & Monuments from the Bounds of Minisink patent on the Fish Kill or Main branch of Delaware River many miles below the forks of [14]Shehawkin proceeds to ascertain the 4th Monument he describes it thus "At the End of those Courses we placed the 4th Monument on a piece of low land full of Timber, a heap of Stones with a flat Stone standing on the Top marked No. 4 by a Butternut Tree marked with a Cross & No. 4 & four Notches." This Monument stands abt. 2 Chains from the River & 18 Chains to the Southward of the [Popaghtonk] or Branch or Crook of the River. Here it seems the Surveyor did not even dream of the West Branch as having any relation to his Survey but calls the Popaghtonk or East Branch simply *the* Branch or Crook of the River. He then proceeds and describes the 5th Monument to be at little distance up the papghtakan [sic] Branch, the sixth further up the said Branch the seventh at Popatonck Indian Village on the East Side which together with their Indian Treaty in 1743 & their two Indian Deeds in 1746 shews that Popakonk was not on the West Side of the Popaghtonk Branch as they have attempted to make appear in Evidence. The surveyor then proceeds to describe his Courses and Monuments up to the Head of the North Branch of the Popaghkonk & when he comes to the 12th Monument at Paghatakan Village he takes Notice of a large River coming from the East which is the River Tweed the Head of which is doubtless the true Boundary intended by the patent should it be tho't proper to admit of an Extension beyond the forks at Shehawkin.

The 17th & last Monument on the East Side of the Popaghtonk he described thus "At the End of all those Courses We came to the head of Paghatakan Branch where we made the 17th Monument *At the old Corner bounds made by Henry Worster.*" Which old Corner Bounds Ebenezer Worster says is a Spruce-pine Tree that had been made by Henry Worster marked with No. 3 & a cross & several other Spruce Trees marked standing by, Where says Ebenezer Worster We made a large Monument of Stone & marked a Flat one on the Top with No. 17 and a cross & 17 Notches. This Monument stands by a Swampside towards the upper End of the Swamp. The Swamp is about 4 Chains wide & near two miles long & is between two high mountains. Against the upper end of the mountains the monumt. stands. Thus it appears that Ebenezer

---

[14] Earlier in the Manuscript this river is called the Shewakin. Ante p. 116.

Worster the very person employed in the final Survey & in the Allotment of the Tract in order to a partition well knew and performed his Work under a Sense that the Popaghtonk Branch was the true Boundary of the patent, for what my Lord could he in any other View possibly mean by calling the placing where he fixed his 17th Monument the *old Corner Bounds of Henry Worster,* which evidently was the Corner Bounds made by him when Peter P. Low in the year 1743 attended him in his Survey up to the Popaghtonk to its head where Ebenezer Worster's 17th Monument is fixed and from thence across to the Head of Cartrix Kill. It is notorious that Henry Worster never attempted in his survey to make an Allotment in order to a decision of the Tract. He did no more than run two of the Outlines of the patent in Exact conformity with the Indian Treaty. In doing this he made his old Corner Bounds at the North head of the Popaghtonk which was Numbered 3 the first probably being at the Bounds of Minisink patent and the second at the Forks of Shewakin. And thus does this very Map of Ebenezer Worster which was made the foundation for a random division of the Lands between the two Branches appear clearly to correspond with the most natural Construction of the Words of the patent and the Sense of the original patentees discovered in Hardenbergh's Complaint to the Justice of Kingston ag[t]. the Indians for obstructing them in their Survey of the outlines of their patent in his Request of a permission from the Indians to run those outlines, their stipulation at the Treaty to permit him to run up the Popaghtonk as one of those uplines, the running of it by Worster in Consequence of that Treaty, & in the two Indian deeds to Hardenbergh & Company obtained after that Treaty. In Short my Lord, Ebenezer Worster's Map mentions not a syllable either of the West Branch or the Lands between the two Branches, & contains no Delineation of those Lands or of the West Branch. It appears to be properly & only a Survey of the Lands lying on the East side of the Popaghtonk. Of which [survey] the present proprietors have availed themselves by an Extension of the Lines of Allotment of those Lands so as to make a random Division of the Lands between the two Branches, on a supposed right which they never avowed but by their deed of partition executed between them above 40 years after the date of the patent & contrary to the their own prior & solemn declared sense in their Complaints, Treaties, Indian deeds & Surveys.

Had the Evidence been closed here on the former Hearing the Ballance would have stood Thus; On our Side the natural Construct[ion] of the patent itself, supported by solemn Action of the parties, a public Treaty with the Indians in the presence of a general meeting of the Magistrates, two Indian purchases clearly explanatory of Our Opponents Sense of the Bounds & repeated Surveys, all corresponding with those other pieces of Evidence; On their side only one insidious attempt by Ebenezer Worster in his last survey to make a survey down the West Branch, & a random partition of the Lands between the two Branches made without actual Survey & at the distance of upwards of 40 years after their patent issued. Which way upon this state of Evidence, the Ballance would preponderate they clearly saw. To cast therefore a little more Weight on their side of the scale they were prepared in the sundry Affidavits wearing the most suspicious Marks of Fraud which need not now be enumerated as their untoward appearance occasioned their total rejection, and this rejection the Opportunity of examining Witnesses *ore tenus* at this day on a single point of fact. But my Lord before I proceed to weigh this part of the Evidence I beg leave to observe (1) that if the persons[15] whose names were subscribed to those Affidavits really did swear to them, their Testimony even had it now come up to what they before swore would be much lessened in point of Credit because a regard to their Reputation would in some Measure oblige them to observe a consistency.

2dly That their Testimony depending on their Memories ought not to have equal Credit with the clear written Testimony on our part, especially as

3dly Their Testimony to have full Weight ought to go back to the Date of the patent which is upwards of 60 years old & this is absolutely impossible &

4thly because what they swear to can only be Matter of Information of a much later date furnished to them by Indians, whose Integrity is too weak to resist a Bribe, and we have proof that the Proprs. of the patent in Question have had it in Contemplation for many years past agt. their own most public, solemn & repeated [acts], to claim the Lands between the two forks which could only be performed by giving the name of the Fish Kill or Main Branch of Delaware River to the Mohawk Branch.

Under the influence of those observations I proceed as summarily as is possible to remark on the oral Testimony of this day[16].

[Summary of argument for Col. Bradstreet.] The Sum of this important controversy my Lord we take to be this. On our part we have been at the Expense of an Indian purchase regularly made of one of the Six Nations, whose property

---

[15] The names of Peter Kuydendal and Jacob Westfall are given in the margin at this point and appear to be the names of the witnesses testifying.

[16] A page of the manuscript is left vacant at this point to call the attention of the attorney to the oral testimony which may be submitted. He then summarizes his argument for Bradstreet.

we say the Lands in Controversy originally were. Our opponents claim a Right to them solely by patent & Indian purchases made near forty years after their patent, While it has been the invariable practice of the Govt. to make an Indian purchase precede a patent. We found the propriety of our Indian purchase upon a clear admission by deed of the Indians of whom they purchased, that the lands between the two Branches Belonged to the Mohawks, (2) On the known History of the Country, & on public Treaties all which shew clearly that the victorious Confederate Nations with the Mohawks at their Head have gained all the original property of the River Indians by Right of Conquest & that it was customary for the Conquerors to permit the Conquered to remain their Tenants at will but especially denied them the priviledge of Sale. On their part they have only shewn that the Indians or some of them of whom they purchased had merely a Residence on the Lands in Controversy and this Residence is not only consistent with the Supposition of the Right of Property in other Conquerors but can furnish no Argument that is not utterly annihilated by the express allowance in their deed of the Right of the Mohawks notwithstanding their Sale. And even were the two Indian Rights doubtful we have the Countenance of Govt. in a purchase regularly made by us at a great Expense to entitle to a preference.

Again tho' our Opponents ground their Claim of present Title solely on their patent we have shewn that this patent in the manner in which it was obtained was so irregular & unauthorized if not fraudulent as to be null & void, or at least to be justly subject from its Suspicious Circumstances to the most rigid Construction. That were it otherwise circumstanced our Construction of the Words of the patent would be confirmed by the Clearest Rules of Law which manifestly require that every patent granted upon the suggestion & petition of the party shall be construed most favorably for the Crown, that the Fish Kill is the Main Branch of the River below the forks of Shewakin, that at this place it divides itself into two Branches the West Commonly called the Mohawk or Cookhouse Sepoos, and Machach Sepoos, the East the Papataghan or Popaghtonk Sepoos. That therefore the Head of the Fishkill is properly at the forks of Shewakin which Construction is most favorable to the Crown. That should a less favorable Construction be adopted, the Fishkill will then appear to have several heads, that the East Branch consists of a union of three large Streams the North Branch, the River Tweed & the Beaver Kill, that tho its most distant Source is not quite so northerly as that of the West Branch yet not only from our Testimony but also from that of Mr Cockburn whom our Opponents sent up to make the Experiment the East Branch is larger swifter & discharges more water into the Main Body. That the Words of the patent "to the Head thereof" does not say which Head & it has several, if the forks at Shehawkin is not the proper Head. That therefore the most favorable construction for the Crown if we are to quit those forks will be furnished by the Head of the Tweed, that even should not the Crown be so favored yet the most northerly source of the East Branch, which Leaves all the Lands in Controversy vacant ought undoubtedly to be the Boundary. That this last Construction falls in with the clearest Weight of Evidence from without, & besides other proof, with their Indian Treaty their two Indian Deeds, their repeated Surveys and particularly their Map of the last Survey, & with their full & declared Sense & Construction for at least forty years after the date of their patent.

To stem all this Torrent of Evidence they have opposed nothing more than one attempt by Ebenezer Worster in his last survey to make a stolen survey of the West Branch contrary to the parts of the Treaty entered into with the Indians in presence of a large Assembly of Magistrates; their random partition after all those Transactions, which in itself is not Evidence, & finally the parol, [i. e., verbal] Testimony of some Witnesses speaking from their Memory about facts gained only on Hearsay & of much later date than the patent and probably gained entirely either directly or indirectly from Indians whose words are of little Weight & who may have been, as they all on any occasion may be, bribed to propagate forged names of places to Suit the Designs of a party; and finally as this lose [loose] heresay & uncertain Evidence stands opposed to the natural face of the Country, the Testimony of other Witnesses, the Words of the patent in the legal Construction, and a train of solemn public & notorious facts furnished by our Opponents & most of them standing on Record as a lasting Memorial of their Truth we flatter ourselves that the Ballance of evidence is clearly in our favor & if so, as the most liberal Construction that can be given to the patent in Question will confine our Opponents to the northern most head of the Popaghtonk Branch in which Case the Lands in Controversy must be vacant, We humbly pray that we may be favored with his Majesty's Letters patent for them upon the usual Terms & Conditions.

ADDITIONAL MANUSCRIPTS
OF THE FRENCH AND INDIAN WAR.

To any person in Springfield or Elsewhere that has the money major Ball Deliverd for Inlisting men for y̆ Ensuing Campaign. Be pleasd to pay it being Two thousand Dollars of Two hundred forty Pound notes making Twelve hundred pound of in the whole Eighteen hundred pound Lawful money to major John Buck who will Give Security to save you harmless of office of Humbl Sers

Timo Ruggles

March 13th 1760

PROCLAMATION BY BRIG. GENL. TIMOTHY RUGGLES. (See page 158.)

ADDITIONAL MANUSCRIPTS OF THE FRENCH AND INDIAN WAR.

1754. Shirley, W[illiam]. Boston. Commission to John
Sept. 10. Burk as Ensign in the Militia Regiment of Col. Israel Williams. Countersigned J[oseph] Willard. D. S. 1p.

1754. Williams, Israel. [Hatfield?] Letter to [John]
Sept. 10. Burk. Directions as to guarding Greenfield, Colrain and Fall Town; scouts to be maintained and information forwarded. A. L. S. 1p.

> The name Fall Town or Falltown was changed to Bernardstown or Bernardston, Mar. 6, 1762. The name Burk seems to have been changed to Burke by some members of the family after the close of the French war in 1763. The signature appears originally as John Burk and is so retained in this calendar.

1755. Shirley, W[illiam]. Council Chamber. [Boston].
Feb. 13. Message to the Council and House of Representatives of Massachusetts. Considers the times favorable for an expedition against Crown Point; attention of French divided between Nova Scotia and Ohio country; advantage to New England and New York of holding Crown Point; calls upon the two houses for a generous effort; promises his own regiment and all that he can do as chief executive of colony; suggests a feint attack by the Kennebec or Chaudiere river as likely to divide the French yet further. Cont. Copy in ms. of and attested by Thomas Clarke, Dpty. Secy. 3pp.

> Enclosed: Shirley, William. Instructions to Robert Hale, Feb. 22, 1755. Printed under date of Feb. 12 and

with other slight variations: N. H. Prov. Papers, Manchester, 1872, VI, 358; Penna. Col. Records, Harrisburg, 1851, VI, 314.

1755. **Massachusetts, General Court.** [Boston]. Com-
Feb. 18. mittee report on Messages of Gov. William Shirley with action of General Court thereon. Approve plan in messages of Feb. 13 and 15 for erecting fortress near Crown Point; consider an army of 5000 necessary for expedition; recommend that Governor request aid from other colonies in following proportion: New Hampshire 400, Connecticut 1000, Rhode Island 400 and New York 800 men; request employment of regiments of Shirley and [Sir William] Pepperrell; provisions for enlistment and pay for 1200 men from Massachusetts; application to be made to New Jersey for men; Gov. Shirley to appoint commander-in-chief and to notify British Government. "By Order J[ohn] Osborne." Report approved by House of Representatives, "T[homas] Hubbard, Spkr." and by Council, "Thomas Clarke Dpty. Secy." Cont. Copy in ms. of and attested by Clarke. 3pp.

> Enclosed: Shirley, William. Instructions to Robert Hale Feb. 22, 1755. Printed with slight changes N. H. Prov. Papers, Manchester 1872, VI, 359. Pa. Col. Records, Harrisburg 1851, VI, 316.

1755. **Shirley,** W[illiam]. Boston, Mass. To Robert
Feb. 22. Hale. Commissions Hale in the name of Massachusetts to apply to the Government of New Hampshire for aid in promoting the expedition [against Crown Point] approved by the Council and House of Representatives; will give more explicit instructions as to method of procedure. "By His Excellency's Command. J[osiah] Willard." Seal. D. S. 1p.

1755. **Shirley,** W[illiam]. Boston. To Robert Hale.
Feb. 22. "Instructions for soliciting" the Government of

Additional French War Manuscripts. 137

[Feb. 27.] New Hampshire to unite with Massachusetts, Rhode Island and Connecticut in an expedition against Crown Point: Is to present Shirley's message to Mass. Assembly [Feb. 13] and reply of that body [Feb. 18] to authorities of New Hampshire and urge coöperation; if colony will not agree to terms set forth in above documents Hale is to ascertain how much it will do and reasons for non agreement with plans as made; report to be made at Boston. P. S. Encloses vote of [Mass.] Assembly of Feb. 27 to be used if a larger number of men can be obtained thereby. L. S. with autograph postscript. 2pp.

1755. Shirley, W[illiam]. Boston. Letter to Gov. [Ben-
Feb. 25. ning Wentworth] of New Hampshire. Attitude of the French toward the English colonies in America; measures of retaliation authorized by the London government; proposed movements outlined in writer's message to the Massachusetts Assembly and reply received; encloses copies of these documents and Robert Hale will give further explanations if desired. L. S. 6pp.

See Message of Shirley of Feb. 13 and action on same Feb. 18 ante. p. 135.

1755. Massachusetts, General Court. [Boston]. Vote
Feb. 27. regarding Crown Point Expedition. In case Governments of New Hampshire, Rhode Island and Connecticut consent to proposed expedition against Crown Point desire Gov. [William Shirley] to issue proclamation for raising 4000 men as quota of Massachusetts; New York to be relied on for 800 men or proportionate share of provisions and other war stores in default of men; upon issuance of proclamation oath of secrecy removed from members of Assembly. "T[homas] Hubbard Spkr." "In Council—— read and concurred Thomas Clarke Dpty. Secy.

Consented to W[illiam] Shirley." Cont. Copy in ms. of and attested by Clarke. 1p.

<small>Enclosed in Shirley, William to Robert Hale Feb. 22-27, 1755.</small>

1755. **Wentworth,** [Benning]. Portsmouth. Letter to
Feb. 28. Gov. William Shirley. Acknowledges letters received giving plans against the French; agrees in the main with Shirley's proposals; asks advice as to best method of raising desired amount of money. Cont. Copy inclosed in Shirley to Robert Hale Mar. 4. 2pp.

<small>In Sir William Johnson Manuscripts ante p. 9.</small>

1755. **S[hirley],** W[illiam]. Boston. Letter to Gov.
Mar. 4. [Benning Wentworth]. Is gratified at Wentworth's approval of plans against Crown Point; outlines further plans against the French and Indians; hopes all the colonies involved may act in unison; united colonial troops to be under Sir William Johnson; [Maj.] General [Edward] Braddock to command British forces. Cont. Copy enclosed in Shirley to Robert Hale of equal date. 3pp.

<small>In Sir William Johnson Manuscripts ante p. 10.</small>

1755. **Shirley,** W[illiam]. Boston. Letter to Col.
Mar. 4. [Robert] Hale. Considers it advantageous for Hale to have copies of Gov. [Benning] Wentworth's letter [of Feb. 28] and his [Shirley's] reply [of Mar. 4] so encloses same; has "taken care of your friend Capt. [Jonathan] Bagley"; Commissioners for Rhode Island, [Thomas] Hutchinson, for New York and New Jersey [Thomas Pownall] and for Pennsylvania [Josiah Quincy] have gone to obtain aid from those colonies; thinks Gov. [Benning] Wentworth will be ready to see him [Hale] by the time the latter reaches Portsmouth and hopes visit will be a profitable one. A. L. S. 1p.

Additional French War Manuscripts. 139

1755. **Welles,** Samuel and John **Choat.** [Hartford, Conn.]
Mar. 14. Letter to [Josiah] Willard, Secy. of Massachusetts. On Mar. 13 presented to Gov. [Thomas Fitch] and both branches of Assembly of Connecticut the plan proposed by Massachusetts for the expedition against Crown Point; having received from [Thomas] Hutchinson news of the favorable actions of Rhode Island presented that among other arguments for action by Connecticut but did not show the Rhode Island act; expect to obtain full quota and possibly more from the Assembly. Cont. Copy in ms. of and attested by Thomas Clarke Dpty. Secy. P. S. Auto. Note of Gov. William Shirley, by whom this copy is forwarded to Robert Hale, stating what portion of letter had been forwarded to Gov. Wentworth of N. H. 2pp.

Welles and Choate had been sent to Connecticut by the Massachusetts General Court as commissioners to advance the cause of the expedition mentioned. For names of Commissioners to other colonies see preceding entry. The spelling Choat is that of the manuscript and has been followed in title.

1755. [**Hale,** Robert]. Portsmouth. Letter to [Gov.
Mar. 14. William Shirley]. Upon receipt of Shirley's letter [of Mar. 4] Hale started for Portsmouth Mar. 8 and arrived Mar. 9; [Gov. Benning] Wentworth unwilling that he see any legislators except the Secy. [Theodore Atkinson] until the Assembly met [Mar. 12]; reports progress made as to raising troops for service; in 1745 New Hampshire had but 7000 rateable polls and the state considers herself on the same footing as Rhode Island; no disposition to make allowance for what "we" [Massachusetts] did in 1754; thinks New Hampshire will provide 300 troops if kept in garrison; pleased that R. I. has come up to her quota; difficulties caused by counterfeit colonial paper; fears that much other aid

is not to be obtained from N. H.; reasons for hoping that [John] Titcomb will be given post of Lt. Col. A. L. 2pp. Incomplete.

1755. H[ale], R[obert]. Portsmouth. Letter [to Gov.
Mar. 15. William Shirley]. Acknowledges letters of Shirley dated Mar. 14; laid enclosures before Gov. [Benning] Wentworth and his secretary; effect of Shirley's message upon the legislature; Hale's personal efforts with [Peter] Gilman, [Theodore] Atkinson and others; expects a report on 17th favoring 600 men with subsistence to point of rendezvous; will move for more men conditional on New York furnishing subsistence; many think New Hampshire should not be asked for half so many men as Massachusetts; doubts if so many can be secured with population but one-sixth as large; all wonder why the General Court of Massachusetts considered itself warranted in fixing the quota each colony should raise. A. L. S. 3pp.

1755. Shirley, W[illiam]. Boston. Letter to Col. [Robert]
Mar. 16. Hale. Acknowledges letters of 14th from Hale and from Gov. [Benning] Wentworth; encloses copy of answer to latter; opinion on proposed feint along the Chaudiere; hints regarding boundary dispute between Massachusetts and New Hampshire; thinks latter colony more interested in solution of troubles with French than is Rhode Island so her quota for Crown Point expedition placed at a larger number; has perfect confidence in Hale's judgment; desires that copies of letters forwarded him be returned as originals have been mislaid. A. L. S. 3pp.

[1755]. H[ale]. R[obert. Portsmouth]. Letter [to Gov.
[Mar. 18]. William Shirley.] From conversation with Col. [Timothy] Ruggles and Capt. [Jonathan] Bagley

has concluded that salaries paid colonial army officers are much too small; bad results of policy; more attention must be paid to forwarding ammunition and supplies; hopes Shirley will look into matters himself; lack of supplies noted by Capt. [John] Osborne; no cannon at Albany until Aug. 2; welcomes [Maj. Genl. John] Winslow as commander [of Massachusetts troops]; praises appointments of Col. [John] Plaisted and Col. [Richard] Gridley; desires no command for himself and asks that his nephew R[obert] H. Chipman may not be compelled to serve as he is in poor health; recommends Capt. John Lee jr. of Manchester. Auto. Draft Signed. 3pp. Incomplete.

1755. Shirley, William. Boston. Letter to Col. [Robert]
Mar. 19. Hale. Regrets difficulty with Col. [Peter] Gilman mentioned in letter of 14th [15th]; knows nothing of Lt. [Richard] Emery but thinks he "may be an officer of Sir William Pepperrell's Regiment"; hopes that obstacles will be removed [as regards raising men for campaign]; will give up such men as [Joseph] Malcolm has obtained; has directed [Ephraim] Berry to adjourn Inferior Court as requested. A. L. S. 1p.

1755. Hale, Robert. Portsmouth. Letter to [Gov.
Mar. 21. William Shirley]. Assembly passed report of committee on raising men [for campaign against Crown Point] but agreed to 400 troops only; difficulties as to procuring appropriation for expenses of expedition; personal efforts with officials raised the number to 500; encloses copy of resolution to that effect just signed by Gov. [Benning Wentworth]; is gratified that so many were secured when length of boundary of New Hampshire is considered and when compared with contribution of Connecticut. A. L. S. 2pp.

1755. New York, Assembly. New York. Committee
Mar. 27. report on message of Lt. Gov. [James DeLancey]
with action of Assembly thereon. Matter considered is expedition against Crown Point;
report made by [William] Nicoll[s] chairman of
Committee; Committee united with Committee
of Council in consideration of message of Mar.
26; approve plan proposed by Gov. [William]
Shirley of Mass. and explained by Lt. Gov.
[De Lancey] and Thomas Pownall; recommend
that colony supply 800 men if British Commander in Chief [Sir William Johnson] approve
and if Mass. raise and subsist 1400 men or 1200
for Crown Point and 200 for a diversion up the
Kennebec; Assembly agreed unanimously as
did the Council and joint committee appointed
to report to Lt. Gov. DeLancey. "By Abrm.
Lott jr. Clk. Assem." Copy in ms. of and
attested by Thomas Clarke. 2pp.

It is possible that by "British Commander in Chief"
Maj. Genl. Edward Braddock is meant. See: Shirley
to Wentworth, Mar. 4, 1755. Ante p. 10.

1755. Massachusetts, General Court. [Boston]. Action
Mar. 29. regarding Crown Point Expedition. In Council:
Committee of War authorized to appoint one or
more delegates to meet in conference with
delegates from other colonies interested; conference to apportion stores necessary for expedition against Crown Point among several Colonies; "sent down for Concurrence T[homas]
Clarke, Dpty. Secry." In the House of Representatives: "Read and Concur'd T[homas] Hubbard Spkr." "Consented to, W[illiam] Shirley."
Copy signed and attested by Clarke. 1p.

1755. Shirley, W[illiam]. Boston. To John Burk.
Mar. 29. Commission as Capt-Lieut. in regiment of Col.
Ephraim Williams. Countersigned J[oseph]
Willard. D. S. 1p.

Additional French War Manuscripts. 143

1755. **Massachusetts, General Court, Committee.** Boston.
Apr. 10. To [Robert] Hale. Consider it necessary for Hale to go to Portsmouth at once; is to inform New Hampshire Assembly that by reason of encouragement given by that body, Massachusetts and other governments have engaged for the expedition against Crown Point; Massachusetts has voted to raise 1500 men in place of the 1200 at first proposed and Committee hope New Hampshire will exert herself correspondingly. L. S. "J[ohn] Osborne In the Name of the Committee." 1p.

1755. **Williams**, Ephraim. Deerfield. Letter to John
Apr. 11. Burk. Offers Burk position of Capt–Lieut. in his regiment for expedition against Crown Point; desires that only good men be enlisted; Simeon Wells to be sergeant of company; conditions of enlistment for privates; wishes early reply and names of men going to join Col. [Israel] Williams at Hatfield. A. L. S. 1p.

> The important officers of this regiment were Col. Ephraim Williams, Lt. Col. Seth Pomeroy, Maj. Noah Ashley, Surg. Thomas Williams, Surg. mate Perez Marsh, Chaplain Stephen Williams, Commissary Eleazer Burt, Adjutant Philip Richardson, Armorer John P. Bull.

1755. **Williams**, Israel. [Hatfield.] Letter to John Burk.
May 1. Consents to dismissal of Sergt. [William] Patrick from service and suggests that [Ebenezer] Sheldon succeed him; present rank of latter can be no higher than Corporal; outlines conduct expected in the office. A. L. S. 1p.

1755. **Williams**, Elijah. [Stockbridge, Mass.] To Col-
Jun. 17. ony of Massachusetts. Account for expenses in building Fort Williams Sep. 1754–Apr. 1755. Account amounts to £11. 14s. 1¾d. and is attested before Joseph Dwight, Justice of Peace of Hampshire Co. It is addressed to Lt. Samuel Brown or Col. Joseph Dwight. A. D. S. 1p.

1755.　[**Williams,** Israel.] To Moses Emerson. Receipt
Jul. 15.　for powder and supplies received Jul. 1–15 at
　　　　the hands of John Burk. A. D. 1p.

1755.　**Orme,** [Robert]. [Fort Cumberland.] To Com-
Jul. 18.　modore Augustus Keppel. Account of the
　　　　battle on the Monongahela Jul. 9. Account
　　　　describes behavior of officers and soldiers on
　　　　English side and gives estimates of losses. In
　　　　ms. of Keppel's secretary. 4pp.

　　　　Enclosed: Keppel to Gov. Charles Lawrence, Jul. 26, 1755.

[1755.]　[**Shirley,** William. Fort Cumberland. To Com-
[Jul. 18.]　modore Augustus Keppel.] "A List of the
　　　　Officers who were present and of those killed
　　　　and wounded in the action on the banks of the
　　　　Monongahela." List contains 86 names headed
　　　　by that of "His Excelency Edwd. Braddock—
　　　　Died of his wounds." Of the officers 63 are
　　　　noted as killed or wounded and this is followed
　　　　by the statement: "About 600 men killed and
　　　　wounded." Cont. Copy in hand of James
　　　　Bradford Secy. to Shirley. 3pp.

　　　　Enclosed: Keppel to Gov. Charles Lawrence Jul. 26, 1755. Contemporary lists differing however in the spelling of names are found in the Minutes of the Provincial Council of Pennsylvania for Jul. 24, 1755, the Pennsylvania Gazette of Jul. 31 and elsewhere. In none are full names given.

1755.　**Keppel,** A[ugustus]. *Sea Horse* at Sea. To Gov.
Jul. 26.　[Charles] Lawrence of Nova Scotia. Acknowl-
　　　　edges letters received; is kept from visiting him
　　　　by defeat of [Maj. Genl. Edward] Braddock;
　　　　encloses letters of [George] Washington and others
　　　　giving details; loss of prestige to British arms;
　　　　other comment; congratulates Lawrence on his
　　　　success in expedition across the bay. A. L. S. 2pp.

　　　　This letter and its enclosures are printed in full on p. 171 ff., where are supplied the full names of officers mentioned in Shirley's list.

Additional French War Manuscripts. 145

1755. **Stebbings,** John. Lake George. Receipt for mil-
Sep. 22. itary outfit belonging to late Robert Royan,
with enumeration of goods received. D. S. 1p.

1755. **Massachusetts,** House of Representatives. Order
Dec. 11. naming a committee of five to which the Council
may join others to consider the affairs of the
French inhabitants of Nova Scotia who have
been brought into this Government. On verso is
oath required from inhabitants in 1761. Cont.
ms. 1p.

1756. **Sinclair,** Sir John. New York. Receipt Book
Mar. 16-24. giving an account of the men employed in the
batteau service in America. The volume contains
lists of 24 companies and signed receipts of 1039
officers and men; these persons "acknowledge
to have voluntarily enlisted for the transporting
of provisions for His Majesty's service in battoes according to the advertisement published
by [Maj.] Genl. [William] Shirley dated Jan. 19,
1756" and they further acknowledge "to have
received from Sir John St. Clair [Sinclair] Dep.
Q. M. Genl. twenty days pay—the Captains
at eight shillings, the Assistants at six and the
Battoe men at four shillings a day." 1039
signatures: 24 and 30pp., 1 vol.

> The names of the captains of the companies follow in
> the order of their signatures: Daniel De Normandie,
> Daniel Sutton, Jonathan Woodroff, James Cusick, Abra-
> ham Van Duerson, William Line, Peter Jaquet, John
> Salmon, John McDougall, John Ten Broek, John Lawrence,
> Thomas Deare, Samuel Neilson, Samuel Askwith, Jacobus
> Wyncoop, George Knaggs, Isaiah Valleau, Joseph Riggs,
> John Egan, Hendrick Seydam, John Brown, John Emott,
> and John Atkins.

1756. **White,** Jonathan; **Richardson,** Philip and John
May 6. **Stebbings.** Boston. Bond to Massachusetts
Colony. Amount of warrants received by each
from the treasurer of the province "to subsist

our respective companies to Albany"; agree to return to Committee of War list of names of men in respective companies and surplus of money if number is not equal to that stated. A. D. S. of White. D. S. of others. 2pp.

<small>The signers were Captains in the regiment of Col. Timothy Ruggles.</small>

1756.
Jun. 5.
Winslow, J[ohn.] Camp at Half Moon. [Albany.] Return of troops. A return of the Provincial troops raised by the Governments of Massachusetts Bay, Connecticut, New York and Rhode Island with the numbers stationed at certain named posts. The troops were raised for the reduction of Crown Point and the posts given are Fort William Henry, Fort Edward, Upper Saratoga, Lower Saratoga, Stillwater and Half Moon; reports other men under Lt. Col. [Jonathan?] Hoar and Maj. [Jonathan] Star as yet on the road. The total is 4170 with artillery. D. S. 1p.

1756.
Jun. 22.
Gridley, Isaac. [Fall Town.] To John Burk. Account of clothing furnished Burk's Company. Account amounts to £ 51. 17 s. 2 d. On verso in ms. of Burk are notes of various additions and deductions to account of Commissary Gridley. A. D. S. 1p.

1755–6.
Crown Point Expedition. [Boston.] Two Tables for computing the wages of the officers and soldiers [from Massachusetts] in the Crown Point expedition. With these tables are two manuscripts classifying the number of officers and men [from Massachusetts] taking part in the Crown Point Expedition with pay of each group. 5pp. with attached slips.

1757.
Jan. 14.
Massachusetts, General Court. To the Committee on the Muster rolls. Resolution of the House

Additional French War Manuscripts. 147

Jan. 17. of Representatives providing method for computing wages of officers and soldiers who enlisted for the expedition [of 1755] against Crown Point sent up for concurrence of Council. T[homas] Hubbard Spkr. In Council: Read and concurred. Thos. Clarke Dpty. Secy. Consented to S[pencer] Phips. Copy examined, A[ndrew] Oliver, Secy. 2pp.

1757. **Burk,** John. Boston, [Mass.] Muster roll of com-
Feb. 23. pany under command of. 36 names on roll, among them 3 deserters and 4 Indians. The list appears to include but a section of Burk's full company and as frequently is the case in these early rolls the word deserter has not the full significance of later days often meaning no more than absent at time of roll call. Cont. Copy. 1p.

1757. **Partridge,** Oliver. Hatfield. Letter to John Burk.
Mar. 30. Has received commission of Captain in [Massachusetts] service for Burk and of Lieutenant for Selah Barnard; requests Burk to notify latter and both to repair to Hatfield [to take oath of service]. A. L. S. 1p.

1757. [**Burk,** John. Fall Town?] List of men to form
Mar. portion of Command of. A list of the names of men raised from the northern regiment in the county of Hampshire for his majesty's service under the command of the Earl of Loudon; 70 names with place of residence. Cont. Copy. 1p.

1757. **Denny,** William. Philadelphia. To Archibald
Aug. 13. Kennedy. Acknowledges receipt of two letters, latter informing him of surrender of Fort William Henry and attack on Fort Edward; Pennsylvania has no militia but will recommend to the Assembly that assistance be given him. Cont. Copy. 1p.

1757.   Winslow, John. [Boston.] Letter to Maj. Elipha-
Aug. 17.   let Pond. Orders Pond to march with his
detachment to Springfield where he is to place
himself under the direction of Sir William
Pepperell; postscript directs Pond to halt at
Worcester for camp on evening of August 18.
L. S. with autograph postscript. 1p.

1757.   Pownall, Thomas. Boston. To Benjamin Hallo-
Aug. 27.   well jr. Commission as Captain of His Majesty's
ship *King George*. D. S. of Pownall certified
by Thomas Clarke, Dep. Secy. 1p.

1757.   Newhall, Jonathan. Stockbridge, [Mass.] Certifi-
Sep. 5.   cate that 31 men have been billeted on inhabitants of Stockbridge, for three weeks; men were
from the regiment of Col. John Chandler jr
D. S. 1p.

1757.   Hale, Robert. Chronicle of the War against the
Oct. 30.   French and Indians. This chronicle is stated
as beginning Jul. 1, 1755 but rough notes of
occurrences as early as Oct. 18, 1748 are given.
Important events of the war against the French
and Indians are noted as also summaries of
legislative proceedings and popular feeling;
occurrences in New England and the North are
followed with more detail than corresponding
movements in the South and West. The Chronicle continues until Oct. 30, 1757 and is continued by a second part Nov. 1, 1757—April
30, 1761, and a third covering May 1, 1761—
Oct. 30, 1762. See entry under later of given
dates for each volume. A. D. 56 pp.; 1 vol.

1757.   Woodbridge, Timothy. [Worcester.] To the pro-
Nov. 7.   vince [of Massachusetts]. Amounts due to 13
named persons; expenses for billeting soldiers
under command of Capt. [Jonathan] Newhall

until troops were ordered by Sir William Pepper[r]ell; total is £18. 12 s. D. S. 1p.

[1757].
[Nov. 17.]
Burk, John. Boston.] Muster roll of Company under command of. 23 names on roll, among whom are noted the men who have been enrolled since Feb. 12, two who never joined and five deserters. The list appears to include but a section of Burk's company. Cont. Copy. 1p.

1757.
Dec. 26.
Lane, Edmund. [Fort Cumberland.] Court Martial of. Record of Court Martial proceedings in case of Edmund Lane of Capt. [Benoni] Danks company of rangers in regiment of Lt. Col. Hunt Walsh. Court of six members, Capt. Theodore Augustus Spann, President; Lane found guilty of fighting and making a disturbance, and sentenced to 100 lashes. Sentence confirmed by "Hunt Walsh Lieut. Col." D. S. of Spann 1p.

1757.
[**Massachusetts.**] Clothing supplied for provincial troops. List of coats, blankets etc. sent to Worcester by various persons to provide for troops at that place. Cont. ms. 1p.

[1757?]
Worthington, [John.] List of certain men in regiment of. "A List of those absent, sick, deserted, absent by leave etc. raised in Col. Worthington's regiment." 32 names. Endorsed: List of soldiers left behind. Cont. ms. 1p.

1758.
Aug. 4.
Danks, Benoni. Fort Cumberland. Roll of Company of. Roll contains names of 57 men of whom 42 are privates. See: Danks, Benoni, Roll Feb. 20, 1761. Cont. ms. 1p. Mutilated.

1758.
Aug. 20–
Sep. 11.
Bagley, Jonathan. Orderly Book of the Massachusetts regiment commanded by Col. Bagley when in provincial camp at Lake George. 34pp. 1 vol.

1758.　**Herres,** William.　Holden, [Mass.] Certificate of
Sep. 15.　service of son. Certifies that his son Valentine
Herres enlisted in Capt. [John] Patton's Company of Gov. [William] Shirley's regiment and
was captured at Oswego. A. D. S. 1p.

1758.　**Williams,** Israel. Hatfield. Letter to John Burk.
Sep. 29.　Death of [John] Catlin makes Capt. Burk the
senior captain on the frontier service [in regiment]; directs him to repair to Colrain and
other frontier posts to see that service is maintained; other directions. A. L. S. 1p.

1758.　**Fort William Henry,** Diary of a soldier stationed
Sep. 15–　at. The record begins with an account of life
Nov. 15.　at the fort; describes such incidents of the war
as the arrival and departure of troops, actions
between opposing forces and rumors of movements by the French or Indians. The volume
contains descriptions of Courts-martial, notes
of frontier life and closes with the record of a
march from Fort William Henry to Albany by
way of Fort Edward, Saratoga, Stillwater and
Half Moon. 12pp. Bound with a Diary of an
Expedition to Louisburgh etc. May 15, 1759–
Sep. 24, 1760. See entry under latter date
post p. 160.

1758.　**Pynchon,** Joseph. Deerfield. Letter to John Burk.
Nov. 26.　Requests names of men on Burk's roll that commissary's account may be prepared. A. L. S. 1p.

1759.　**Hutchinson,** Israel. [Boston?] To Gov. Thomas
Mar. 1.　Pownall and the General Court of Massachusetts.
Petitioner was a Lieut. in company of Capt.
Andrew Fuller and regiment of Col. Jonathan
Bagley in expedition of 1758 against Canada;
mishaps suffered at "Ticondaroga" form basis
of petition for relief; certificates offered to
support claim. A. D. S. 1p.

Additional French War Manuscripts. 151

[1759]. Fellows, [John] and others. "A List of the men
Feb. 23– enlisted above the Green Woods" by Capt.
Mar. 6. Fellows, [Paul] Dewey, [William] King and
[Josiah] Church. 70 names are given and mention is made of one deserter. Cont. ms. 1p.

1759. Ruggles, Timothy. [Boston.] Letter to Capt.
Mar. 27. John Burk. Has appointed Burk Captain in his own regiment; directs him to apply to Col. Israel Williams of the militia for 90 men; latter will raise this number and turn them over to Burk who will be accountable for them thereafter. L. S. 1p.

> On verso in the manuscript of Burk is a Table giving expenses of travel from Springfield to Boston May 17-21, with notes of stopping places on way.

1759. Pownall, T[homas]. Boston. Commissions to
Mar. 31. Cornelius Stowell and William Henshaw as 1st and 2d Lieutenants respectively in companies of Capts. William Paige and Jeduthan Baldwin of regiment commanded by Brig. Genl. Timothy Ruggles. Ds. S. Certified by A[ndrew] Oliver, Secy. 1p. each.

1759. Pierce, Benjamin. Hampshire County. Enlist-
Apr. 2. ment papers. Acknowledgment of enlistment in service for invasion of Canada. Countersigned by Joseph Hawley, Justice of Peace of County of Hampshire. D. S. 1p.

[1759.] Ingersoll, Joseph. Boston. Letter to William
Apr. [10.] Henshaw. Notifies him that he has been appointed a Lieutenant under Brig. Genl. [Timothy] Ruggles for the campaign against Canada, and directs him to repair to Worcester for orders. A. L. S. 1p.

1759. Waldo, Samuel jr. Falmouth. [Portland Me.]
Apr. 13. Letter to William Brattle. Encloses regimental

return; 50 men for Canada of whom four are in navy; expects 150 are with the Penobscot expedition. A. L. S. 1p.

1759. Henshaw, Jonathan. [Leicester.] To William
Apr. 14. Henshaw. Account for military equipment to sum of £ 14. 12 s. 4 d. for which a note has been received. In ms. of William Henshaw. 1p.

1759. [Burk, John. Deerfield, Mass.] Billeting roll of
May 1. company under command of. 29 names [constituting the last division of company by alphabetical arrangement] with cost of billeting from date of enlistment to Apr. 30, 1759; date of enlistment varies in different cases. Cont. Copy. 1p.

1759. Pownall, T[homas]. Boston. To Jonathan Hol-
May 11. man. Commission as 1st Lieutenant in company of Jeremiah Learnard of regiment commanded by Col. Abijah Willard. D. S. of Pownall, certified by A[ndrew] Oliver. In absence
May 18. of Gov. Pownall Lt. Gov. Thomas Hutchinson certifies that Holman took the oaths required by Parliament and Provincial law. A. N. S. 1p.

[1759.] Burk, John. [Deerfield, Mass.] Billeting roll of
May 13. company under command of. 102 names with amount due for billeting each from date of enlistment to May 13. See Ruggles to Burk
Jun. 1. Mar. 27, 1759. A similar roll compiled Jun. 1 follows giving amounts due to May 26 and containing many signatures apparently as receipts for sums named. A. Ds. S. 3pp. and 1p.

1759. Whiting, Leonard. Detachment at Fort Edward.
Jun. 13. List of men detached from regiment of Brig. Genl. Timothy Ruggles on garrison duty at Fort Edward. 91 names. In ms. of William Henshaw. 1p.

Additional French War Manuscripts. 153

1759.　**Henshaw,** Daniel. Leicester. Letter to William
Jun. 23.　Henshaw. Acknowledges letter of Jun. 13 and
is pleased to know of his continued good health;
war news that has reached Leicester; capture
of French Man of War. A. L. S. 1p.

1759.　**Whiting,** Leonard. Fort Edward. Proceedings of
Jul. 10.　a garrison Court Martial consisting of Capt.
Whiting and four others in the cases of Donald
Curry, Thomas Muffett and Jacob Jones. Cont.
Copy by William Henshaw. 2pp.

1759.　**Kenfield,** George and others. Camp at Lake
Jul. 11.　George. To John Burk. Receipt for one King's
arm to each person. D. S. George Kenfield,
Aaron Petty, Ephraim Smith. 1p.

1759.　**Burk,** John. Lake George. To Josiah Brewer.
Jul. 12.　Order on Brewer for goods to value of three
shillings in favor of Joshua Gibbs. Similar
orders of Jul. 28 and 31 are drawn by Burk on
Brewer in favor of William Gray and John Rugg
respectively. A. Ds. S. 1p. each.

1759.　**Baldwin,** Jeduthan. [Fort Edward.] Troops com-
[July.]　manded by. A List of officers and privates
under Capt. Jeduthan Baldwin enlisted in the
first battalion of [Brig.] Genl. [Timothy] Ruggles
of which battalion Lt. Col. Joseph Ingersoll
was commander. Names of three additional
commissioned officers and 58 non commissioned
officers and privates are given. Cont. Copy. 1p.

1759.　**Elmer,** Samuel. Fort Edward. To John Burk.
Aug. 3.　Order upon Burk to amount of £ 1. 12 s. 5 d.
to be stopped from Elmer's wages in favor of
Josiah Brewer and in payment of enclosed note
to Brewer for above amount. Benjamin Edgell
is witness to both note and order. Ds. S.
1p. each.

1759. **Burk,** John. Crown Point. To Josiah Brewer.
Aug. 10. Order upon Brewer for goods to value of twelve shillings in favor of John Rugg. A. D. S. of Ebenezer Bardwell "in behalf of Capt. John Burk." 1p.

1759. **Partridge,** Oliver. Hatfield. Letter to John Burk.
Aug. 10. Congratulates Burk on successes thus far obtained; requests forwarding of news; mentions reduction of Niagara, progress of [James] Wolfe, affairs in Virginia and visit from Lt. [Ebenezer] Sheldon. A. L. S. 1p.

1759. **Williams,** Israel. Hatfield. Letter to John Burk.
Aug. 13. Acknowledges letters and congratulates Burk on success at Crown Point; "this may be the day of vengeance upon our enemies;" no news from [Maj.] Genl. [Daniel] Webb; fragments of news from Europe; troops leaving No. 4 [Charlestown, N. H.] presumably for Burk's support; hopes there will be no trouble between reenforcements and former men. A. L. S. 2pp.

1759. **Wyer,** David. Annapolis Royal. Letter to Samuel Curwen. Account of skirmishing and conflicts in and near Annapolis. A. L. S. 2pp.
Aug. 29.

1759. **Whiting,** Leonard. Fort Edward. Proceedings of a garrison Court Martial consisting of Capt. Whiting and four others in case of John Munn. Cont. Copy by William Henshaw. 1p.
Sep. 2.

[1759.] **Henshaw,** William. [Fort Edward.] Return of 49 men under command of Lieut. Henshaw with names and limited description of persons in company. A. D. S. 1p. Mutilated.
Sep. [26].

1759. **Curtis,** Zacheus. Plymouth. To Gov. Thomas Pownall and the General Court of Massachusetts. Petitions for remuneration for loss of his appren-
Oct. 3.

Additional French War Manuscripts. 155

tice Francis Finney for two years; Finney enlisted in company of Capt. Samuel Nicols Nelson for expedition against Crown Point; was captured at Fort William Henry and kidnapped by Indians; broke away in 1759; came to Ticonderoga and on capture of that post was allowed by Sir [Jeffery] Amherst to return to Plymouth; result is loss of two years' service and other extra expense. A. D. S. Finney's oath to truth of statement is attested before Thomas Foster, Justice of Peace. A. N. S. of Foster. 1p.

1759. [Henshaw, William.] Fort Edward. Return of
Oct. 24. garrison at Fort Edward. A monthly return of the state of the Garrison at Fort Edward; portions of eight regiments given making 344 men of all classes in the Garrison. A. D. 1p.

1759. Whiting, Leonard. Fort Edward. Proceedings of
Oct. 30. a garrison Court Martial consisting of Capt. Whiting and four others in cases of Thomas Moffett and Mathias Duyce. Cont. Copy by William Henshaw. 1p.

1759. Lawrence, Sir Charles. Halifax. To Capt-Lieut. John
Nov. 15. Walker. Directs Walker to proceed with Capt. [Benoni] Dank's company of rangers and relieve Capt. [Jotham] Gay with his provincials at Fort Edward; is to obtain from Capt. Gay account of stores etc. belonging to garrison and give receipt therefor; one-third of company to be on duty each day; further directions. Countersigned Archd. Hinshelwood Secy. D. S. 2pp.

1759. Henshaw, William. Orderly Book for the expedi-
May 9- tion to Fort Edward with later notes. The
Nov. 28. volume has a list of the officers and men of Capt. Jeduthan Baldwin's Company in which Henshaw served as 2d Lieut., begins with the

regimental orders at Worcester May 9, and follows the march until the arrival at Fort Edward Jun. 5, 1759. After this date are found orders as issued at Fort Edward [N. Y.] until Nov. 9, together with many of Henshaw's private notes. During November the location of camp varies as the expedition against Crown Point is assumed, and the final entry of the war is dated at Rutland, Mass., Nov. 28, when the company broke ranks. Later notes to 1773 are of a miscellaneous character. A. D. 174 and 42pp. 1 vol.

A facsimile reproduction of two pages of this Orderly Book faces p. 181 where begins the print of the manuscript.

1759. **Crown Point,** Diary of a soldier stationed at.
May 16– The record begins with an account of conditions
Nov. 28. at Albany and notes of the march from Springfield thither; this is followed by notes of march to Saratoga and description of local events about Crown Point; the most common entry until November being "nothing extraordinary." Appended to the diary proper are various orders for the first battalion of Brig. Genl. [Timothy] Ruggles's regiment by [Cornelius Stowell and] Joseph Ingersoll; other entries of a later date and disconnected with the Crown Point campaign follow. 43pp. 1 vol.

1759. **Massachusetts,** "Book of Balances". This volume
[Dec.] contains the names of soldiers representing the colony of Massachusetts in the French and Indian war during 1759 and to whom there is money yet due. In some cases the individual names of privates are omitted but total company numbers are given. The volume contains also receipts from officers and from many privates for monies received. 25pp. 1 vol.

Additional French War Manuscripts. 157

[1759]. [**Burk,** John. Crown Point?] A List of men that came in Maj. [John] Hawks detachment. This list gives the names of 27 men belonging to Brig. Genl. Timothy Ruggles's regiment who accompanied Hawks by the road to No. 4 with accounts of billeting, etc. On verso is receipt of William Jennison to John Burk for money received for Thomas Haywood [Heywood.] A. D. 1p.

[1759.] **Burk,** John. [Fall Town.] Roll of company under command of. This roll gives the names of 101 men including officers, with date of enlistment and occasional notes as to the 97 privates. Cont. mss. 4pp.

[1759.] [**Burk,** John. Fall Town.] Account of money disbursed. "Account of the 2d billeting money which I have paid out & to whome." 9 officers mentioned as receiving money and goods with amount given each. Auto. ms. 1p.

[1759.] **Hawks,** G[ershom. Fort Charlemont.] List of soldiers at Fort Charlemont under command of. List comprises names of 11 men under Hawks and 10 men of "Taylor's garrison" under command of Sergt. Othniel Taylor. Cont. ms. 1p.

1760.   **Willard,** Nahum. Worcester. To the Colony of
Jan. 29.   Massachusetts. Bill for services as physician and surgeon to Colonial troops Dec. 25, 1758 to Aug. 10, 1759, 119 cases. Sworn to before Jacob Wendell, Boston, Jan 31, 1760. A. D. S. of Willard with A. N. S. of Wendell. 11pp.

1760.   **Dimuck,** Gideon. [Springfield.] Enlistment papers.
Feb. 19.   Acknowledgment of enlistment in provincial service and receipt of bounty money from Capt. Trastrum [Tristram] Davis with signed

attestation of John Worthington dated Mar. 5 D. S. 1p.

> Similar enlistment papers for Luke Day, Benjamin Knight, George Larkin, Edmond Murphy and Josiah Ward jr. are in this collection. All are attested by Worthington.

1760. **Warner,** Ichabod. [Fall Town?] Enlistment papers.
Feb. 24. Acknowledgment of enlistment in provincial service and receipt of bounty money from John Burk with signed attestation of Israel Williams dated Mar. 5. D. S. 1p.

> Similar enlistment papers for Thomas Elgar and Thomas Stanley are in this collection. Both are attested by Williams.

1760. **Ruggles,** Timothy. [Springfield.] Proclamation.
Mar. 13. Notifies any person having money received by Maj. [Francis] Ball for enlistments to pay same to Maj. John Burk. A. D. S. 1p.

> This proclamation is reproduced in facsimile facing p. 135.

1760. **Ruggles,** Timothy. Boston. Letter to John Burk.
Mar. 31. All men enlisted in Hampshire County to hold themselves ready to march at shortest notice to rendezvous selected; that provision for commissions and supplies may be made, return of numbers enlisted by various officers and account of previous service to be forwarded at once; time for enlistment extended to Apr. 15. L. S. 1p.

1760. **Ruggles,** Timothy. Boston. Letter to John Burk.
Apr. 2. Exhaustion of bounty money by supplying recruiting officers; directs Burk to call upon such of their number as have funds remaining in case of enlistment of additional new recruits. L. S. 1p.

1760. **Harris,** John. [Springfield.] Enlistment papers.
Apr. 15. Acknowledgment of enlistment in provincial service and receipt of bounty money from Lieut.

Joseph Thompson, with signed attestation of John Worthington dated Apr. 24, D. S. 1p.

1760. Goffe, John. Camp. [N. H.] Letter to Lt. John
[Apr.] 23. Parker. Need of provisions as movements are extended away from the [Connecticut] river; urges that wagons loaded with both flour and meat be hurried on from Number 4 [Charlestown, N. H.] and that nothing but king's stores be allowed on the wagons; Lt. [Othniel] Taylor should be allowed ten days provisions; is to communicate instructions to Lt. Timothy Bedloe. A. L. S. 1p.

1760. Paine, Timothy. Worcester. To [John] Burk.
Apr. 29. Sends blankets etc. by [Benjamin] Peirce and [Asa] Flagg; receipt to be signed and returned; additional stores to be obtained from Capt. [Luke] Bliss [jr.] of Springfield or from Capt. [Moses] Marsh of Hadley. Copy. 1p.

1760. Gray, Harrison, jr. Worcester. Letter to John
Apr. 30. Burk. Is unable to leave Worcester himself but sends £ 112 sterling for equipment of troops etc.; asks to be informed if more is needed. A. L. S. 1p.

1760. Williams, [Israel]. [Hatfield.] Roll of regiment
Feb. 21– under command of. Roll gives names of 113
May 12. men with dates of enlistment and muster; names are arranged under names of officers by whom men were enlisted. Auto. draft. 2pp.

1760. Ruggles, Timothy. Boston. To Abijah Willard.
May 19. Urges that provincial troops be hurried to Albany; is to forward letter or copy to John Burk. Copy by Willard on page with following letter.

[1760.] Willard, Abijah. [Worcester.] Letter to John
[May 21.] Burk. Has sent bounty notes by Lt. John

Bailey and will send more if needed; [Harrison] Gray [jr.] will send money requested by first opportunity. A. L. S. 1p.

1760.
May 22. **Gray,** Harrison, jr. Worcester. Letter to John Burk. Sends him £ 31. 41 s. 8 d. as desired; asks if money sent earlier has been received. A. L. S. 1p. See Gray's letter of Apr. 30 ante.

1760.
Jun. 7. **Torrence,** Thomas. Leicester. To William Henshaw. Receipt to Henshaw for money in full for services of John Cannon and one other [in the campaign of 1759.] D. S. 1p.

1760.
Aug. 23. **Pitt,** William. Whitehall. To Gov. [Stephen Hopkins] and the Company of Rhode Island. Has heard through British officers in America of illegal commerce between the King's subjects and the French settlements on the continent and islands; this commerce alone enables the French to continue the war in America especially by means of the money paid for French products; strict inquiry to be made and punishment meted out to all persons guilty of maintaining these trade relations. Cont. Copy. 2pp.

This letter was a circular one addressed to the various Governors in America. See N. J. Archives, ser. I, vol. 9, p. 240; Newark 1885; where is given the reply of Gov. Thomas Boone.

1759–
1760.
May 15–
Sep. 24. **Louisburgh.** Diary of an expedition to Louisburgh with account of life on the coast of Cape Breton. The record begins with the departure from Nantasket for Louisburgh [in the *Oliver*], and the author is the same as that of the diary Sep. 15–Nov. 15. 1758 (ante p. 22) with which this record is bound. Reaching Louisburgh May 24 the author mounts guard for the first time Jun. 10; on Jul. 9 sail is made on the *Oliver* for Spanish River [Cape Breton's Island]; account of events

Additional French War Manuscripts. 161

follows detailing movements of troops as well as of vessels; the volume closes with scattered orders after Jun. 1, 1760 and the announcement on Sep. 24 of the surrender on Sep. 8 of Montreal with all Canada to Genl. Amherst. 38pp. 1 vol.

1760. **Saturday,** Jacob. Half Moon. To Jesse Bellows. Order
Nov. 10. upon Bellows for sum of wages due to date. D. S. 1p.

1759– **Henshaw,** William. Account Book. Accounts at
1760. Fort Edward and at Leicester for various articles
May 26– purchased from individuals named. There are
Dec. 4. also occasional notes of money borrowed or loaned and events occurring within the writer's knowledge bearing upon the progress of the war. A. D. 14pp. 1 vol.

> In addition to this volume there are in the collection many notes and accounts of Henshaw during the war for which no entries have been included in this calendar. Some are but fuller statements of items given in this Account Book and others refer to matters covered by the Henshaw Orderly Book listed on p. 155.

1760. **Willard,** Nahum. Worcester. To the Colony of
Dec. 22. Massachusetts. Bill for services as physician and surgeon to Colonial troops, Jan. 21, 1760 to Dec. 1, 1760; 103 cases. A. D. S. 8pp.

1761. **Leake,** Robert. Albany. To Samuel Mather.
Jan. 11. Need of a deputy commissary at Fort Detroit; duties and salary of the position; offers it to Mather; if accepted latter is to meet writer in New York to receive further detailed instructions proceeding thence to post via Philadelphia and Pittsburg. A. L. S. 2pp.

1761. **Danks,** Benoni. Fort Cumberland. Roll of Com-
Feb. 20. pany of. List of men in company of Capt. Benoni Danks; roll contains the names of 7 officers and 93 privates. Cont. ms. 1p.

1761.   **Stiles,** Jacob. Leicester. To William Henshaw.
Apr. 25.   Receipt to Henshaw for money in full for services of Ephraim Gibson and one other [in the campaign of 1759]. D. S. 1p.

1761.   **Hale,** Robert. Chronicle of the War against the
Apr. 30.   French and Indians. This volume continues the chronicle begun in vol. I (Jul. 1, 1755-Oct. 30, 1757) and contains similar notes to Apr. 30, 1761. It is followed by a third continuing the record from May 1, 1761 to Oct. 30, 1762. See entries under date Oct. 30, 1757 and Oct. 30, 1762. A. D. 66pp. 1 vol.

1761.   **Bernard,** Francis. Boston. To Benjamin Hallo-
May 26.   well jr. Commission as Captain of His Majesty's ship *King George*. D. S. of Bernard. Certified by A[ndrew] Oliver Secy. 1p.

1761.   **Wethered,** Samuel. Fort Cumberland, To John
Jun. 8.   Walker. Receipt for £ 15. 11 d. Nova Scotia currency in full of account to date; account is in large part for war stores of various kinds. A. D. S. 1p.

1761.   **Scott,** John; **Barritt,** William and Levi **Fletcher.**
Jun. 30.   [Dunstable, Mass.] To John Tyng. Order upon Tyng in favor of Thomas Farrington for £ 3. 14 s. 8 d. each, this sum being the amount remaining due to each from the Colony of Massachusetts as bounty money for enlistment in the French war. On verso is Farrington's receipt of even date to John Tyng for payment of several amounts above stated. D. S. 1p.

1761.   **Cheever,** Ezekiel and five others. Westford, [Mass.]
Jul. 1.   To John Tyng. Order upon Tyng in favor of Leonard Whiting for £ 3. 14 s. 8 d. each, this sum being the amount remaining due each from the Colony as bounty money. Signed:

Ezekiel Cheever, Amborry [Ambrose?] Emery, Thomas Green, Nathaniel Emery, William Belknap, Nathenel Harmen [Nathaniel Harriman?]. On verso is Whiting's receipt of Jul. 2 to John Tyng for payment of several amounts above stated. D. S. 2pp.

<small>A like order upon Tyng in favor of Capt. Whiting signed by William Hunt and receipted by Whiting follows in the collection.</small>

1761. [Tyng, John. Dunstable.] Return of Enlist-
[Jul. 2.] ments in Massachusetts Provincial Service. Return of men enlisted for His Majesty's service for the protection and security of His Majesty's dominions and conquests in North America. Roll contains names of 44 persons enlisted by Capts. William Barron, Thomas Farrington, Moses Parker, Leonard Whiting and Samuel Berry with time of enlistment and various details regarding same. On verso are receipts to John Tyng for provincial bounty received by men enlisting. In ms. of John Tyng. 44 signatures. 2pp.

1761. [Tyng, John. Dunstable.] Return of Enlistments
[Jul. 4.] in Massachusetts Provincial Service. Return of men enlisted for His Majesty's service for the protection and security of His Majesty's dominions and conquests in North America. Roll contains names of three persons enlisted by Capt. Thomas Farrington with time of enlistment and various details regarding same. On verso are receipts to John Tyng witnessed by Jacob McDaniel for provincial bounty received by men enlisting. In ms. of John Tyng. 3 signatures. 2pp.

1761. [Tyng, John. Dunstable.] Notes of Money on
Jul. 4. hand. Rough notes as to money of province on hand [and due various persons as bounty

money for enlistment in Massachusetts provincial service.] A. D. 1p.

1761. [Tyng, John. Dunstable.] Note of men enlisted
[Jul. 4.] in companies of Capts. Moses Parker, May 1 and 5, and Leonard Whiting, Apr. 29 [to whom bounty money is due.] A. D. 1p.

1761. Goldthwait, Thomas. Boston. Receipt for enlist-
Jul. 8. ments. Receipt for enlistments of men in companies of Capts. [Thomas] Farrington, [Leonard] Whiting and [Oliver] Barrons. A. D. S. 1p.

1761. Whiting, [Leonard]. List of men under command
Jul. 2–14. of. List of 18 men under Capt. [Leonard] Whiting with amounts of money paid various individuals. In ms. of John Tyng. 2pp.

1761. Berry, Samuel. Dunstable. To John Tyng.
Jul. 14. Receipt for £3. 14s. 8d. due to Zechariah Flagg jr., Samuel Farley jr. and Benjamin Cory, being the amount due each as bounty money from the Colony. Individual receipts signed by each of the above men are in the collection. These are dated Jul. 11, are witnessed by Samuel Berry and Hugh Floyd and were delivered to Berry. A. D. S. 1p.

1761. [Tyng, John. Dunstable.] Note of money paid.
Jul. 14. Note of £11. 4s. paid Samuel Berry in satisfaction of claim of Zechariah Flagg [jr.], Samuel Farley [jr.] and Benjamin Cory for remainder of bounty money due each. A. D. 1p.
  See preceding entry.

1761. Cobb, Silvanus. Halifax. Receipt for various
Sep. 16. supplies. Supplies and stores received on board sloop *York & Halifax* and to be delivered to Capt. Walmough at Fort Frederick, St. Johns river. "John Merserum, Witness." D. S. 1p.

1761.   **Knap,** John, Salem.   To Francis Bernard.   Knap's
Nov. 11.   son John served under Capt. John Tapley at Fort
William Henry; captured and taken to England
he died in Dec. 1757; father petitions for customary wages of son till date of death.   D. S.   1p.

<blockquote>Attached is certificate of John Okeman to service and capture of Knap and of William Rackley to date of his death.</blockquote>

1762.   [**Tyng,** John.   Dunstable.]   Enlistments in Massa-
[Mar. 22.]   chusetts Provincial Service.   Return of 41 men enlisted for His Majesty's service by Capt. [William] Barron, Lt. [Ezekiel] Brown, and Lt. [Benjamin] Byram; time of enlistment and details regarding the men enlisting.   A. D.   1p.

1762.   [**Tyng,** John.   Dunstable.]   Enlistments in Massa-
[Mar. 27.]   chusetts Provincial Service.   Return of 44 men enlisted for His Majesty's service by Capt. Benjamin Edwards, Lts. Benjamin Byram, [Thomas] Maxwell and Ensign Leo Butterfield; time of enlistment and details regarding men enlisting. A. D.   1p.

1762.   **Dixson,** Thomas.   Fort Cumberland.   Letter to
Apr. 9.   John Walker. Acknowledges letters of Jan. 4 by Capt. [David] Dickey; family matters; rumor of troops at Fort Cumberland about to be sent to the West Indies or to the Mississippi; refers him to Capt. [Benoni] Danks for further information; severity of previous winter and poor prospects for crops of present year.   A. L. S.   2pp.

1762.   **Walker,** John.   Fort Frederick.   To Col. [William]
Apr.   Forster. Encloses monthly returns of garrison for February and March; sent those for November, December and January by a French courier to Fort Cumberland and hopes Forster has received them; reports as to accidents and desertions from fort; gives names of seven deserters and account of their capture; asks

instructions as to their treatment; plenty of guns and ammunition at fort but small supply of flints. Auto. Copy Signed. 2pp.

1762. [May 15]. [**Tyng,** John. Dunstable.] Return of Enlistments in Massachusetts Provincial Service. Return of men enlisted for His Majesty's service for the protection and security of His Majesty's dominions and conquests in North America. Roll contains names of 40 soldiers enlisted by Capts. Benjamin Edwards and Thomas Farrington, Lts. Ezekiel Brown, Benjamin Byram, [Thomas] Maxwell and Henry Woods, with time of enlistment and various details regarding men enlisting. A. D. 1p.

1762. Oct. 30. **Hale,** Robert. Chronicle of the War against the French and Indians. This volume concludes the chronicle begun in Vol I, (Jul. 1, 1755-Oct. 30, 1757) and continued in Vol. II, (Nov. 1, 1757-Apr. 30, 1761) carrying it from May 1, 1761 to Oct. 30, 1762. It is of the same character as the preceding volumes already described, giving outlines of important legislative and military happenings during the period covered although especial emphasis is given to the northern and eastern fields. See entries under dates Oct. 30, 1757 and Apr. 30, 1761. A. D. 32pp. 1 vol.

1763. Mar. 1. [**Bernard,** Francis.] Boston. To Tarrant Putnam. Commission as Capt. of 3d military company from Sutton. D. S. John Cotton, Depy. Secy. On verso is signature of John Chandler and Edward Davis attesting to oath taken by Putnam. 1p.

1763. Oct. **Stone,** Joseph. Leicester. To William Henshaw. Receipt in full to Henshaw for money due for services at Fort Edward in 1759. D. S. by mark. 1p.

1766–   **Rogers,** Robert. Journal of Proceedings with the
1767.   Indians. This manuscript furnishes an account
Sep. 21– of the proceedings of Maj. Rogers with the
Feb. 1. Indians in the district of "Michillimackinac"
during the period immediately following the
French and Indian war. The events here
chronicled are a result of that war and should
not be separated from it. 28 and 30pp.

THE KEPPEL MANUSCRIPTS
DESCRIPTIVE OF THE DEFEAT OF
MAJOR-GENERAL EDWARD BRADDOCK.

Commodore Augustus Keppel to Gov. Sir Charles Lawrence.

Sir: SEA HORSE AT SEA July 26th, 1755.

I have received the favour of several different letters from you upon his Majesties service & was upon the point of sailing to your port, but first the melancholly report of the defeat of the Kings troops under General Braddock stop't me and imediatly after receiving Admiral Boscawen's orders, I am prevented having the pleasure of seeing you, but I must give you joy of your being so much more effectually guarded.

Between the first report of the General's death & any confirmation of the story, there was a space of ten days which gave me flattering hopes that it was only report, but the day before yesterday, I received a confirmation of it by express from Wills creek, I imagine altho' its a melancholly subject you wou'd be glad of the particulars & have inclosed you a list of the killed and wounded, a copy of a letter from Mr. Orme, General Braddocks Aid de Camp, to me and a copy of Mr. Washingtons (who was likewise the General's Aid de Camp) to Governor Dinwiddie. Great blame & shame is laid to the charge of the private men of poor Sir Peter Halkett, & Col. Dunbars regiment that was upon the spot. The loss of the artillery is irretrievable as it enables the French to fortify themselves so strongly, and I fear very much the Credit of the British Arms among the Indians will now be lost. A number of unhappy circumstances will attend this defeat. It may effect Govr. Shirley in his attack against Niagara, as well as many other operations that were proposed.

I give you joy that your expedition up the Bay has succeeded so well & I wish Sir you may always be as successful. I am to far off to receive your comands for England & Am Sir

Your most Obed. & most
humble Servant,

To Gov. Lawrence. A. KEPPEL.

Endorsed: Commodore Keppel, Sea Horse at Sea July 26, 1755, enclosing copys of Capt. Orme's letter to Mr. Keppel, Majr. Washington's to Mr. Dinwidee & a list of officers at the action under Gen. Braddock on the Monongahela. recd. by Capt. Barrington, Aug. 11.

See note on p. 177.

Officers present at the Battle of Fort DuQuesne.

A List of the Officers who were present and of those Killed & Wounded in the Action on the Banks of the Monongahela the 9th July 1755.

Staff.

His Excelency Edwd. Braddock Esq. Genl and Commander in Chief of his Maj^s. Forces in North America, Died of his..Wounds.

Robert Orme   ⎫
Roger Morris   ⎬ Esqs. Aids de Camp....... ⎫ Wounded.
√Geo. Washington   ⎭   ⎭
Willm. Shirley Esqr. Secretary...................Killed.
Sir Jno. St. Clair Deputy Quar. Master General..Wounded.
Mattw. Lessley Gentn., [Lieut. serving as] Assistant
  to the Quart. Mastr. Genl......................Wounded
√Francis Halket Esqr. Major of Brigade................

44TH REGIMENT.

Sir Peter Halket Colonel........................Killed.
Lieut. Col. [Thomas] Gage.............Slightly Wounded.
Captn. [Charles] Tatton.........................Killed.
√[Samuel] Hobson.................................
√[John] Beckworth[1].............................
[Capt.-Lieut. Richard] Gethins...................Killed.

Subalterns.
⎧ √Lieut. [Thomas] Faulkner[2]..................
⎪ [William] Litteler[3]..........Wounded.
⎪ √[Richard] Baylie[4]....................
⎪ [William] Dunbar..........Wounded.
⎪ √[James] Potinger[5]...................
⎪ [James] Halket................Killed.
⎪ [John] Treby...   ....Wounded.
⎨ [James] Allen[6].................Killed.
⎪ [Andrew] Simpson[6]......⎫
⎪ [Robert] Lock[6]..........⎬
⎪ [Ensign Daniel] Disney ....⎬ Wounded.
⎪ [Quinton] Kennedy[7].....⎭
⎪ [Robert] Townsend............Killed.
⎪ √[William] Preston....................
⎪ [Francis] Nartlow[8]............Killed.
⎩ [George] Penington[8].........Wounded.

[1] The name of this officer is usually given as Capt. John Beckwith, but 1 follow the text. Similar inaccuracies in spelling show that this list was made from no official report but from memory or from other than official information.

[2] Faulkner's name is often given as Falconer. He was promoted to a company Nov. 5, 1755.

[3] More correctly spelled Littler.

[4] This officer is sometimes confused with Alexander Baillie but is more probably the Richard Bailey who obtained his Lieutenancy Apr. 3, 1750.

[5] More accurately Pottinger.

[6] Lt. Simpson had been promoted from the rank of Ensign Jun. 26, 1755, and Lock on the 27th. Allen is here given as killed, but a James Allen was commissioned Lt. of the 44th on Nov. 9, 1755, and it is probable that he was but wounded at this time.

[7] Winthrop Sargent in his History of Braddock's Expedition, Philadelphia, 1855, gives this officer as Primrose Kennedy.

[8] Unless this be Francis Nartloo, later Ensign and Lieutenant of the 55th Foot, I have been unable to identify him. The name Nartlow or Nortlow does not appear among the officers of the 44th in the Army List of 1755. The later lists do not contain his name, nor would they owing to his death, but he would have been commissioned probably as early as Penington, who dated from Jun. 6, 1755.

Additional French War Manuscripts. 173

48TH REGIMENT.

Lieut. Col. [Ralph] Burton[9].....................Wounded.
Major [William] Sparks...............Slightly Wounded.
√Captn. [Robert] Dobson..............................
    [Robert] Chulmley.........................Killed.
    [Richard] Bowyer................... ⎱
    [Robert] Ross..................... ⎰ Wounded.
Capt. Lieut. [William] Morris...........................
  [Lieut. Theodore] Barbut................... ⎱ Wounded.
    [John] Walsham...................... ⎰
    [Waterhouse] Crimble..................⎞
    [William] Wideman[10]...................⎬ Killed.
    [John] Hansard ....⎠
    [Henry] Gladwin.......................Wounded.
√[John] Hathorn.................................
    [William] Edmiston......................Wounded.
√[John] Cope.....................................
    [Percival] Brereton[11]................... ⎱ Killed.
    [John] Hart............................ ⎰
    [John] Montreseur.....................Wounded.
√[John] Dunbar....................................
√[Ensign Thomas] Harrison[12]............................
  √[Joseph] Cowhart [Cowart]......................
    [Alexander] McMulen [McMullen].......⎞
    [Richard] Crow.....................⎬ Wounded.
    [Robert] Sterling...................⎠

ARTILLERY.

√Captn. [Thomas] Orde ....
Captn. Lieutn. [Robert] Smith.....................Killed.
Lieut. [Francis James] Buckhanon...........⎞
    [William] McCloud [McLeod] ....⎬ Wounded.
    [Patrick] McCuller ....⎠

ENGINEERS.

Peter McKeller.... ⎞ ....⎞
Robt. Gordon...... ⎬ Esqrs...............⎬ Wounded.
[Adam] Williamson ⎠ ....⎠

---

[9] The Army List for 1755 gives the name Robert Burton but this is an error.

[10] In several cases spelling of names differs. Thus Wideman is better Widman, Hansard should be Handsard; Edmiston should be Edmondston, etc.

[11] Brereton and Hart are given as Ensigns in the Army List for 1755, and their death prevents further mention. Dunbar and Montresor were commissioned Lieutenants on July 3 and 4 respectively.

[12] Thomas Harrison appears to have been transferred from the 36th Regt. of Foot shortly before this campaign.

DETACHMENT OF SAILORS.

Lieutn. Spendelow............................Killed.
√Mr. Haynes } Midshipmen.
Mr. Talbot }   ....Killed.
Captn. [William] Stone of Gen. [Peregrine] Lascells
  Regement...............................Killed.
[Scot] Floyer of [Maj.] Gen. [Hugh] Warbur-
  tons Regement..........................Wounded.

INDEPENDENT COMPANIES OF NEW YORK.

Captn. [Horatio] Gates........................Wounded.
Lieutn. [Simon] Sumain........................Killed.
√[Richard] Miller..................................
Howarth of Capt. Demaris Indept. Compy. } Wounded.
[Robert] Gray, of the same Company .. }

VIRGINIA TROOPS.

Capt. [Adam] Stevens... ....Wounded.
√[John] Wagoner[18]..............................
[William] Poulson....................... } Killed.
Peronie [Peyroney]...................... }
√[Robert] Stewart...............................
[John] Hamilton...........................Killed.
√[Henry] Woodward..............................
√[John] Wright ....
[Carolus Gustavus de] Splitdorff...................Killed.
[Walter] Stewart..........................Wounded.
[Edmond] Wagoner..........................Killed.
√[John] McNeal.................................

According to the most exact return we can as yet get about 600 men killed and wounded.

Those marked √against their names received no hurt.

Capt. Robert Orme to Commodore Augustus Keppel.

Extract of a Letter from Capt. Orme (Aid de Camp to his late Excellency Genl. Braddock) to the Honble. Augustus Keppel dated at Fort Cumberland the 18th July 1755.

At the Little Meadows a place about Twenty Miles from this, we found it unavoidable to alter our disposition of march, it being impossible to proceed with such a Train of Carriages. A detachment was therefore made of twelve hundred men, ten pieces of ordnance, ammunition and provisions calculated

---

[18] The spellings in this Virginia list are defective. Wagoner should be Waggoner in each case; Poulson is probably Polson and McNeal should be McNeill; possibly Hector in place of John.

for reducing the Fort and our subsistance. With this we proceeded very fast and in great spirits till about one o'clock on the 9th Instant. The French with some Indians, the number of both unknown, had taken a very strong post about half a mile from the Banks of Monongahela; our advanced party, consisting of 300 men began a very irregular & confused attack; they were ill sustained by 200 in their rear, and the whole fell back upon the van of [the] main body, commanded by the General, whilst he was moving forward to their assistance. From this time all was anarchy, no order, no discipline, no subordination; the General with the Officers endeavored to bring the men back to a sense of their duty, but all efforts were vain.

This Confusion lasted about two hours and a half, and then the whole ran off crying the devil take the hindmost. Our guns, ammunition provisions and baggage remained in the hands of the enemy, and the General was with the greatest difficulty brought off being so much wounded as to be quite helpless. The General had five horses shot under him and at last received a shot through his lungs of which he died the 13th Instant at night. His Family were prettily pickled, Shirley killed in the field, Morris and myself much wounded, Washington alone escaped tho' no man deserved a wound better, his whole Behavior being extremely gallant. Burton sends his compliments and is now lying by me, with an extreme bad wound in his hip, but it is hoped he will recover.

Never did Officers behave so well. They got themselves murder'd by distinguishing themselves in leading their men on. 28 Officers are dead, 35 wounded, many of which will not recover, and about 600 Men Killed & Wounded according to the best accounts we have yet been able to get. Your Guard behaved very well. Spendelow & Talbot are no more, and if you should see Palliser, tell him his nephew behaved particularly well, advancing with the colours and innocently asking if the men would not go along with him.

I could talk to you an hour in this manner, but I am too weak to continue it long, but as my strength increases, I will write frequent and long letters. As soon as I am able, I shall go to Philadelphia and from thence to England.

George Washington to Gov. Robert Dinwiddie.

FORT CUMBERLAND, July 18, 1755.

Honbl. Sir:

As I am favored with an opportunity, I should think myself inexcusable was I to omit giving you some account of our late Engagement with the French on the Monongahela, the 9th instant.

We continued our March from Fort Cumberland to Frazier's (which is within 7 miles of Duquesne) without meeting any extraordinary event, having only a straggler or two picked up by the French Indians. When we came to this place, we were attacked (very unexpectedly) by about three hundred French and Indians. Our numbers consisted of about thirteen hundred well armed men, chiefly Regulars, who were immediately struck with such an inconceivable panick, that nothing but confusion and disobedience of orders prevailed among them. The officers in general, behaved with incomparable bravery, for which they greatly suffered, there being near 60 killed and wounded—a large proportion, out of the number we had!

The Virginia companies behaved like men and died like soldiers; for I believe out of three companies that were on the ground that day scarce thirty were left alive. Capt. Peyroney and all his officers down to a corporal, were killed; Captn. Polson had almost as hard a fate, for only one of his escaped. In short, the dastardly behaviour of the Regular troops (so-called) exposed those who were inclined to do their duty to almost certain death; and, at length, in despite of every effort to the contrary, broke and ran as sheep before hounds, leaving the artillery, ammunition, provisions, baggage, and, in short, everything a prey to the enemy. And when we endeavoured to rally them, in hopes of regaining the ground and what we had left upon it, it was with as little success as if we had attempted to have stopped the wild bears of the mountains, or rivulets with our feet; for they would break by, in despite of every effort that could be made to prevent it.

The General [Edward Braddock] was wounded in the shoulder and breast, of which he died three days after; his two aids-de-camp were both wounded, but are in a fair way of recovery; Colo. [Ralph] Burton and Sr John St. Clair [Sinclair] are also wounded, and I hope will get over it; Sir Peter Halket, with many other brave officers, were killed in the field. It is supposed that we had three hundred or more killed; about that number we brought off wounded, and it is conjectured (I believe with much truth) that two-thirds of both received their shot from our own cowardly Regulars, who gathered themselves into a body, contrary to orders, ten or twelve deep, would then level, fire and shoot down the men before them.

I tremble at the consequences that this defeat may have upon our back settlers, who, I suppose, will all leave their habitations unless there are proper measures taken for their security.

Colo. [Thomas] Dunbar, who commands at present, intends, as soon as his men are recruited at this place, to continue his

Additional French War Manuscripts.

march to Philadelphia for winter quarters; consequently there will be no men left here, unless it is the shattered remains of the Virginia troops, who are totally inadequate to the protection of the frontiers.***

The copy of Washington's letter mentioned as an enclosure by Keppel is not with the letter of that officer in the collections of this Society but there is a contemporary copy in the Library of Congress at Washington. The copy printed above is from Ford: Writings of Washington I, 173. New York, 1889.

Friday First Edward Sepr. 14th 1759
Parole Boyne
Capt. of the Day for to Morrow Capt.
Whiting for Guard —— Lt. Pillo
To Visit the Barracks —— Lt. Henshaw
the Royal Blockhouse Island & Island
Number N:o 1 & 3 to be Relievd to Morrow
the Wood Cutting party to Continue—
1 Subs Batto & party to Morrow Capt. Love
the Whole of those Imployd this Day to
parade at 8 oClock to Morrow to
Repair the Bridge alonge the Creek

Saturday 15 Sepr. 1759
Parole Dungannon
Capt. of the Day for to Morrow Capt. Love
for Guard —— Lt. Henshaw
To Visit the Barracks —— Ens: Lr. Baker
the Bridge & Block House Do No 1 & 2
Releivd to Morrow—the Wood Cutting
party to Continue till further Orders
A Sub? 2 Corpl? 2 (or Lt 46 privates
to go to Morrow for provissions
for their Duty—Lt. Gibs

A Garrison Court Martial to sit
at 10 oClock to Morrow
Capt. Whiting President
Lt. Dayton   } Members   { Lt. Scott
Ens: Lr. Baker   Ens: Mr. Price
who the Draftsman to be Aquainted
and all Evidences to Attend

Sunday First Edward Sepr 16:1759,
Parole Milborry
Capt. of the Day for to Morrow
Capt. Williams for Guard — Ens: Lr. Baker
To Visit the Barracks Lt. Dayton
the Royal Blockhouse Island &
Block Houses No 1 & 3 to be Releivd
to Morrow—the Wood Cutting party
to Continue—No Battoe party to Morrow—

16th Sunday Do Releivd the Guard
James Genl: 2 Col. Carolina Rifferd
from Crown Point & prisoner, 1
days for a Boat over to the Island

THE ORDERLY BOOK OF
LIEUT. WILLIAM HENSHAW.

WILLIAM HENSHAW'S

ORDERLY & JOURNAL BOOK

BOUGHT AT FORT EDWARD

June th13 – 1759: price 4/6 York Currency

GIVEN BY COL. WILLM. HENSHAW
TO HIS SON
HORATIO GATES HENSHAW.–
AND BY HORATIO G. HENSHAW
GIVEN TO HIS DAUGHTER
HARRIET ELIZABETH HENSHAW.

A LIST OF CAPTAIN BALDWINS COMPANY

Capt. Jedun. Baldwin
Lieut Natl. Ingersol
Lieut William Henshaw
Ensn. Nathaniel Bond

John Allen
John Blunt Serjt.
Andrew Blunt
Isaac Bolster Serjt.
Jona. Buck
John Bogle
Josiah Baldwin
John Ballard
Abner Blanchard
Solomon Cummings
John Dunkin
Pomp' Funnel
Benja. Garfield
Nehemiah Gale Corpl.
Joseph Googins
Abijah Gale
Sippio Gates
Saml. How Corpl.
Silas Hooker
James Hull
Willm. Hatfield
Danl. Hovey
Nathan Howard
James Johnson
Thias Johnson
Willm. Lackey Serjt.
Abel Levens
Elijah Learnad
Ebenezer Marsh

Nathan Moore Corpll.
Richard Moore
Adam Martin
Aquilla Moffit
Joseph Moffit
Aaron Martin
Abel Mason
Amariah Parks
Ebenr. Putnam
Jona Phillips
Abraham Pratt
John Rumble
Asa Roberts
Ichabod Robbins
John Streeter
Jona. Streeter
Peter Shumway
Zebulon Streeter
Saml. Streeter
Ebenr. Tucker Serjt.
David Town
Elijah Town
Moses Town
Phineas Walker
Danl. Wyman Serjt.
Josiah Walker
Ebenr. Whitney
Ephraim Watkins Corpll.
Willm. Parkman

THE ORDERLY BOOK OF LIEUT. WILLIAM HENSHAW.

Regimental Orders Worcester May th.9, 1759

That all the troops belonging to General Ruggles Regiment that have past Muster by the Regular Genl. Muster Master to gett themselves Ready to March to Morrow Morning by Sun rise; the Capts. are to make a Victualling Return Immediately to the Adjutant for four days provision, & to Receive the same, so as to have all things Ready to March to Morrow morning—the Capts. will apply to Colo. John Chandler for Carriages for there men — Capts Baldwin Reed & [Ebenezer] Cox two Carrages, Capts [John] Nixon [Abijah] Willard & [Job] Williams two, Capt [Leonard] Whiting[1] one, Capt. [Samuel Clark] Paine one, Capt Furnace one, Capt Mainor one & Capt [Leonard] Butterfield one; it is Expected they See their Carriages ready this day so as to load them by Day Break to Morrow morning—J[oseph] Ingersol, L. Colo.

Thursday May 10–1759 Set out from Leicester. Stopt at [Thomas] Sergeants pd the Billeting Roll £14 – 8 – 6 Sterling; bought an Old horse, 4 Dollars, went to B[rother Samuel] Dennys & Lodged F[air] W[eather].[2]

---

[1] After the union of the forces from Connecticut and Rhode Island with those from Massachusetts, there appear to have been two other Captain Whitings in this expedition: Capt. John Whiting of Rhode Island, Capt. Charles Whiting of Connecticut, and later a Col. Nathan Whiting also of Connecticut. Capt. Leonard Whiting was, however, more closely connected with Henshaw at all times.

[2] Whenever possible the given names of persons are supplied at the time of their first mention. In case of a second mention, the first name has rarely been inserted. Following the same rule it has been considered unnecessary to explain these single letter notes as to weather conditions in further instances.

Fryday. 11. Set out. F. W. Stopt at [Benjamin?] Flags & Overtook the Company. Went to [Benjamin] Reeds at Weston & Lodg'd. – 30/³

Saturday May 12. Cloudy set out Went to Springfield Village & Lodgd at Mr. [Moses] Blis's

13 Sabbath Day Stayed in the Village at Mr. [Luke] Hitchcocks Went to Meeting heard Mr Merrick;⁴ Lodg'd here 20/

14 Monday Set out Went in to Sprg'd Town Stopt & Sup'd at [Cornelius] Jones in Springfield Town 10/

15 Tuesday Made the Muster Roll. Staid here all Day at Mr. Jones 15/

16 Wednesday Muster'd at 4 °Clock in Afternoon set out Went to Westfield Lod'g at Deacon [Eldad] Taylor's – 15/

17 Thursday Set out Left a Man Sick on the Mountains, Jona Phillip. Went into Glasgow Lodg'd at Mr. Mortons 10/

18 Fryday Rainy Set out through the Green Woods at 10 °Clock Lodg'd at Shaddocks at No. 1 15/

19 Saturday Staid here all Day & Lodg'd 30/

20 Sabbath FW: Set out Stop'd at Sheffield Meeting heard a Sermon, provided a Team to Forward our Baggage to Green Bush, Lodg'd at a private house 10/

21 Monday F. W. Set out from Sheffield. Stopd in the Contending lands, Stopt at [Daniel] Lovejoys in the Land of Contention Heard the News of Capt. [Abijah] Burbanks being taken with a scouting party of about 30 Men at the Narrows by the Indians. Stop'd at [Thomas] Ingersols Esqr. Stop'd at Christian Rays in Spencer Town

---

³ This sign is used to denote shillings, possibly as a simpler form for the script *f*. Similar entries will be found noting the writer's expense account on various days.

⁴ This is probably John Merrick. The regular pastor of the Church at Springfield at the time was Rev. Robert Breck.

The Orderly Book of Lieut. William Henshaw. 187

& Lodg'd 14 Mes. from Sheffield. Spencer Alias Claverick alias land of Contention 18/

22 Tuesday F W: Set out – Stopt at Stone house, from thence into Kenderkook Lodg'd by the Meeting house 22/6

23 Wednesday Do: Set out & Stopt at the half way house 12 M. thence into Green Bush & Lodg'd at Justice [Ezra] Taylor Sutler in G Bush 15/

24 Thursday Stay'd at Green Bush & Din'd at Capt. [William] Dowes. 6/. then Set out in Battoes & Cross'd the River into Albany Draw'd Tents & provision Encamp'd on the Hill 100 Rods from the City Lost my Cape brought from home.

25 Fryday Do. Orders for Fatigue: some to pick Oakum others to clear the parade to Encamp on. Serjt. [William] Lackey taken up for Desertion. Went & Lodg'd at Capt. [Philip] Lansings 10/

Albany May 24th, 1759 – Parole Liverpool –

The Order for Desertion to be read to ye[5] Provincials for which Purpose, the Commanding Officer of ye Royal Regt. will have their Men Under Arms & Read the same to them & to assure the Men that ye Genll. is Determined not to pardon any one Deserter from any of the Troops During the Campaign; as he is to Reward the Men to ye Utmost of his Power when their good Behaviour Deserve it –

Camp Near Albany 25th. May 1759 – Parole Glascow –

Rhode Island Regt. to be Ready to March at ye Least Notice, Surgeon [John] McColm of the Royal to attend the Hospital at Fort Edward & Mr. [Edward] Bray mate of the Hospital to do Duty with ye Royal as a Surgeon; the Massachusetts Troops to furnish out Twenty five Teamsters, that they may be sent Immediately to Colo. [John] Bradstreet – a Working party of a Hund. Men with 2 Sub[altern]s,

---

[5] The y in this word and in following cases is, of course, the old Saxon character for th and is retained in the printed text as the nearest equivalent to that character. It will be noticed that at this point the Orderly Book really begins. Before this there has been merely a Journal found hereafter in the secondary entry for the day.

2 serjts. 2 Corplls. ye 1st Battn. to find One Sub One Serjt. one Corpll. & 60 Privates –

25 May 1759 F W. [John] Bogle went to Oxford for Serjt. Lackey's Discharge Encamp'd in Regular Order Swap'd Sword & Buckles with Capt Paine. I had 2 & ½ Dolls. between Buckles; & 12 & ½ Dolls. Between Swords to Boot 22/6

Camp Albany Hill: 26 May – 1759 – Parole Guernsey –

The Provential Regts. to be Very Exact when they send any Man to ye Kings Hospital that they Have proper Certificates of their Names, Regt. & Compy. Sign'd by an Officer of ye Comp: Specify'g the Regt. they Belong to – As Waggons are now Wanted for the service of ye Troops, all Sutlers, Merchts. &c. are to Have passes to Follow ye Army [and] they are for ye Future to make Use of Only Ox Carts in the same Manner as Regimental Sutlers – Orders have Been sent to the Different Posts to stop all Waggons. Officers are to pay for any Horses they Press when their Duty Requires it; those of ye Regt. are to Apply to ye Majr. of Brigade, the Artillery to their Own Commanding Officer, the Engineer to ye Chief Engineer, ye Hospital to ye Director of ye Hospital for ye Payments of which, Accompts. are to be laid before ye Commander in Chief to Allow ye same if Reasonable. Officers not to Neglect Giving Proper Certificates to ye Drivers of Carts Employ'd to Carry Baggage for ye Troops Mentioning the time they have been Employ'd, Complaint having been Made Heretofore of their Omission: – the Genll. Court Martial [of which] Colo. [James] Grant is Pressident to set again to Morrow Morng. at 8 °Clock – Baggage & Forage Money to be paid to ye Sevrll. Regt. Immediately – As ye Provincials Arive, ye Commanding Officers are to Apply to Mr. Lake[6] for Provisions that they may be Enabled when ye Whole of Each Regt. Arive so to proportion ye Delivery of Provision thatt hey may all Receive to ye same Day – an Officer & 25 Men of ye Royal Highland Regt with a Weeks Provision to be sent to the Widow McGinnesses House to Protect that Settlement, – 2 Subs. 2 serjts. 2 Corpll. & 100

---

[6] Robert Leake Commissary at Albany. See p. 161.

The Orderly Book of Lieut. William Henshaw.

Privates of Colo. Ruggles Regt for Work to Morrow at 6 °Clock; 2 Serjts. 2 Corpll. & 24 Men for ye Town Guard.

27 of May – 1759 Do. Went to the English Church in Forenoon – Carried J[eduthan] Baldwin to the Grand Hospital, in Aftern Wrote a Letter home No 1 post pay, 2/

Camp on Albany Hill 28th May – 1759 – Parole Massac –

The Following Detacht. to be made of ye Following Troops, they are to be proper Men for ye Battoe Service –

C^7	S	S	Privates	
1	4	5	120	Massachusets
2	7	10	240	Connecticut
1	3	4	140	New Jersey
1	1	2	54	Rhode Island

This Detachment is to Parade to Morrow Morng. at 5 °Clock on ye Right of ye Rhode Island Troops & wait till Major [Alexander] Moneypenny see them March off. They are to take their Arms, A Proportion of Camp Necessaries and as many Days Provision at they have Recd.–Waggons will be Allowed[8] – for ye Connecticut Troops – 2 for ye Massachusets – 2 for N Jersey & 1 for Rhode Island troops, for Carrying Victuals,[8] for sending to Lieut. [George] Coventry DQM Genll.[8] this Detacht Perhaps to Remain out some Months & ye Officers & Men when Employ'd as Battoe Men will be paid as in the Orders of the 23d. May; this Detachment to March to Morrow Morng. to Schenactada; an Officer of Each Core will go Forward when ye Detacht Marches & Apply to Capt. [Allen] Mc Clean at Schenactada who has Orders to Mark out their Encampmt. The Commanding Officer of Each Core will Receive Particular Orders when they will March from thence; all ye Provenll. Troops are to Provide themselves Immediately with Everything they want to Carry with them that the Men be ready to March at the Least Notice –

---

[7] The abbreviations are for Commissioned Officers, Subalterns and Sergeants. They occur frequently in the manuscript text of the volume.

[8] No number is given but four wagons appear to have been the Connecticut allotment, with one for food and one for Lieut. Coventry.

Albany May th28 – 1759 Monday Showry I Went on Fatigue Clearg Lands, News that 3 Men Kill'd & two Wounded between Albany & Senactada View'd the Kings Garden on the Island a Highland [er] Whip'd 300 L[ashes;] 5 of Our Compy. Draw'd out for Battoing.

May 28th After Orders – The Genl. Court Martial of wch. Colo. Grant is Pressident is Dissolved The Genll has Allow'd ye Following Sentences of ye Genl. Court Martial: Jno Holden in Capt. [Thomas] Burkets Compy in R Island Regt is to Receive 1000 Lashes with a Cat of Nine Tails, Wm Gray Soldier in Wallis's[9] Compy. in ye Royal Regt. Being Accused of Death of Jno Mc Clean in sd. Compy. is found not Guilty of Wilful Murder & is Acquitted, Malcolm McDaniel Soldier in Capt. [Charles] Grahams Compy. of ye R H Regt Accused of being Accesary to ye Death of Peter Canada is found not Guilty of Wilful Murder & is Acquitted. David Roggers Corpl in Capt. Ross's [Samuel Rose's] Compy. of ye R. Island Regt Found Guilty of Desertion Laid to his charge & is to suffer Death: Samll. Harris Soldier in ye R. Island Regt. & in Colo. [Henry] Babcocks Compy found Guilty of Desertion Laid to his Charge & is to Suffer Death, Peter McMartin soldier in Colo. ———[10] Regt found Guilty of Desertion Laid to his Charge & is to suffer Death –

The R[oyal] H[ighland] Regt. Massachusets, New Jersey, Connecticut, & R[hode] Island Troops to be Out to Morrow Morng. at 5 ⁰Clock. Leaving Proper Guards with care of ye Camp [they] are to March Immediatly to ye Ground that will be Markt out for them by the Q. Master of ye Highland Regt at 6 ⁰Clock this Evening, for wch. purpose a Quar Master of Each of ye Provencial Regts. will attend. The Troops are to be Drawn up, the Highlanders on ye Right the Massachusets & Connecticut on ye Left of the R. H. Regt – New Jersey on the Right of the Massachusets, R. Island in ye Center – the Detachment Order'd for Schenactada is not to March till the Execution is over &

---

[9] This is probably a mis-statement for Capt. James Wall's company.
[10] The name of the Colonel is omitted in the text.

is to be Drawn up on the Left of the Massachusets Troops. They will afterwards March & where the Majr. of Brigade Moneypenny will Direct them. A Platoon of ye R Island Regt. to be Drawn up on ye Front of those Regts. [and] to be Loaded with Ball Ready for ye Execution; the Provost Guard to March the Prisoners David Rogers & Samll. Harris at 6 °Clock to Morrow Morng. from ye Prison to ye Right of ye Line & in ye Front of the Center to where the Execution is. A Chaplain to Attend on ye Prisoner. Colo. Grant, Colo. of ye Day for to Morrow, Brigadeer [Genl. Thomas] Gage to Command the Whole.

Tuesday   Albany   29th of May 1759

Regimental Orders for the 1st Battalion of Brigr. Ruggells Regt. – That a Return of Each Compy. be made of what arms & Accoutrt are wanting to Compleat the Regiment; Likewise that a Victualling Return be made Immediately – that the place of Cooking be on the Side of the Hill & no where Else (Excepting Officers) – That the Men Attend every Eveng. at the Beating the Retreat & that an Officer from Each Compy Likewise Attend the Same at Roll call –

Orders th29 May – Parole Amsterdam. All the proventials Regts. to be drawn up Without Arms in the Front of their several Encampments at 1°Clock – the Commanding Officer to have Returns Ready of their Numbers Now hear & of those they Expect to Joyn them which they will give to the Genll. –

Any Soldier that is found out of Camp after Retreat Beating will be severely punished –

29 Raw Cold   Paraded the Men at 5 °Clock in Morng. to See two Men Shot. [Samuel] Harris was Shot Dead – [David] Rogers was pardon'd. Paraded at 1 °Clock to be Viewd. Bot. a pair of pumps £4-10   15/

Camp on Albany Hill 30th May 1759

Regimental Orders for the 1st. Battalion of Brigr. Ruggels Regiment – It is Expected that no Capt. or Subaltern are out of Camp Excepting [they] leave Word where they shall

be found, on any pretence whatever – It is further Expected that Every Capt. see that Everyman in their Respective Compy. be Acquipt with Arms & Accoutrement without any Delay – And to have every thing Ready to March at a Moments Warning As I Expect Orders to March Every Moment. – I Expect these Orders be strickly Obey'd
Joseph Ingersol Lt Colo.

Parole Albany – The Rhode Island Regiment to March to Morrow to F[ort] Edward; they will strike there Tents at 5 °Clock; there Baggage will go by Water; they will apply to Colo. Bradstreet for that purpose; they will take with them 20 Battoes Loaded with provision which they are to load this Evening, the Regt to be Compleated with 6 Days provision – A Detachment of 200 Men are to take Battoes this Afternoon at 4 °Clock which they will load to Morrow Morning at 5 °Clock & proceed with them to half Moon where they will Deliver them to the Commanding Officer & then Return in Scows if there be any their to Albany –

For this Detachment:

	Capt	Subs	Serjt.	R File
N Jersey	1	4	4	100
Massachust.	1	2	3	80
Connecticut		2	2	50

th30 May Wednesday – Election 1759 – Mr. Louder from Boston brought a packet. Recd. 4 Tents for the Officers Bought a Fryg. pan   30/

Camp on Albany hill 31st of May

1st Battalion Orders – That the Capt. or Commanding Officers of Companies see that the Balls fit the Mens Guns so that they run down the Barrels & to have Every thing Ready to March to Morrow morning by 5 °Clock. Those that have not got Cartridges boxes must break their Cartridges & put there powder into there horns – It is Further Expected that all the mens arms are Clean & in good Order – An Officer from Each Compa. to see it Done as soon as may be – the Commanding Officers of Each Compa. to give in a Return of all their Effective Able Men to the Adjutant Immediately –

Jos. Ingersol: Lt. Colo.

A Regimental Court Martial to be held at 9 ºClock this Morning For the Tryal of John Williams, Henry Moncel, Elias Peters & Levi Doricke for theft

Capt [John] Nixon Pressident
Lt. [John] Worthington
Lt Coburn [John Cockburne]
Lt. David Joy
Ensn. [Daniel] Wheeler
} Members

Parole Somerset – Genll. Orders All the guards of the Royal Highlnd Regt. to be Reliev'd by the Connecticut Troops & they to March to Morrow Morning at 5 ºClock to the Half Moon where they will take the Artillery under their Care & Escort the same to F. Edward – one Waggon for a Company, one for the Commandg. Officer & one for the Staffs be Allow'd – The Regt. to take 6 Days provision the Women be Allow'd 4d pr Day in Lieu of provision which will be paid On Applying to Lieut Coventry as D. Q. M. G.- The Massachusetts Troops to take up 80 Battoes with them at 3 ºClock Loading them with provision Reserving 6 for the tents & Baggage – which they will load to Morrow at 5 ºClock & proceed to F Edward. They are to take 9 Days provision with them – Colo. Ruggels will leave Careful Officers here to bring up those he Expects to Join him – Majr. Dod to put the Artillery & Stores into Scows this Evening which are to Proceed to Half Moon & be Escorted to Fort Edward:— the Regt. of Colo. [Phineas] Lyman, [Eleazer] Fitch & Schyler [Peter Schuyler][11] to be ready to March at the First Notice Colo. Lyman & Fitch will Leave proper Officers hear to bring up the Men which are Left here –

Camp at Albany May 31th 1759 Each Officer Commanding a Compy. to Return their Sick who are unable to March into the Kings Hospitals Taking Great care that the Genlls.

---

[11] This is clearly Col. Peter Schuyler of New Jersey although at other places in the text Col. Philip Schuyler of New York may be intended.

Orders are Observ'd Respecting the leaving Certificates. A Commission Officer to be in every Battoe to take care that no Damage be Done or Disorder Committed – A Serjt. 1 Corpl. 12 privates for a Guard near the Battoes this Night. The tents to be struck & Remov'd on Board the Battoes to Morrow Morning by Sun rise – A Serjt. Commanding the guard to Reserve for the Tents & Officers Baggage a Battoe. A Daily Return [to be made] of the State of the Mens Arms
Timothy Ruggles

31 of May 1759 F W Thursday   Recd our Guns [and] Ammunition, Recd of Capt Saml. Clarke Paine 6 Dolls. in part.   Left in Green Bush with Capt [William] Dowes a Coat Jacket & Breeches Sword & Belt   3 Strops   Tobacco & buckle Brush – all Except the Sword in Majr [John] Hawks Chest at Capt Dowes   Sent home a Letter No 2 by Benja Richardson

Fryday 1 of June Rainy. Struck our tents by 5 °Clock Wrote to B[rother] Benja by Justice Taylor of Middletown, Went on Board the Battoes & Set sail. Carried 20 Barrels in Each Battoe   Went a shore at half Moon & Encamped 11 Miles from Albany   22/

2 Do. Saturday   Set out at 6 °Clock   Very hard going up the Rifts.   Ariv at Capt. [William] Lamsons at the 3 Mile house in the Rifts   Pitch'd Tents – 9/

3 Do. Sabbath   Set out   Made an Attempt to go up the Rifts but In Vain   Came Down stream   Unloaded the Chest & Set out & Landed at Still Water   Left my Knife at the Sutlers   Came to Still Water & Encamp'd 13 Miles from half moon   14/

4 Monday   A pleasant Day, Nothing Remarkable Encamp'd at Saratoga 12 Miles from Still water   15/ In Pro Cu[12]

5 Tuesday went over the Falls & Loaded Went to Fort Miller   Unloaded   Draw'd our Battoes by Land ½ Mile Loaded   J—n Poor Whip'd 23L. for Impudence Arrivd

---

[12] In Pro Cu. In provincial currency.

at F Edward at 7 °Clock   25/   14 M. from Saratoga – paraded. Call'd up to Mount guard –

Fort Edward Wednesday th6 of June 1759 –
– Parole Guadalope –

Lieutenant Colonel [Beverly] Robinson will mark out the Ground for Encamping to Morrow morning at 5 °Clock that the Regts. may take up the ground as they Arrive The Regiments are to Camp – the first Brigd. the Royal on the Right, Iniskilling [or 27th regiment] on the Left, [John] Prideaux in the Center; 2d Brigd. [John] Forbes on the Left, Royal Highlands on the Right, Mongomery [Alexander Montgomery's Highlanders] in ye Center. The Grenadiers & light Infantry will form 2 Battalions apart & will be posted from Right to Left by Seniority of Regiments –

A Camp will be Marked for those Corpes & the Companies will March to the Camps as they Arrive. The Proventials are to be Encampt – the Massachusets on the left, Jerseys on the Left, [Center?] N Hampshire on the Right, the Massachusets & Connecticut on the Left of the Jerseys, Rhode Islands on the Left of Connecticut's, this is the Order of Battle for the Troops – They may be Altered in their Camp according to the Situation of the ground – the Houses of Officers to be made in the Front as the Deputy Q Master General shall Direct – All Beatings to be Taken from the Right to the Left – the Pick[et] is to turn out at the Retreats Beating the Arms to be Examined & the men of the Picquet are to lye in the Front Tents that they may be ready to turn at any time at a moments Notice – a Serjt. & 16 men of the Royal Highlands to take the Grenadiers guard –

6 Wednesday   Releas'd the Guard   View'd the Works at F Edward. [John] Bogle came up with Lakes Discharge 24/

Thursday June th7 – 1759 Parole Prideaux –

The Regs. are not to change their Encampment until the Ground is quite dry – The Regs. at there Arrival are to give in a Return to what time they have Recd. Provision that the particular time for the Delivery of Each Corps may be hereafter Regulated. It Having been Reported to me by the Comissary that it [there?] has been a Waste & as the Daily Allowance of Each man as Followeth is Sufficient – If any have been Drawn for & Expected more then the Allowance, they must make it good in having the Overplus Deducted in the Allowance they are hereafter to Receive –

The Regs. are to take for there Effectives Only. The Commandg. Officers are to Certify the Number of these of there Respective Companies on the Issuing the Provision, & the Officer Commandg. Regt. to Examine & be Answerable that the Whole is Just – Spruce Beer will soon be Brew'd it is hop'd Sufficient for the Whole & will cost the Men but a Very Moderate price –

7 Thursy. Cold Rain all Day Kept Close to my Tent No news only a No. of French & Indians at the Lake a Searching for Cannon balls, Ammunition which our people Hid last Year.

Fort Edward Fryday th8 of June – Parole Falmouth –

Field Officer for Picquet this day Lt. Colo. Salsonstall [Richard Saltonstall,] for to Morrow Lt. Colo. Ingersol – The Field Officer Will go the Rounds as Usual & Report to the D Q M G Before Orderly time – 1 Sub & 30 Men for the Genl. guard– No men [to] go beyond the Centries of the Blockhouses upon any Account Whatever Except when sent out with a Covering party A Serjt. & 12 Men to mount guard at Each of the Provision sheds 1 Subn. & 30 Men as a guard over the Battoes the Regt. to change their Encampments at 1 ºClock –

8 E[ast] W[ind] Went to the R Encampments at the Falls our Men a Cleaning & Discharging their Guns Alarum'd us at the Forts. Orders to stand to your Arms our Regt was Draw'd up in 3 Mins. in a few Mins. 1000 G Dischar^d Sent to the Genl for Orders to follow sent word that it was our men firing by his leave

Camp at F Edward 9th of June – Parole Plymouth –

Field Officer for the picquet this Day Lt. Colo. Ingersol for to Morrow Majr. Grayham [Gordon Graham] – A Detachment of the Royals in Garrison to Encamp at 5 ºClock this

Afternoon On the Left of the light Infantry of the Royal Highland Regiment Which is the Ground the Royal Regt is to Encamp on – All Sutlers who have passes & are not attach'd to any Regt. are to be Encamp'd together on the ground the D Q M G will mark out this day at 1 °Clock which ground is to be the Centre of the Army & the Market to be Kept there for Selling whatever the Sutlers shall bring for the Support of the Camp – The Provost guards shall Encamp around them to keep good Order no lights are Suffer'd at Night; None of the Soldiers are allowed or Permitted to be there after the Retreats Beating; the Sutlers are to Encamp on this ground at 4 °Clock this day & none permitted to stay on the Glasssees [Glacis] of the Fort; the light Infantry of the Royal Highland Regt is to Fire Ball to Morrow morng. at 6 °Clock near the Royal Block house on the other Side of the River the Camps not to be Alarm'd –

The Subn. Guard over the Battoes to be taken of & 2 Guards to be plac'd in Lieu thereof – A Serjt & 15 Men on this Side of the River – It is a standing Order that no Dropping Shots be Made or Fired. Whenever there is a Firelock that will not Draw a Report is to be made therof that they may be Collected together & Fired off when the Camps are Advertized of it that there may be no Unnecessary alarm - the Indians to be particularly Acquainted with these Orders which if they Disobey they will be severely punished –

9th of June Saturday – Fair & P. Last Night a Frost this day Clearing; the parade & Encamp'd in Regular Order   10/

Camp at F Edward 10th June Sabbath – Parole Gersey –

Field Officer for the Picquet this Night Major Graham for to Morrow Majr. Crombwell Colo. for the Day Colo. [James] Grant – All Reports from the First Officer of the Picquet & Extraordinary's that may happen in Camp are to be made to the Colo of the Day who will Report at Orderly time to the Commander in Chief – all Guards are to turn out to the Colo. of the Day General Officers guard Excepted – he will go the Rounds to see & Visit all Guards & Outposts To see if the Whole [be] Alert, & Inform the Colo. who Relieves him of the several Guards & outposts & times he Visited them – Divine Service to be performed Every Sunday at the head of the Regiments – A General Court Martial to Set ToMorrow Morning at 8 °Clock to try such prisoners as are Under the provost Guard – all Evidences must attend – President for sd. Court Colo. Mon[tgomery.] Lt Colo. Ingersol, Majr. Ball, 1 Capt. of the Royals, 2 Capts. Each from the Royal Highlands, Pruddocks[13] & Montgomery – 2 from the Massachusets 1 from Rhode Island [to be] Members; Lt. Genl. George Burton of the Royal [to be] Deputy Judge Advocate to whom the Members Names & Dates of their Commission – & Evidence's Names are to be sent at 6 °Clock this Afternoon – A Marker to be posted at the Centre of the Line where the Court Martial will Assemble & a Serjt. & 12 Men of Montgomerys. Regt. to Serve as a Guard while the Court Martial is Sitting – Royal Highlands in Montgomerys Regt. To send as many Men This Afternoon at 4 °Clock as is Necessary to Clear the Ground where the light Infantry is to Encamp – Lieut Colo. Robinson will take them to the Ground – they will Rece. Axes & Apply to the store Keeper in ye Fort who will attend them, which they will Return when the Work is Finis'd; the Serjt Guard over the Battoes on ye Island to be Reduced to a Corpl. & Six Men. As by Order of the 7th. Inst. Spruce Beer will be Brew'd for the Army it is not Intended to hinder any People from Bruing Small Beer – All Sutlers are to keep Bruing Whatever they have a Mind to – The Genl. guard Artillery Magazine Provost & Battoe Guards are to be Reliev'd every 18 hours.

10 of June Sunday Fair 1759 The two Battalions of Colo Rugg[s] Regt. (Except few to Keep tents) to go to F Miller for provisions, Went over the Island at 10 °Clock Returnd; the Neat scow [became] full [and] sunk, the Men sav'd Clearing Parade this Afternoon The scows Returnd from Fort Miller 8 Ms. from F Edwd. [Joseph] Charles 11/3

11 Monday Do. The Men Clearing Parade[ground] Drawing of Logs, Clearing a Road to the Blockhouse,

---

[13] Probably John Prideaux, the error in spelling being a natural one.

Wrote a Letter home No. 3 by Doct. [George] Young. No News

12 Tuesday Wet Nothing Remarkable, our Men a Diging & Clearing of Stumps Wrote home No. 4 by Doct. Young–[14]

13 of June Wednesday – Rhode I[sland] Man Whip'd 400 L[ashes.] In the Afternoon Draw'd Lots to go to F[ort] E[dward] to keep it 220 of the Massachusets Forces [and] 90 of the Jersey Blues Station'd there; 200 of the bay Men sent to half Way Brook 150 Gone to Battoeing 25 a Teaming about 300 in Camp & 600 Invalids not yet Join'd–

14 Thursday. Do. Draw'd a List of Our Men in F E[15] two R I Men Whip'd one 1000 the other 500 Lashes, bot. 2 lb of Brown Sugar – 18/

Parole Norfolk F E-dd June th11, 1759

Colo. for ye Day Colo. Grant, for toMorrow Colo Schuyler – Field Officer of ye Picquet Major Kimball, for to Morrow Lt Colo. [Samuel] Hunt. Each Regt will make a path to their Front for their Picquet to Advance when anything may be Extraory. The Genl. will shew the Commanding Officer where he would have those Picquets Advance to & in Case of any Alarm in ye Night No Regt. on any Acco^{nt} Whatever to fire a Shot from ye Lines but ye Picquet will be Order'd out & will be Supported. Spruce Beer will be Brew'd for ye Health & Conveniency of ye Troops which will be sold at ye prime Cost 5 quarts of Molasses will be put into Each Barrl of Spruce Beer. Each Gallo. will Cost near 3 Coppers, the Q Mastr. of ye Regts Regulars & provincials is to give Notice this Evening to Lt Colo. Roberson [Beverly Robinson] of ye Quantity Each Corps is Desirous to Receive for which they are to give Receipts & to pay ye Money before ye Regt. March's. – Each Regt. to send a Man Acquainted with the Brewing, or that is Best Capable of Assisting ye Brewer, to Brewing to Morrow Morng. at

---

[14] This letter is acknowledged as of June 13. See reply of David Henshaw dated June 23. Ante p. 153.
[15] See Whiting, Leonard. Detachment at Fort Edward. Ante p. 152.

6 °Clock at ye Rivalock at ye Left on Mongomerys. These Men are to Remain & to be paid at ye Rate of One shillg. & 6 pence p Day Currency; a Serjt. of ye Regulars & of the Provincials to Superintend the Brewing Who will be paid at the same Rate. Spruce Beer will be Deliver'd to ye Regts. on Thursday Evening or Friday Morng. – To Morrow Morng. 1 Sub[altern] 1 Serjt. 3 Corpll. 32 Men to Mount a Guard on ye Island. He will Detach a Corpl. & 6 Men to take Care of ye Battoes & a Corpl. & 6 Men to take Care of ye Whale Boats this Guard to be Releiv'd every 48 hours: ye Whole to take there Tents & Provision with them & ye Guards at ye Island to Come of at Orderly times at 10 °Clock in ye Morng. & ye Adjutant to attend at 6 in the Evening forever After Orders these may be the Genl. guard to Morrow – Colo. Montgomerys ye Picquet & out Guards to Load with Roustring Ball that there may be no Waste of Ammunition Every Officer of Guards to take Care this Order is Fulfill'd.[16]

Fort Edward June th14, 1759   Parole Lancaster –

Field Officer of the Day to Morrow Colo. Montgomery – Capt. for the Day Capt. [Job] Williams. An Officer to Visit the Barracks to see that the Men keep them Clean & that they Sweep under their Beds & that they Report it to the Officer of the Day & to Examine the Buckets of the Well & Report them – The Officer of the Guard to go his Rounds at the Dawn of the Day & if any of the Centries be found asleep, Confine him Immediat^y. or be Absent from there post find them out & Confine them – No Fires to be Suffer'd in the Mens Barracks but to Cook there Victuals the Officer of the Guards to Visit the Mens Rooms to see that there Fires are put out at the Tattoes Beating – No Dirt or Nastiness to be thrown out in the Fort. * * * * * The Commanding Officer of the Guard to see that these Orders are Strickly Comply'd with & that all Orders Relating to the Men are Read to them that None can plead Ignorance –

---

[16] This entry is succeeded by two blank pages. The difference in dates suggests that Lt. Henshaw expected further news or orders for these two days than are given on p. 198 and reserved a place for them.

He hath Determd to punish the first Man that is found guilty with the Utmost Severity – the Capt. of the Guards to go his Rounds any time betwixt the hours of 10 and 12 at Night.

Evening Orders: Capt. for the Day to Morrow Capt. Whiting – to Visit the Barracks Lt. [Elias] Dayton. For Guard to Morrow Lt. Gibs, [Joshua Gibbs] & Lieut [Amos] Styles – 3 Serjts. 6 Corpll. & 72 Privates –

Fort Edward June th15 – 1759 Parole Sussex:

Field Officer for the Picquet Lt. Colo. Ingersol – For Guard to-Morrow Lieut Henshaw & Ensn. [Elijah] Baker – Capt. of the Day to Morrow Capt. [Zephaniah] Luse – To Visit the Barrs. toMorrow Massachusets 3 Serjts 4 Corpls. 52 Privates – Jersey Blues 1 Serjt. 2 Corpls. & 20 privates.

15 Friday Do. 3 Regs. of Highlands March'd to the Lake – 200 of Invalids Join'd us –

16 Fort Edward June th16 1759 Parole Boston:

Eveng. Orders For Guard to Morrow Lt. Dayton & Ensn. Force – Capt. for the day to Morrow Capt. Whiting to Visit the Barracks Lt. Gibbs for Guards 2 Serjts. 3 Corpls. & 52 privates

16 Saturday F W – Went to the Camps to see a Man shot; but he was Reprieved after the Cap was pull'd over his Eyes. At 9 °Clock went with a Guard to the Royal Block house

Fort Edward June 17th. 1759 Parole London –

Capt of the Day to Morrow Capt Whiting – For Guard to Morrow Lt. Gibbs & Lt. Scot [Charles Scott] – to Visit the Barracks Ensn. Freeman. A Court Martial to sett to morrow Morning at 10 °Clock: President Capt. [Zephaniah] Luses. (Lt. [John] Cambell Lt Dayton Ensign Gordon & Ensn. Freeman Members.) The Prisoners to be Acquainted and all Evidences to Attend –

17 Sunday Relievd at the R Blockhouse Went to the Fort Rainy Weather Nothing Extraordinary

Fort Edward June 18th – 1759 Parole Westminster –

Capt of the Day to Morrow Capt Luse. For Guard Lt Styles & Ensn. Freeman – To Visit the Barracks Lt. Henshaw. For Guard 2 Serjt. 3 Corpls. & 52 Privates

18 Monday F. The 1st Battalion set out at 5 ^{O}Clock for half Way Brook. Extream hard Rain at Night when I was in Colo Ruggles Tent – Bought of Mr Forsey

	York Currency.		
A Tea pot.	£0 8	=	0
½ lb of Tea @ 12/6 pound.	6	=	3
2 lb of Sugar @ 1/6 pound.	3	=	
3 Cups & Sawcers.	2	=	6
1 Cake of Chocolate.	3	=	6
2 lb of Sugar.	3	=	0
1 Spoon 1/ 2 quarts of Milk: 8d.	1	=	8
	£1 = 7	=	11

Fort Edward June th19. 1759 Parole Gravesend

Capt of the day to Morrow Capt Williams – For Guards to Morrow Lt. Henshaw & Ensn. Baker – To Visit the Barracks Lt. Dayton, 2 Serjts. 4 Corpls. & 52 privates

19 Do. Tuesday Do – New Hampshire Troops Arrivd A packet came in but have not heard what news – Yesterday a Flag of Truce Came from Ticonderoga, came to our Block house was Examind & Let go: Draw'd Flow'r, Meat, Rice, & Butter, all which was very good

20 Wednesday Do. Went with the Guard to the Royal Blockhouse 3 Compas. of the Last Recruits came up

20 of June Wednesday   Parole Southwark

Capt of the Day for to Morrow Capt Whiting – For Guard Lt. Dayton & Ensn. Force To Visit the Barracks Lt.

The Orderly Book of Lieut. William Henshaw. 203

Gibbs For Guard to Morrow 1 Officer 2 Serjts 3 Corplls. & 36 Privates

	S	C	P
The Island Guard.............	1 –	1 –	12
Block house West of the Bridge...........		1 –	6
Block house East end Do................	1 –	1 –	9
No 1............................		1 –	6
No 2............................		1 –	6
No 3............................		1 –	6
No. 4............................		1 –	6
No. 5............................		1 –	6
Ravellene Guard......................	1–	1 –	12
Garden Guard.........................		1 –	3
Total	3 =	10 =	72

21 Thursday Do. the Army to the No. of about 8000 Men Marcht for the Lake this Morning Bought a side of Venison of an Indian Weigh'd 50 lb sold 1 Quarter for 8 Dolls. 3 lb. for 16/10

Fort Edward June th21. 1759 – Parole Amherst –

Capt of the Day for to Morrow Capt. Luse. For Guard to Morrow Ensn. Force. To Visit the Barracks Lt. Scott. The Same Number of Men to be Warned for Duty to Morrow as this Day and an Orderly Man for the Governour–the Commanding Officers of Compys. to make up a Regular Roll of their Comps. & give them in to Morrow – & to give in a true State of their Compys. Every Morning

22 Friday Do. Serjt. Blunt Came up Wrote a Letter to Ensn. Bond: Bott 8 lb of Sugar –

Fort Edward June th22 – 1759 – Parole Montgomery –

Capt of the Day for to Morrow Capt. Williams For Guard Lt. Gibbs – to Visit the Barracks Ensn. Freeman the Royal Blockhouse & Island to be 48 Hours Guards till Further Orders. Capt Luses Compy. gives the Royal Block house Guard & Capt Williams Compy. the Island Guard –

Fort Edward June th23 – 1759 – Parole Great Britain –

Capt of the Day For to Morrow Capt. Whiting For Guard Lt. Scott To Visit the Barracks Lt. Stiles

23 Saturday June 23 Do 1759 a Regular Corpll. Confd. for Strikg. Serjt Wyer. A Chaplain of the Jersey Regt. went to prayer in Garrison.

Fort Edward June 24 – Parole Edinburgh –

Capt of the Day to Morrow Capt Luse For Guard to Morrow Ensn. Freeman – To Visit the Barracks Lt. Henshaw the Royal Blockhouse & the Island Guard to be Reliev'd to Morrow; Capt Williams Compy. gives the Royal Blockhouse Guard & Capt Whitings the Island guard; a Corpl. & 15 Men For Fatigue at 6 °Clock to Morrow Morning – Serjt. [William] Ferguson of the Royal Highlands will show them what they have to do – No Man belonging to the Garrison to lye out of the Fort on any Account –

24 Sunday Do. A Highland[er] Shot Accidently through the thigh. Read the Boston prints of the 11 Inst. Lieut. [John] Martin of the Rangers came from Ticonderoga with a Scouting party Reports they are Very Numerous Several Officers Arriv'd this Day Lt [Nathaniel] Ingersol Lt. Dunlap Ensn Ward Watkins – Memoranter. Jno Knower

Fort Edward June 25th 1759 – Parole Glasgow –

Capt. of the Day for to Morrow Capt. Williams, For Guard Lieut. Henshaw, to Visit the Barracks, Ensn. Baker –

25 Monday Very warm Visited ye Barracks Walk'd out of the Fort & heard Mr. [William] Crawford go to prayer & sing Psalms in Colo. Willards Regt. 11/3

Fort Edward June 26th. 1759 – Parole Prussia –

Capt. of the day to Morrow – Capt. Whiting for guard Ensn. Baker To Visit the Barracks Lt. Dayton. an Officer pr. Compa. to Attend Roll Call every Eveng. & to see that there Men be properly Warn'd for Duty & to be upon the Parade Every Morng. when the guards Mount that they may Answer for any thing Deficient – In Case of an Alarm by Day or Night the Garrison is to parade in the Following Manner – Capt Luses Compa. upon the Royal Bastion. Capt. Williams on the Snook Bastion. Capt. Whiting on the Magazine Bastion – the Invalids of the 55th. & 80th. Regts. on the Water Bastion – the Officer of the guard to be Very Alert & keep his Guard ready to turn out at the first Call. The Rolls to be Call'd for the Future upon the Alarm posts: the Royal Blockhouse & Island Guards to be Reliev'd to Morrow – Capt Whitings Compa. Gives the Royal Blockhouse guard & Capt Luse the Island guard – The Garrison is to draw 2 Days fresh provision to Morrow Morng. at 9 ^{O}Clock

26 Tuesday Do. Reliev'd the Main Guard Serjt. [of] the Jerseys Confd. for being Drunk & Absent from Duty. Removed to North Side of the Fort.

Fort Edward June th27, 1759 – Parole Berlin –

Capt of the Day to Morrow Capt. Luse for Guard Lt. Dayton to Visit the Barracks Lt. Gibbs.

27 Wednesday Do. Lieut. Ingersol went to Join our Compa. at half Way Brook 200 of the Invalids March'd with him – Wrote to Capt. Furness

Fort Edward June th28 – 1759 – Parole Air –

Capt. of the Day to Morrow Capt. Williams – for Guard Lt. Gibbs, to Visit the Barracks Lt. Scott – the Royal Blockhouse and Island Guards to be Releiv'd to Morrow – Capt. Luse's Compa. gives the Royal Blockhouse guard & Capt William's the Island Guard

28 Thursday Do. N Extraordinary. The Main guard of the Fort & Guards depending Consists of about 150 Men –

Fort Edward June th29. 1759 – Parole Eglinton –

Capt. of the day to Morrow Capt. Whiting – For guard Lieut. Scott to Visit the Barracks Ensn. Freeman Capt Luse's Compa. to parade on the Alarm Posts to Morrow Morng. at 7 ^{O}Clock in Order to have there Arms Ammunition & Accoutrements Inspected. A Garrison Court Martial to Set to Morrow Morng. at 10 °Clock to try such of there prisoners as shall be brought before them.

Capt Williams Pressident
Lieut. Gibbs   Lieut. Henshaw } Members
Lieut. Scott   Ensn. Freeman

29 Friday Do. this Morng. at Sun Rise heard the Report of Cannon & platoons at the Lake which Continued 2 hours & Alarm'd the Fort & B Houses: Colo Mongomery sent 300 Men: Colo Willard 150 to the Lake to know the Ocasion - the Men Return'd & Reported they were Clearing there Peices

Fort Edward June th30 - 1759 - Parole Argyle -

Capt of the day to Morrow Capt Luse for Guard Ensn. Freeman to Visit the Barracks Lt. Stiles. No person belonging to the Garison to Carry Spirituous Liquors of any Kind to the Sick in the Hospital Under the pain of being Severely Punished. Capt Williams Compa to parade on their Alarm posts at 7 °Clock to Morrow Morng. in Order to have there Arms & Accoutrements Inspected - the Royal Block house & Island Guard to be Reliev'd to Morrow - Capt Williams Compa. Gives the Royal B House Guard & Whitings the Island Guard

30 Saturday This Morning [Rev. Edward Eells of Middletown] the Chaplain of Colo. [Nathan] Whitings Regt. of Connecticut Went to prayer in Fort - Set on a Garrison Court Martial to try two prisoners of the Jersey Regt. one for being Drunk & Neglect of Duty the other For being drunk & Quitting his post when on Centinel -

Fort Edward July th1 1759 - Parole New York -

Capt. of the [day] for to Morrow Capt Williams - For Guard Lt. Stiles to Visit the Barracks Lt. Henshaw; the Invalids of the Royal 55th & 80th Regts. to attend Roll Call Regularly On the Water Bastion -

1 Sunday Misty Day took a Walk towards the Falls [Wind] N E -

The Orderly Book of Lieut. William Henshaw. 207

Fort Edward July - 2 - 1759 - Parole Philadelphia -

Capt. of the Day for to Morrow Capt. Whiting: for Guard Lieut. Henshaw to Visit the Barracks Ensn. Baker; the Royal Blockhouse & Island Guards to be Reliev'd to Morrow Capt. Whitings Compa. Gives the Royal Blockhouse Guard & Capt Luse the Island Guard

2 Monday Do. Visited the Barracks   Made Report N E -

Fort Edward July th3 - 1759 - Parole Boston -

Capt. of the day for to Morrow Capt Luse - For Guard Ensn. Baker; to Visit the Barracks Lt. Dayton; a Picquet Consisting of a Subaltern 1 Serjt. 1 Corpll. & 24 Privates to mount at Retreats Beating this Evening & hereafter till Further Orders; 3 Men from the Picquet to mount as a Guard in Each of the 2 Blockhouses at the provision Sheds & Continue till the ports are Opened. The Serjts. Corplls. & the rest to joyn the Main Guard & Furnish the two Additional Centinels & partys for the Following Rounds Viz: a Serjt. & 4 Privates for the grand Rounds with the Capt. Between 11 & 12 °Clock a Corpl. & 4 Men for the Officer that Visits the Barracks Between 1 & 2 °Clock, the Like Number for the Officer of the Picquet Between 2 & 3 °Clock, And the Officer of the Guard to have his Guard & the picquet under Arms half an Hour before Day & to Continue So till it is Clear Day & take Care that the Serjt. or Corpl. of the Picquet with 2 Men Patrole round the Centries Every half hour.

Ensn. Force for the Picquet - No Man to smoak Tobbacco in the Barracks under the pain of being Severely Punished. The Serjts. & Corpl. to see this Order Comply'd with & to Confine any they find trangressg & to take Care that their is no Fire or Light in the Barracks Rooms after Retreats Beating - the Bridge & Block houses No. 4 & 5 are to be guards of 48 hours till further Orders. Capt Williams Compa. gives the Bridge Guards -

The 3 Day July Tuesday. The Collos. Mongomery Willard & Lovell[17] with there Regts. March'd & Escorted the Cannon

---

[17] Unless this be Zacheus Lovewell I have been unable to identify him.

to the Lake. Heard the News of 16 Jersey Blues Walking from the Lake to get Bark; the Indians fell on them Kill'd & Scalp'd 11. Relieved the Guards.

Fort Edward July th4 – 1759 – Parole Albany –

Capt. of the Day for to Morrow Capt Williams–for Guard Lt Dayton–to Visit the Barracks Ensn. Force – For Picquet Lt. Gibbs – The Royal Blockhouse & Island Guard to be Reliev'd to Morrow Capt Luse's Compa. Gives the Royal Blockhouse guard & Capt Whitings the Island guard – the Blockhouses No. 1–2 & 3 are to be Guards of 48 hours – Capt Luse's Compa. gives the guard for No. 1 Capt. Williams for No. 2 and Capt. Whiting for No. 3 the Garrison are to Receive 4 Days Fresh Provision at 9 °Clock to Morrow from Mr. Washington –

4 Wednesday Do. a party of Rangers brought in several Scalps Taken near Crown point. Bott. 2 lb of Sugar

Fort Edward July th5. 1759 – Parole Newport –

Capt of the Day for to Morrow Capt. Whiting – for guard Ensn. Force – to Visit the Barracks Lt. Gibbs For Picquet Lt. Scott – the Bridge & Blockhouses No. 4 & 5 to be Reliev'd to Morrow Capt Williams Compa. gives the Bridge guards & Capt. Luses Compa. the Guard for No. 4 & Capt Whitings for No. 5 – For Guard – 2 Serjts. – 4 Corpls. – 47 Privas.

5 Thursday Do. 8 Weeks – from – Worcester Orders Given out for Sutler's to Strike their Tents; Bott. of Mr. Cutler

		s	
1 piece of Nanteen [Nankeen] 22/......	£1	– 2	– 0
2 Dozn Butts. at 18d pr Dozn............		3	
Thread 1/.........................		1	
	1 –	6	– 0

Fort Edward July th6 – 1759 – Parole Brunswick –

Capt. of the Day to Morrow Capt. Luse – For Guard Lt. Gibbs – to Visit the Barracks – Lt. Scott – For Picquet – Ensn. Freeman. The Royal Blockhouse Island & block houses No. 1, 2 & 3 to be Releiv'd to Morrow – Capt Luse's Compa. gives the Royal Blockhouse Guard & Capt Whiting the Island

6 Friday Do. Bott. of [Josiah] Brewer 2 lb of Sugar N E – Capt Luse Gives No. 1, Capt Will^s. No. 2 & Capt. Whitings No. 3 [Blockhouse] Guards a Serjt. & 12 Men of the picquet to go at 3 ^{O}Clock to Cut Brooms for Cleaning the parade & Chimneys – all the Chimneys in the Garrison to be Swept to Morrow Morning – For Guard – 2 S – 4 C – 55 P.

Fort Edward July: 7th – 1759 – Parole New Hampshire –

Capt. of the Day For to Morrow Capt. Williams – For Guard Lt. Scott – to Visit the Barracks Ensn. Freeman. For Picquet – Lt. Stiles. The Bridge & Blockhouses No. 4 & 5 Guards to be Releiv'd to Morrow – Capt. Williams Compa. gives the Bridge Guard, Capt Whitings No. 4 & 5 – for Guard – 2 S – 5 C – 52 P.

7 Saturday Do. Went & Wash'd in the River – Aaron Smith of Rhodetown Died th5 Inst. His Cloathing priz'd £3 – 12 – 0.

Fort Edward July th8 – 1759 – Parole Newark –

Capt. of the Day for to Morrow Capt. Whiting – For Guard Ensn. Freeman – to Visit the Barracks, Lieut. Stiles For the Picquet – Lieut. Henshaw – the Royal Blockhouse Island, Blockhouses No. 1–2 & 3 Guards to be Releiv'd to Morrow – the Officers of the Company's that hear the Roll Call'd to see the Men of their Compa. Paraded for the Guards & Picquet & to Examine their Arms & Ammunition & See that the Men are properly Drest – For Guard: 2 S – 5 C – 49 P.

8 Sunday Do. the Picquet turn'd out to look after Cattle.– Releiv'd the Picquet.–

Fort Edward July th9. 1759. – Parole Huck –

Capt. of the Day to Morrow Capt. Luse – For Guard Lt. Stiles – To Visit the Barracks Lt. Henshaw. For Picquet

Ensn. Baker. The Bridge guards & Blockhouses No. 4 & 5 to be Reliev'd to Morrow. A Garrison Court Martial to sett at 10. °Clock to Morrow Morning

Capt. Whiting Pressident
Lieut. Dayton   Lt. Gibbs   } Members.
Ensn. Baker   Ensn. Force   }

The Prisoners to be Acquainted and all Evidences to attend.[18] For Guard – 2 S – 5 C – 49 P

9th Monday: Bott. a Nankeen Jacket 14/ 1 pr of Indian Stockings 4/ Dr. Lt. Gibbs to ½ a piece Nankeen 13/

Fort Edward July th10 – 1759 – Parole Burlington –

Capt of the Day to Morrow Capt. Williams. For Guard Lieut. Henshaw – To Visit the Barracks Ensn. Baker. For Picquet Lieut. Dayton. The Royal Blockhouse – Island & Blockhouses No. 1 – 2 & 3 Guards to be Reliev'd to Morrow. For Guard – 3 S – 5 C – 49 P

10 Tuesday Rainy – Draw'd Flour, 707 lb. Meat & Butter for 3 Days – Visited the Barracks. –

Fort Edward July th11, 1759 – Parole Charlestown –

Capt of the Day for to Morrow Capt. Whiting For Guard Ensn. Baker To Visit the Barracks Lt. Dayton – For Picquet Ensn. Force. The Bridge Guards and Block Houses No. 4 & 5 to be Releiv'd to Morrow.

11 Wednesday Fair – Reliev'd the Guard Several Prisoners brought from Saratoga Absent at G[enl.] R[uggles] Very Cold at Night Wrote to Boston to B[rother] Jos[eph] –

Fort Edward July th 12 – 1759 – Parole Amboy –

Capt. of the Day for to Morrow Capt. Luse – For Guard Lt. Dayton to Visit the Barracks Ensn. Force for Picquet Lieut Gibbs. the Royal Blockhouse Island & Block houses No. 1 2 & 3 to be Reliev'd to Morrow –

---

[18] For record of proceedings, see entry under Jul. 10 . Ante p. 153.

12 Thursday – Do – Ensn. Force Officer of the Picquet Orderd to Escort a Prisoner & some Waggons to the falls – Several Indians Discoverd Last Night at the Falls – Block houses No. 3 & 4 Fir'd. Each of them at 10 or 12 at Night. Alarmed the Garrison heard that Majr. [Robert] Rogers had an Engagement at the lake Early this Morning – At Night he Returnd with the Loss of 1 Serjt. Killd. & 1 Wounded.

Fort Edward July th 13. 1759 – Parole Boston –

Capt. For the Day to Morrow Capt. Williams For Guard Ensn. Force, To Visit the Barracks Lt. Gibbs For Picquet Lt. Scott The Bridge & Blockhouses No. 4 & 5 to be Releiv'd to Morrow.

13 Friday Do. Lieut. Gibbs Officer of the Picquet Order'd to the Falls to Escort 6 Prisoners Dutch Waggoners for stealing Old Iron Bott. 2 lb of Sugar at Night the Garrison Alarmd at the Firing two Guns from Bridge Blockhouse –

Fort Edward July 14 – 1759 – Parole Pittsburgh –

Capt of the Day for to Morrow Capt. Whiting, For Guard Lt. Gibbs, To Visit the Barracks Lt Scott, For Picquet Ensn. Freeman. The Royal Blockhouse & Island Blockhouses No. 1 2 & 3 to be Releiv'd to Morrow – A Garrison Court Martial to Set to Morrow at 10 ºClock –

Capt. Luse Pressident –
Lt. Scott   Lt. Henshaw } Members
Lt. Stiles   Lt. Freeman }

the Prisoners to be Acquainted & all Evidences to Attend –

14 Saturday Very Hot – Rain Last Night. A Compa. of the last Recruits came up Jona. Phillips Arriv'd 2 or 3 Comp Highlands Ariv'd from Ohio the Fort Alarm'd this Night the Royal Fir'd at an Indian –

Fort Edward July th 15, 1759 – Parole Louisbourgh –

Capt. of the Day for to Morrow Capt. Luse, for Guard Lt. Scott – to Visit the Barracks Ensn. Freeman, For

Picquet, Lt. Stiles – the Bridge guard & Blockhouses No. 4 & 5 to be Releiv'd to Morrow – the Sick in the Garrison to be Carried over to Island at 9 °Clock to Morrow Morning to be seen by the Doctors

15 Sunday Rain. Two prisoners of the 80th. Regt. Try'd for Stelth, One more tried for Quitting his Post; A Waggoner Came to Fort & Reported that he saw a No. of Indians & Ran away & Left his Waggon. A party of Voluntiers [went to investigate]   Capt. Whiting & Lt. Dayton Headed the party. Returned m[orning.]

Fort Edward July th16 – 1759 – Parole Ligoneer –

Capt. of the Day for to Morrow Capt. Williams – For Guard Ensn. Freeman – To Visit the Barracks Lieut. Stiles For the Picquet Lieut. Henshaw– The Royal Block house & Island & Block houses No. 1: 2 & 3 to be Releiv'd to Morrow Morning   For Guard: 3 S – 5 C – 49 P

16 Monday Rainy – 3 Compa. of Colo. Fitch's Regt Arived – Colo. Lymans Chaplain [Rev. George Beckwith] Preach'd a sermon in Fort   Went the Rounds between 2 & 3 °Clock at Night – one of the Centinals not Alert

Fort Edward July th17. 1759 – Parole Perth –

Capt. of the Day for to Morrow Capt. Whiting – For Guard Lt. Stiles – To Visit the Barracks Lt. Henshaw For Picquet Ensn. Baker   the Bridge & Block houses No. 4 & 5 to be Releiv'd to Morrow, Guard 2 S – 4 C – 52 P–

17 Tuesday Fair – Drawed our Allowance of all Species for a Week – 4 Days fresh Beef – 3 Days of Salt pork – 3 Days of Butter – 7 Days of Flower – for 100 Men – Vizt. 700 lb of Flower pr Week 400 lb fresh Beef &c.

Fort Edward July th18. 1759 – Parole Montrose –

Capt. of the Day to Morrow Capt Luse – For Guard Lieut. Henshaw   To Visit the Barracks Ensn. Baker   For Picquet Lieut   Dayton The Royal Blockhouse Island & Block house

Guards to be Releiv'd to Morrow. Vizt. No. 1 – 2 & 3
For Guard 3 S – 5 C – 49 P

18 Wednesday Do. Visited the Barracks

Fort Edward July th19 – 1759

A Garrison Court Martial to sett at 10 °Clock this Forenoon

Capt Williams Pressident
Ensn. Baker,   Lieut Dayton   } Members
Ensn. Force   & Lieut Gibbs }
the Prisoners to be Acquainted & all Evidences to Attend –

July th19 – Afternoon Orders – Parole Elgin –

Capt of the Day for to Morrow Capt Williams – For Guard – Ensn. Baker To Visit the Barracks Lt. Dayton For Picquet Ensn. Force the Bridge & Block houses – No. 4 & 5 to be Releiv'd to Morrow   For Guard 2 S – 4 C – 52 P

19 Thursday Do.– Releiv'd the Guard this Morng. the Govr. of So. Carolina[19] Ariv'd here Last Night. Set off this Day for the Lake – Came to see the Proceedings of Genl. Amherst – Attended with 2 Negro Servants. [He is] a tall Man upwards of 50 Years of age. A prisoner Comited to the Guard for Desertion

Fort Edward July th20 – 1759 – Parole Falkirk –

Capt. of the Day for to Morrow Capt Whiting – For Guard – Lt. Dayton To Visit the Barracks Ensn. Force For Picquet – Lt. Gibbs – The Royal Blockhouse Island & Blockhouses No. 1: 2 & 3 to be Releivd to Morrow – [For guard] 3 S – 5 C – 53 P

20 Friday Do. Wrote a Letter home sent by Capt. Doolittle – the Battoes all Loaded to Sail at the First Notice, One of Capt Paines Men Confin'd for Desertion – 3 Men Whip'dt of 80th [regt.] 2 for Stealing – one for a False Alarm; 2 of the 80th Regt. Sentenc'd 750 [Lashes] Recd. one 400, the

---
[19] William H. Lyttleton was governor of South Carolina at this time. See post p. 234.

other 300 Lashes; the Jersey Blue sentenc'd 100 Recd. 50 – for False Alarm – Nothing Further Extraordinary –

Fort Edward July 21 – 1759 – Parole Linlethgow –

Capt. of the Day for to Morrow Capt. Luse – For Guard Lt. Gibbs – To Visit the Barracks Lt. Scott – For Picquet Ensn. Freeman – sick, [replaced by] Lt. Stiles – The Bridge & Blockhouses No. 4 & 5 To be Releiv'd to Morrow

21 Saturday By a Man who came From the Lake this Morning I was Inform'd that the Orders was for the Army to strike their tents by 2 ºClock in Morning – at 3 ºClock they was all Embarkd & Sail'd for Ticonderoga. About 200 of the Connecticut Forces Ariv'd to Day

Fort Edward 22d. of July 1759 – Parole Dumfreis –

Capt of the Day to Morrow Capt. Williams – For Guard Lt. Scott – To Visit the Barracks Ensn. Freeman For Picquet Lt Henshaw – The Royal Blockhouse Island & Blockhouses No 1 – 2 & 3 to be Releiv'd to Morrow No person to throw Water or any Filth out of their Barrack Windows under pain of being Severely punished –

22 Sunday Do. 7 or 8 of Connecticut Troops Ariv'd – N Extraordinary

23d. of July – 1759 – Parole Paisly –

Capt. of the Day for to Morrow Capt Whiting – For Guard Ensn. Freeman To Visit the Barracks Lt. Henshaw For Picquet – Ensn. Baker. The Bridge & Block houses – No. 4 & 5 to be Releivd to Morrow For Guard: 3 S – 5 C – 55 P

23 Day of July – 1759 Monday. Bott of Cutler one Silk Handkerch 1 pr. of Buckles recd the Boston Gazette of the 16 Inst. read the News of Saml. Lynds house blown over – by a Huricane also the Death of Sir Wm. Pepperell Lt–Griggs – In the Evening heard a sermon preach'd by Mr. [Benjamin] Pomroy – Chaplain of one of the Connecticut Regts. [He] Lodg'd with us at Night Nothing Further Remarkable

Fort Edward the 24th of July – 1759 – Parole Peebles –

A Garrison Court Martial to sett Immediately.

Capt Whiting Pressident
  Lieut. Scott   Lieut Stiles ⎫
  Lieut Henshaw Ensn. Baker ⎬ Members
                ⎭

The Prisoners to be Acquainted and all evidences to attend

Capt. of the Day for to Morrow Capt Luse, For Guard Lieut. Henshaw, To Visit the Barracks Ensn. Baker, For Picquet Lieut. Dayton, The Royal Blockhouse Island and Blockhouses No. 1 – 2 & 3 to be Releiv'd to Morrow –

24 Tuesday Do. Orders for a Court Martial to set Immediately for the tryal of 2 prisoners one for Striking a Waggon Master the other a Delirious Fellow, For Alarming the Garrison. Pass'd Sentence & Carried it in. Orders to try them again. Our Opinion the same. Bott of Brewer 2 lb Sugar.

Wednesday Fort Edward July 25 – 1759 – Parole Berline –

Capt. of the Day for to Morrow Capt. Williams For Guard Ensn. Baker To Visit the Barracks Lt. Dayton For Picquet Lt. Gibbs – The Bridge & Blockhouses No. 4 & 5 to be Releiv'd to Morrow all the Axes in the Fort to be Given in this Evening to Mr. Man –

25 Wednesday Do. Reliev'd the Main guard. Letters from Ticonderoga says our Men all safe Landed – One Kill'd 13 or 14 Wounded – Dr. to Brewer 2/6 Dd Jno Allen to 2 lb Sugar–

Fort Edward July 26 – 1759 –

A Garrison Court Martial to set Immediately.

Capt. Luse Pressident
  Lieut Dayton Lt. Gibbs   ⎫
  Lieut Scott   Ensn. Freeman ⎬ Members
                ⎭

the prisoners to be Acquainted and all Evidences to attend

– After Orders – Parole Potsdam –

Capt. of the Day for to Morrow Capt Whiting for Guard Lt. Dayton – to Visit the Barracks Lt. Gibbs – For Picquet Lt Scott – The Royal Blockhouse Island & Blockhouses No. 1: 2 & 3 to be Reliev'd to Morrow. For Guard: 3 S – 5 C – 55 P

26 Thursday Do. Capt [Cornelius?] Higgins in a Battoe with 8 Men on the Lake; the Capt. with 5 Men Kill'd & Scalp'd the Other three, dont know wt. became of them. A Court Martial Set to try 4 prisoners: 1 provincial Sent. 500 [lashes] Recd none; 1 for Defaming Lt. Dayton Sent. 200 R[eceived] N[one]. 1 for Knocking a Man Down Sent. 500 Recd None; one for refusing to do his Duty Sent. 100 Recd None; all Cleard for the Taking Ticonderoga. N. Hamps [troops] sent from Ticonderoga to Join our Forces up Mohawk River

Fort Edward the 27th of July 1759 Parole Dresden –

Capt of the Day For to Morrow Capt Luse – For Guard – Lt Gibbs – To Visit the Barracks Lt. Scott – For Picquet – Ensn. Freeman – the Capt. of the Day to give in Every Day a Written Report Specifiing the prisoners & their Crimes & any thing Extraordinary that Happens. The Bridge & Block houses No. 4 & 5 to be Releiv'd to Morrow- [For guard] 2 S – 4 C – 52 privs.

27 Friday Colo. [George] Townsend Adjut. Genll. was Kill'd at Ticonderoga. As he was Reconoitring the Ground with one or two more, he was shot from th Fort with a Cannon Ball through the Body & Liv'd about a Min^t. told them to Carry him of the Ground; his Body was Embalm'd & Fetch'd down to day & Escorted to Albany – 15 Wounded men came Down & [were] carried into the Hospital on the Island 2 French Prisoners Came Down & Carried to Fort Miller

Fort Edward July th28 1759

A Garrison Court Martial to Set Immediately Capt Williams Pressident

Lt. Stiles   Lt. Henshaw } Members
Ensn. Baker Lt. Dayton   }

The prisoners to be Acquainted and all Evidences to attend–

Afternoon Orders – Parole Ticonderoga –

Capt. of the Day for to Morrow Capt. Williams, For Guard Lt. Scott to Visit the Barracks Ensn. Freeman – For Picquet Lt. Stiles – the Royal Blockhouse Island & Blockhouses No. 1: 2 & 3 to be Releivd to Morrow For Guard – 2 S – 4 C – 55 P

July th28 – 1759 Saturday. News by Colo. Amherst that Ticonderoga is in the Hands of the English. The 26 Inst. in the Night the French Deserted it after Blowing up one End & Setting it on Fire but the English soon Extinguish'd the Fire; the French made their Escape in Battoes. Information thereof: Rogers Raingers Pursued them, took about Twenty Prisoners & some Plunder. Sett on a Court Martial to Try two Teamsters for stealing the Kings Flower-Sentd. 200 [lashes] Each, 1 pardoned the other Recd. 75 Lashes – the Prisoners Pardon'd at the News of Ticon[a]. being taken this Afternoon 20 prisoners Came in; the Picquet escorted them to F Miller Dr. to Brewr. To 1 Bottl. Wine to 2 pints, Do. – Went to hear prayers at Night Nothing Further Remarkable, Bott. ½ lb Tobacco

Sunday Fort Edward the 29th July – 1759 – Parole Amherst –

Capt of the Day for to Morrow Capt Whiting, for guard Ensn. Freeman, To Visit the Barracks Lt. Stiles, For Picquet Lt. Henshaw – The Bridge & Blockhouses No 4 & 5 to be Releiv'd to Morrow. Only 4 Men & a Corpll. to mount guard in Each Blockhouse till further Orders & they are to keep 1 Sentry by Day & 2 by Night till further Orders – For Guard 2 S – 3 C – 44 P

29 Sunday Report that the Army is getting Battoes into Lake Champlain & preparing to Besiege Crown point – 2 or 3 of Connecticut Men came in Wounded

Fort Edward July 30th. 1759 – Parole Gage –

Capt. of the Day for to Morrow Capt. Luse, for Guard Lt. Stiles, To Visit the Barracks Lt. Henshaw, For Picquet Ensn. Baker – the Royal Blockhouse Island & Blockhouses No. 1 – 2 & 3 to be Releiv'd to Morrow; a Serjt. & 10 Men to Mount Guard in the Royal Block house & a Corpl. & 4 Men in Each of the other Blockhouses –

30 Monday Rainy – this Day I was for Picquet. Brigd. Genll. Gage Came from Ticonderoga this Afternoon

July 31th – 1759 Fort Edward – Parole Wolfe –

Capt of the Day for to Morrow Capt. Williams – For Guard Lieut. Henshaw – To Visit the Barracks Ensn. Baker – For Picquet Lieut Dayton – The Bridge & Blockhouses No. 4 & 5 to be Releiv'd to Morrow For Guard 2 S – 4 C – 48 P

31 Tuesday Do. Brigd. Genll. Gage Set out for Niagara to take the Command there, he was Guarded by the Picquet to Fort Miller – Lieut [Edward] Church Came in from Fort Massachusets No. 4 with 5 Men 5 Days a Coming across the woods – Visited the Barracks

Fort Edward the 1st. of August, 1759 – Parole Pitt –

Capt. of the Day for to Morrow – Capt Whiting, for guard Ensn Baker, To Visit the Barracks Lt. Dayton, For Picquet – Lt. Gibbs the Royal Blockhouse Island & Blockhouses No. 1 – 2 & 3 to be Releiv'd to Morrow –

1st. Wednesday Fair & Warm Releiv'd the Guard Lt Church Set out for Ticonderoga to Carry a Lettr. to the Genll. from thence he is to go through the woods to No 4 Wrote a Lettr. to No. 4 by him Wrote a Lettr. by Mr. Rice home No 6 –

Fort Edward th 2d – of Augt. 1759 – Parole Chesterfield –

Capt of the Day for to Morrow Capt. Luse for guard Lt Dayton – To Visit the Barracks Lt Gibbs For Picquet Lt. Scott – the Bridge & Blockhouses No. 4 & 5 to be Releiv'd to Morrow [For guard] 2 S – 4 C – 48 P

2d. Thursday Rainy – This Afternoon Informed that a party of ours went on a scout from Ticonderoga to Crown point They report the French had blown up one Magazene set it a Fire & Deserted it so they took possession –

The Orderly Book of Lieut. William Henshaw. 219

Fort Edward 3d. of Augt 1759 Friday – Parole Litchfield –

Capt of the Day for to Morrow Capt. Williams For Guard Lt. Gibbs To Visit the Barracks Lt. Scott No Picquet to mount till further Orders 9 Men to mount at Retreats Beating this Evening & Joyn the Main guard which till further Orders is to Consist of 33 Privates no guard to Mount at the Provision sheds till Ordered: the Blockhouse Guards No. 1: 2: 3 – 4 & 5 to Consist of a Corpll. & 3 Men, the Royal Blockhouse Island & B: house No. 1: 2 & 3 to be Releiv'd to Morrow: a subaltern 2 Serjts. 2 Corplls. & 55 privates to go to Morrow Morning with 15 Battoes to Fort Miller, the Battoes to be Compleated in Oars & Paddles – For this Duty Ensn. Freeman –

3d Augt. 1759 Friday (Fair weather)[20] This Morning at 3 ^{O}Clock an Express Ariv'd which gives an Account of Reduction of Niagara & 600 of the Enemy made Prisoners – also a French Man the Chief Sagamore of the Indians who always Instigated them to Murder & Scalp there prisoners

Fort Edward Augt. 4th. 1759 – Parole Niagara –

Capt of the Day for to Morrow Capt Whiting for guard Lt. Scott To Visit the Barracks Ensn. Freeman the Bridge & Blockhouses No. 4 & 5 to be Releiv'd to Morrow – a Corpll. & 4 Privates to mount guard on the West End of the Bridge For Guard 2 S – 4 C – 53 P

4th Augt 1759 Saturday – Do. Walk'd into the Woods to see the Working party Chop Wood in the Afternoon Went a Hunting with Capt Williams –

Fort Edward Augt. 5, 1759 – Parole Pyrna –

Capt of the Day for to Morrow Capt. Luse for Guard Ensn Freeman To Visit the Barracks Lt. Stiles the Royal B house Island & B house No. 1 – 2 & 3 to be Releiv'd to Morrow a Subaltern 2 Serjts. 2 Corpls & 55 Privates to go to Fort Miller with 15 Battoes to Morrow Morning the Battoes to be got Ready & Compleated with Oars – Paddles

---

[20] These words are erased in the original manuscript indicating changed conditions.

Setting Poles this Night. For this Duty Ensn. Force – For guard 3 S – 5 C – 56 P

5th Augt Sunday Fair – 1759 Eat some Huckleberrys at No. 1: B[lock house.]

Fort Edward Augt. 6th. 1759 – Parole Sheffield –

Capt. of the Day for to Morrow Capt Williams for guard Lieut. Stiles to Visit the Barracks Lieut. Henshaw the Bridge & Blockhouses No. 4 & 5 to be Releivd to Morrow

6th Monday Fair Mr Brewer brought 2 Letters from Albany but through a Mistake Carryed them to the Lake –

Fort Edward Augt. 7th 1759 – Parole Crown Point –

Capt of the day for to Morrow Capt. Whiting For Guard Lt. Henshaw To Visit the Barracks Ensn Baker the Royal Blockhouse Island & Block Houses No. 1 : 2 & 3 to be Releivd to Morrow – for Guard – 2 S – 5 C – & 56 P

7th Augt. Tuesday Fair – 1759 at 5 °Clock this Morng. Set out for the Lake Ariv'd at 10 °Clock Enquir'd for my Lettrs. but could get no Information of them as Mr. Brewer had set out for Ticonderoga; then went & Viewed the Old Fort the French Intrenchments & the place where they Landed round a point of Land. The French Intrench'd within 80 Roods of the Old Fort – View'd the New Fort that is Building: the Walls about 14 feet thick built of Stone & Lime;– Set out Stopt at half way Brook to see Capt Gales [Nehemiah Gale?] of Connecticut who is Station'd there Came to Fort Edward at 8 °Clock in Evening &c –

Fort Edward Augt. 8th. 1759 – Parole Rochester –

Capt. of the Day for to Morrow Capt. Luse for guard Ensn. Baker To Visit the Barracks Lt. Dayton the Bridge & Block houses – No. 4 & 5 to be Releivd to Morrow – [For guard] 2 S – 4 C – 51 P

8th Wednesday Fort Edward 1759 Recd. 2 Letters from Danll. & Jos. Dated July the 26 & 28th Which was

Carry'd to the Lake through a Mistake & Sent Back to Fort Edward Before I Came from the Lake. Releiv'd the Guard: no Prisoners Nothing Extraordinary

Thursday Fort Edward Augt. 9th 1759 – Parole Stillwater –

Capt. of the Day for to Morrow Capt. Williams – For Guard Lt. Dayton – To Visit the Barracks Ensn. Force – the Royal Block house Island & Block Houses No. 1: 2 & 3 to be Releivd to Morrow

Thursday the 9th of Augt. 1759 Bought of Mess. Cutler & Brewer –

		s	d
4 & ½ Yds. of Green Batteen @ 10/ P yd...	£2 –	5	– 0
3 & ½ Yds. of Shalloon @ 4/ P Yd.........		14	–
3 Sticks of Mohair @ 6d Each............		1	– 6
2 hanks of Green Silk @ 1/ Each..........		2	–
½ Yd. Buckram @ 3/ P Yd...............		1	– 6
Green thread 6d. penny Worth............			– 6
2 Dozn. of Buttons @ 4/2d P Dozn............		8	– 4
Total	£3 –	12	–10

Nothing Extraordinary

Friday Fort Edward Augt. 10th. 1759 – Parole Colchester –

Capt. of the Day for to Morrow Capt. Whiting – For guard Ensn. Force To Visit the Barracks Lt. Gibbs the Bridge & Block houses No. 4 & 5 to be Releiv'd to Morrow: [For guard] 2 S – 4 C – 51 P

10th Friday Misty – Capt. [Valentine] Jones: Lieut. Howard & Ensn. Lowder Set off for Crown point, they Arivd here Last Night. took a Walk, N[othing] Extraord[inary] All's Well –

Saturday Fort Edward the 11th. of Augt. 1759
– Parole Dancaster –

Capt. of the Day for to Morrow Capt. Luse – For Guard Lt. Gibbs – to Visit the Barracks – Lt. Scott – the Royal

Blockhouse Island & Blockhouses No. 1: 2 & 3 to be Releivd to Morrow –

11th of Augt. 1759 Saturday Fort Edward Went a Hunting in the Afternoon on the West side of the River – an Express Arriv'd at 11 °Clock at Night with a packet From Crown point to Fort Edward A Man was sent Immediately to Forward it to the Next post, Rain'd hard all Night

Fort Edward Augt. 12th. 1759 Sunday – Parole Dunbarton

Capt of the Day for to Morrow Capt. Williams, for Guard Lt. Scott, To Visit the Barracks Ens. Freeman the Bridge & Block houses No. 4 & 5 to be Releiv'd to Morrow – A Subaltern 1 Serjt. 1 Corpll. & 24 Privates to parade to Morrow Morng. at 6 °Clock to mend all the Bad Steps in the Road from this to Fort Miller they are to get tools of Mr. Mann – for this Duty Lt. Stiles. [Guard] 1 S – 2 C – 20 P

Sunday Fort Edward Augt. 12th. 1759 a Wet Showry Day

Monday Fort Edward Augt. 13th. 1759 – Parole Hamburg –

Capt. of the Day for to Morrow Capt Whiting For Guard Ensn. Freeman To Visit the Barracks Lt. Stiles the Royal Blockhouse Island & Blockhouses No. 1: 2 & 3 to be Releiv'd to Morrow – A Subaltern 1 Serjt. 1 Corpll. & 24 Privates to Parade to Morrow at 6 °Clock to Repair the Roads from this to Fort Miller – for this Duty Lt. Gibbs

13th Monday Fair heard that Colo. Ruggles Regt. is Clearing a Road from Crown point to No. 4 Alias Charlestown

Tuesday Fort Edward Augt. 14th. 1759 – Parole Middleburg –

Capt. of the Day for to Morrow Capt Luse For Guard – Lt. Stiles To Visit the Barracks – Lt. Henshaw the Bridge & Blockhouses No. 4 & 5 to be Releiv'd to Morrow a Subaltern 1 Serjt 1 Corpll & 30 Privates to Parrade to Morrow Morning at 6 °Clock to Work on the Roads; for this Duty Lt. Scott

14th Tuesday Do. – Went over to the Island & Assisted Mr. Cowper in Posting his Books & Setling his Accounts –

Fort Edward ye 15th. Augt. 1759 – Parole Gorham –

Capt of the Day for to Morrow Capt Williams   For Guard Lt. Henshaw   To Visit the Barracks Ensn. Baker Royal Block house Island & Blockhouses No. 1 : 2 & 3 to be Releiv'd to Morrow – a Subaltern 1 Serjt. 1 Corpll. & 30 Privates to parade to Morrow at 6 ^{O}Clock for Repairing the Roads from this to Fort Miller; for this Duty Lt Dayton

Wednesday Augt. 15th 1759 – Was over to the Island all Day & till 10 ^{O}Clock at Night   the Sally ports was Opened for us to Come in   Mr Nichols Went to New England   Omitted Writeing by him – Visited the Barracks –

15th August Fort Edward: 1759   A Court Martial to set at 10 ^{O}Clock to Morrow; Capt. Whiting Pressident;

Ensn. Force   Lt. Gibbs,
Lt. Scott   & Ensn. Freeman   } Members

The Prisoners to be Acquainted & all Evidences to Attend –

Thursday Fort Edward, Augt. 16, 1759 – Parole Camphire –

Capt. of the Day for to Morrow Capt. Whiting, for guard Ensn. Baker, to Visit the Barracks Lt. Dayton   the Bridge & Blockhouses No. 4 & 5 to be Releiv'd to Morrow – the Like party as to Day to parade at the same time to Morrow for the Roads – For this Duty Lt. Gibbs   None of the Men Upon Duty in the Blockhouses to fire their Pieces on any Account; the Serjts. & Corplls. to be Answerable that these Orders are Comply'd with   Guard: 2 Corpl. 20 privates – For Work 1 Serjt. 10 ps.

16 Releiv'd the Guard; 3 prisoners Try'd; all pardon'd.

Friday Fort Edward 17th. Augt. 1759 – Parole Ostend –

Capt. of the Day for to Morrow Capt. Luse   for Guard Lt. Dayton   to Visit the Barracks Ensn. Force   the Royal Blockhouse Island & Blockhouses No. 1, 2 & 3 to be Releiv'd to Morrow; the Like party as to Day to parade to Morrow at the same time for the Roads   for this Duty Lt. Henshaw –

17th Friday Fort Edward wrote all Day at the Island –

Saturday Fort Edward Augt 18th – Parole Cologne –

Capt. of the Day for to Morrow Capt. Williams for Guard Ensn. Force to Visit the Barracks Lt. Gibbs the Bridge & Blockhouses No. 4 & 5 to be Releiv'd to Morrow – A Subaltern to go Early to Morrow morning with the Recover'd Men & Deliver them to the Commanding Officer at the Lake for this Duty Ensn. Baker.

18 Saturday Do. Went to Work on the Road between Fort Edward & Fort Miller with 1 Serjt. 1 Corpll. & 30 Privates Cross'd way'd 90 Yds. 3 Yds. Pr. Man [is a day's] stent –

Sunday Fort Edward Augt. 19th. 1759 – Parole Herenhousen –

Capt. of the Day for to Morrow Capt. Whiting for Guard – Lt. Gibbs to Visit the Barracks Ensn. Freeman the Royal Block House Island & Block houses No. 1: 2 & 3 to be Releiv'd to Morrow – a Subaltern Serjt & Corpl. & 30 privates to parade at 6 °Clock to Morrow morning for the Roads betwixt this & Fort Miller these are to Begin Work where the Last party Left of & make the Road of the same Breadth & Goodness that the party Yesterday Made; for this Duty – Lt Scott – For Guard 1 S – 2 C. – 22 P. for Work 9 P.

19th Sunday: Fair Went to the Island Doct. Steel Came from the Lake Order'd up Mohawk River there to be Station'd at the Little Falls –

Fort Edward ye 20th. Augt. 1759 – Parole Springfield –

Capt. of the Day for to Morrow Capt Luse for Guard Lt. Scott to Visit the Barracks Lt. Henshaw – the Bridge & Blockhouses No. 4 & 5 to be Releiv'd to Morrow; the like party as to Day to parade to Morrow at the same time for the Road & Observe the Directions of Yesterday – for this Duty Lt. Stiles

20th Monday Do. this Morng. Doct. Steel Set out. Walk'd with him 3 or 4 Miles Returnd & went over to the Island wrote all Day, Recd. a Letter from Brother Denny[21] –

---

[21] Brother Denny is Samuel Denny. See under May 10. Ante p. 185.

The Orderly Book of Lieut. William Henshaw. 225

Tuesday Fort Edward 21st. of Augt – 1759 – Parole Antwerp –

Capt. of the Day for to Morrow Capt Williams for Guard Ensn. Freeman to visit the Barracks Ensn. Baker the Royal Blockhouse Island & Blockhouses No. 1: 2 & 3 to be Rel^d. to Morrow; Complaint being made that Milk is Sold at an Extravagant Price it is Order'd that no Sutler or any other Person Exact more than Six pence New Y[ork] Currency for the Future pr. Quart if any Do they'll Immediately be sent of[22] A Subaltern, 2 Serjts. 2 Corpls. & 36 privates to go to Morrow Morng. without Arms with 8 Battoes to Fort Miller where they are to Load their Battoes with provision & Return Immediately here with the Loaded Battoes; they are to take great Care of the Provision & to keep it Dry – they are to be paid for this Duty & the Serjts. are to Give in a List of their Names & Company's upon their Return – for this Duty Lt. Henshaw W[ork] Party – 1 S – 0 C : 11 Privs. For Guard 1 S – 3 C : 22 Privs.

21st. Tuesday Rainy: Wrote a Letter home by Capt. [Jonathan] Carver post pay: 1/ York Currency – went to the Island –

Wednesday Fort Edward: 22d. Augt. 1759 – Parole Harwick –

Capt. of the Day for to Morrow Capt. Whiting for Guard Lt. Stiles To Visit the Barracks Lt. Dayton the Bridge & Block Houses No. 4 & 5 to be Releiv'd to Morrow – As the Battoes were not Ready to Day a Subaltern 2 Serjts. 2 Corplls. & 46 Privates to go Early to Morrow Morning to Fort Miller for provis^n. They are to take such Battoes as are Ready here, & they'll find others at Fort Miller, they are to Observe Yesterday's Orders; for this Duty Lt. Henshaw. A Garrison Court Martial to set at 10 ^{O}Clock to Morrow Morng.

Capt Luse President

Ensn. Baker   Lt Dayton   } Members
Ensn. Force   Lt. Gibbs

The Prisoners to be Acquainted & all Evidences to attend –

---

[22] This is another example of the frequent use of the old spelling of, corresponding to the more recent off.

22 Wednesday Aug. 22d. 1759 Fair – Was Employ'd in Looking after Battoes & Seeing them Corked & Mended.

Thursday Fort Edward: 23d. Augt. 1759 – Parole Seton –

Capt. of the Day for to Morrow Capt. Williams for Guard Ensn. Baker to Visit the Barracks Ensn. Force – The Same party that went to Day to go Early to Morrow Morning to Fort Miller for Provision – the Royal Block House Island & Blockhouses No. 1: 2 & 3 to be Releiv'd to Morrow – for the Future no Blankets Bed or Bed Cloaths to be Air'd or Dry'd on the Ramparts this Order to be Read to the Companys at Roll Call –

23d. Thursday Do. Went Down to Fort Miller with 6 Battoes – & 50 Men Loaded them & Retur'd with 10 Battoes: 97 Casks of Bread in them –

Friday Fort Edward: 24th. Augt. 1759 – Parole Lyon –

Capt. of the Day for to Morrow Capt. Whiting For Guard Lt. Dayton To Visit the Barracks Lt. Gibbs the Bridge & Block houses No. 4 & 5 to be Releiv'd to Morrow. A Subaltern 2 Serjts. 2 Corplls. & 46 Privates to go Early to Morrw. Morng. with 10 Battoes for Provision to Fort Miller – for this Duty Ensn. Force.

24th Friday Went to Fort Miller with 10 Battoes Loaded them & Return'd with one 100 Casks of Bread –

Saturday Fort Edward: 25th. Augt. 1759 – Parole Murray –

Capt. of the Day for to Morrow Capt. Williams for Guard Lt. Gibbs To Visit the Barracks Lt. Scott The Royal Blockhouse Island & Blockhouses No. 1: 2 & 3 to be Releiv'd to Morrow; till further Orders only a Serjt. Corpll. & 6 privates to mount Guard in the Royal Blockhouse; a Serjt. Corpll. & 9 Privates on the Island; a Corpll. & 6 Privates in the Ravaleen & none in Blockhouse No. 2: The same party that went to Day to go Early to Morrow to Fort Miller for Provision – no person to go out a Hunting with out Leave & no Guns to be Fired on any Account within the B[lock] Houses; this Order to be read to the Compa. at Roll Calling this Evening.

25th Saturday Fair – Nothing Remarkable

Sunday Fort Edward Augt. 26th. 1759 – Parole Drummond –

Capt. of the Day for to Morrow Capt. Whiting   For Guard Ensn. Freeman   To Visit the Barracks Lt. Henshaw   the Bridge & B: House No. 4 to be Releiv'd to Morrow – till further Orders only a Serjt. Corpll. & 6 Privates to mount Guard at the East End of the Bridge, a Corpll. & 3 Privates at the West End of the Bridge; they are to assist the Sawyers in Putting Logs on the Saw pitts   a Subaltern 2 Serjts. 2 Corplls. & 46 Privates to Releive the Battoe party   For this Duty Lt. Stiles – A Subaltern 1 Serjt. 1 Corpl. & 30 privates to parrade Early to Morrow Morning for Repairg. the Roads Leading to F; Miller   they are to Begin where the Last party left of & make the Roads of the same Breadth & Goodness   For this Duty Lt. Stiles; Order'd that Lt. Stiles go in the Battoes

26th Sunday Do. 3 French Prisoners Deserted from Niagara taken up at the 4 Mile Picquet & Brought Down to Fort Edward –

Monday Fort Edward: 27th. Augt. 1759 – Parole Graham –

Capt. of the Day for to Morrow Capt Williams for Guard Lt Stiles – to Visit the Barracks Ensn Baker   The Royal Blockhouse Island & B Houses No. 1 & 3 to be Releiv'd to Morrow –

27th Monday Fort Edward: 27th Augt. 1759. Lt. Dayton & Lt. Scott sent out in Search of French Deserters with a party of 30 Men. Recd. a Letter from Benja. by Capt. Stevens[23]   Visited the Barracks –

---

[23] Benjamin Henshaw was a brother of the author of this volume. See entry of Sep. 7, post p. 231, where he is referred to as Brother Benjamin. The bearer of letter was probably Capt. Adam Stevens or Stephens.

Tuesday Fort Edward: 28th Augt. 1759
– Parole Northumberland –

Capt. of the Day for to Morrow – Capt. Whiting; for Guard Lt Henshaw – To Visit the Barracks Lt. Dayton The Bridge & Blockhouse: No. 4 to be Releiv'd to Morrow – a Subaltern 1 Serjt. 1 Corpll. & 30 privs. to parade at 6 °Clock to Morrow to Repair the Road to Fort Miller; they are to Begin where the Last Party left of – for this Duty Ensn. Baker

28th Tuesday Do. Wrote a Letter to Danll. [Henshaw] at Boston by Doct. Hudson of Hooseek The partys that went out Yesterday Returnd without Making any Discoveries

Wednesday Fort Edward: 29th. Augt. 1759
– Parole Durham –

Capt. of the Day for to Morrow Capt. Williams – for Guard Ensn. Baker To Visit the Barracks Lt. Scott – the Royal Blockhouse Island & Blockhouses No. 1 & 3 to be Releiv'd to Morrow – A Subaltern 1 Serjt. 1 Corpll. & 30 Privts. to Repair the Roads, they must Cut the Timber at least 14 Feet long & Begin where the party left of to Day for this Duty – Lt. Gibbs –

29th Wednesday – Do. Releiv'd the Guard – my Coat brough[t] from Albany the Jacket & Breeches taken out of Chest

Fort Edward Thursday: 30th. Augt. 1759
– Parole Cumberland –

Capt of the Day for to Morrow Capt. Whiting; for Guard Lt. Dayton To Visit the Barracks Ensn. Freeman. The Bridge & Block house No. 4 to be Releiv'd to Morrow – the same party that went to Day to go Early to Morrow to Fort Miller for Provision – A Subaltern 1 Serjt. 1 Corp. & 30 Privates for the Road – for this Duty Lt. Scott

30th Thursday Do. Dismiss'd the Guard

The Orderly Book of Lieut. William Henshaw. 229

Friday Fort Edward, 31st. Augt. 1759 – Parole Redney –

Capt. of the Day for to Morrow Capt Luse – For Guard Lt. Gibbs – To Visit the Barracks Lt. Stiles The Royal Blockhouse Island & B Houses No. 1 & 3 to be Releiv'd to Morrow the Battoe party formerly Order'd [is] to go to Fort Miller for provision to Morrow: & if the day is fair the party Order'd Yesterday [is] to go to the Roads –

31st Do. Friday Rainy, staid in Fort all Day –

Saturday Fort Edward: 1st Sept. 1759 – Parole Prussia –

Capt. of the Day for to Morrow Capt Williams; for Guard Lt. Scott; To Visit the Barracks Lt. Henshaw – the Bridge & Block house No. 4 to be Releiv'd to Morrow – a Subaltern 2 Serjts. 2 Corplls & 46 privates to go Early to Morrow morning to Fort Miller for provision – for this Duty Lt. Styles – A Garrison Court Martial to Set at 10 ^{O}Clock to Morrow –

Capt Whiting pressident
Lt. Dayton   Lt. Henshaw   } Members
Ensn. Freeman   & Ensn. Force

The Prisoners to be Acquainted & all Evidences to Attend.

1st. Sept. Saturday Fort Edward Do. 1759 in the Afternoon went a Hunting & Blackberring 5 Miles Down the River

Sunday Fort Edward: 2d. Sept 1759 – Parole Denmark –

Capt. of the Day for to Morrow Capt. Whiting – for Guard Ensn. Frem^n. To Visit the Barracks Ensn. Baker the Royal Blockhouse Island & B: Houses No. 1 & 3 to be Releivd to M. The same party that went this Day to go to Morrow Morng. for provision A Subn. Serjt. Corpll. & 30 privates to Repair the Roads; for this Duty Lt. Henshaw –

2d. Sunday – Cloudy & Rainy – Set on a Court Martial to Try a Man for sleeping on his Post – Pardoned.[24]

---

[24] See entry under this date. Ante p. 154.

Monday Fort Edward Sept. 3 – 1759 – Parole Cronstat –

Capt. of the Day for to Morrow Capt Luse; for Guard Lt. Stiles to Visit the Barracks Lt. Dayton The Bridge & B: House No. 4 to be Releiv'd to Morrow – A Subaltern 2 Serjts. 2 Corplls. & 46 privates to go Early to Morrow for provision for this Duty Lt. Henshaw –

3d Monday Do. at the Island

Tuesday Fort Edward 4 Sept. 1759 – Parole Hampstead –

A Garrison Court Martial to Set Immediately

Lt. Gibbs   Lt. Scott   } Members
Ensn. Freeman & Ensn. Baker }

The prisoners to be Acquainted & all Evidences to Attend.

Capt. of the Day for to Morrow Capt. Williams; for Guard: Ensn. Baker To Visit the Barracks Ensn. Force the Royal B: House Island & B: Houses No. 1 & 3 to be Releiv'd to Morrow – the Same Officer & party that went to Day to go to Morrow for provision. Complaint being made that the Sutlers take an Extravagant Price for their Chees – for the Future no Sutlers is to take or none belonging to the Garrison to give more then One shilling New Y[ork] Currency pr. pound for New Chees Under the pain of being Severly punish'd – this Order to be Read to the Companys & Communicated to ye Sutlers –

4th Tuesday Do. Went down to Fort Miller with 10 Battoes Brought up 72 Barrls. of Flowr. 38 'Barrls. Pork, 2 Tearse Bread & 1 Barrl. Peas. Bought a Tump[25] line, Bullet pouch & Strap 2/ L M

Wednesday Fort Edward: 5th. Sept 1759
– Parole Kensington –

Capt. of the Day for to Morrow Capt Whiting – for Guard Lt. Dayton – to Visit the Barracks Lt. Gibbs – the Bridge & Block house No. 4 to be Releiv'd to Morrow – a Subn.

---

[25] A tump line is a line or strap passing across the forehead and attached to a pack on the back thus aiding the burden bearer. L. M. is, of course, legal money.

2 Serjts. 2 Corplls. & 46 Privates to go Early to Morrow to Fort Miller for Provision for this Duty Ensn. Force

5th Wednesday Cloudy Went to F Miller for provision 50 Men 10 Battoes Brot up 108 Barrls. Flowr. 10 Barrls. Pork the River high.

Thursday Fort Edwd. Sept. 6 1759 – Parole Dumblane –

Capt. of the Day for to Morrow Capt Luse – for Guard Lt. Gibbs – To Visit the Barracks Lt. Scott – the Royal Block house Island & B. Houses No. 1 & 3 to be Releivd to Morrow, the same Officer & party that went this Day to go to Morrow for provision –

6th Thursday Do. Capt. [Adam] Stephens Ariv'd here from Crown point

Friday Fort Edward 7th. Sept. 1759 – Parole Andraseer –

Capt. of the Day for to Morrow Capt. Williams – for Guard Lt. Scott – To Visit the Barracks Ensn. Freeman – the Bridge & Blockhouse No. 4 to be Releiv'd to Morrow – A subaltern 2 Serjts. 2 Corplls. & 56 privates to go to Morrow for provision – for this duty Lt. Stiles

7th Friday Do. Capt. Stevens Set out for home; Wrote a Letter to Brother Benja. by Mr. Smedley of Mansfield in Connecticut.

Saturday Fort Edward 8th Sept. 1759 – Parole Flamborough –

Capt. of the Day for to Morrow Capt. Whiting – for Guard Ensn. Freeman – To Visit the Barracks Lt. Henshaw – the Royal Blockhouse Island & B: Houses No. 1 & 3 to be Releivd to Morrow – the same Officer & party that Went to Day to go to Morrow to Fort Miller for provision.

8 Saturday Fort Edwd. Rainy Over at the Island

Sunday Fort Edward 9th. Sept. 1759 – Parole Stamford –

Capt of the Day for to Morrow Capt Luse for Guard Lt. Henshaw to Visit the Barracks Lt. Dayton the

Bridge & Block house No. 4 to be Releiv'd to Morrow – A Subn. 2 Serjts. 2 Corplls. & 56 privs. to go to Morrow for Provision – for this Duty Ensn. Baker –

9th Sunday Fair. Walk'd with Mr. Bowman to the 4 Mile Picquet the River very High the Scow Bridge Broke –

Monday Fort Edward: 10th Sept. 1759 – Parole Minas –

Capt. of the Day for to Morrow Capt Williams for Guard Lt. Dayton; To Visit the Barracks Ensn. Force the Royal Blockhouse Island & Blockhouses No. 1 & 3 to be Releiv'd to Morrow the Battoe party for this Day Goes to Morrow – 10th Sept. Monday Do. – Releiv'd the Guard –

Tuesday 11th. Sept. 1759 – Parole Werkindam –

Capt. of the Day for to Morrow Capt. Whiting; for guard Ensn. Force to Visit the Barracks Lt. Scott the Bridge & Block house No. 4 to be Releiv'd to Morrow – A Subn. 2 Serjts. 2 Corplls. & 56 privates to go to Morrow for provision – and None but the strong healthy Men abel for the service to be Sent – for this Duty Lt. Gibbs – A Garrison Court Martial to set at 10 ᴼClock to Morrow –

Capt Williams, Pressident
    Lt. Dayton   Lt. Scott
    Lt. Stiles   & Ensn. Freeman } Members

The Prisoners to be Acquainted & all Evidences to Attend –

11th Tuesday Do. Went to the Island –

Wednesday Fort Edward Sept. 12th. 1759 – Parole Waldeck –

Capt. of the Day for to Morrow Capt Luse; for Guard – Lt. Scott To Visit the Barracks Ensn. Freeman the Royal Blockhouse Island & Blockhouse No. 1 & 3 to be Releiv'd to Morrow the Battoe party Continues A Serjt or Corpll. with 30 Privates to Cut Wood to Morrow for Fires the Logs Must be Split & they are to Continue till Further Orders & Cut near the Bridge –

12th Wednesday: Do. two Prisoners try'd one for Insulting an Officer the other for Exacting Money of a Sutler for Lowering the Bridge

Thursday Fort Edward Sept. 13th. 1759
Parole Limbrick –

Capt. of the Day for to Morrow Capt. Williams for Guard Ensn. Freeman To Visit the Barracks Lt. Stiles the Bridge & Blockhouse No. 4 to be Releiv'd to Morrow – the Battoe & Wood Cutting partys to Continue.

13th Thursday Rain in Afternoon Heard that Genl. Wolfe was Retreated to his Former Incampment & that he Lost 500 of the Young Highland Regt. near Quebec in Going to Fetch of Three Hund. Fat Cattle of the Enemy's. –

Friday Fort Edward Sept. 14th. 1759 – Parole Boyne –

Capt. of the Day for to Morrow Capt. Whiting for Guard – Lt. Stiles; to Visit the Barracks – Lt. Henshaw the Royal Blockhouse Island & Blockhouses No. 1 & 3 to be Releiv'd to Morrow the Wood Cutting party to Continue –: No Battoe Party to Morrow but the Whole of those Imploy'd to Day to parade at 8 °Clock to Morrow to Repair the Bridge A cross the Creek – 14th[26] Friday fair Nothing Remarkable.

Saturday: 15 Sept. 1759 – Parole Duncannon –

Capt. of the Day for to Morrow: Capt. Luse – For Guard Lt Henshaw – To Visit the Barracks Ensn. Baker the Bridge & Block house No. 4 to be Releivd to Morrow – the Wood Cutting party to Continue till further Orders A Subn. 2 Serjts. 2 Corpll. & 46 privates to go to Morrow for provision – for this Duty – Lt. Gibbs –

15th[26] Saturday Do. Visited Barracks over at the Island. A garrison Court Martial to set at 10 °Clock to Morrow –

---

[26] This entry for Sep. 14 is separated by a day from the remainder of the notes for the 14th in the original text, as in the second entry for Sep. 15. They are placed in their proper order in this volume.

Capt. Whiting Pressident
Lt. Dayton   Lt. Scott
Ensn. Baker   & Ensn. Force } Members

The Prisoners to be Acquainted and all Evidences to Attend.

Sunday Fort Edward Sept. 16: 1759
– Parole Killkenny –

Capt. of the Day for to Morrow Capt. Williams; for Guard: Ensn. Baker To Visit the Barracks Lt. Dayton The Royal Blockhouse Island & Blockhouses: No. 1 & 3 to be Releiv'd to Morrow – the Wood Cutting party to Continue – No Battoe party to Morrow

16th Sunday Do. Releiv'd the Guard Former Govr. of So. Carolina Return'd from Crown point – 2 prisoners Try'd for a Riot over at the Island.

Monday Fort Edward 17th Sept. 1759 – Parole Airth –

Capt. of the Day for to Morrow Capt Whiting – for Guard Lt. Dayton – To Visit. the Barracks Ensn. Force – the Bridge & Blockhouse No. 4 to be Releiv'd to Morrow – the Battoe party to go to Morrow if the Day is fair the Wood Cutting Continues.

Monday Fort Edward 17 Sept. 1759 Rainy Wet Day; Dismissed the Guard –

Tuesday Fort Edward Sept. 18th. 1759
– Parole Galloway –

Capt. of the Day for to Morrow Capt. Luse – For Guard Ensn. Force – To Visit the Barracks: Lt. Scott; the Royal Blockhouse Island & Blockhouses No. 1 & 3 to be Releivd to Morrow; the Battoe & wood Cutting Continues; No Person Belonging to the Garrison or Hospital to stay at any of the Sutlers after Night fall under the pain of being Severly punished & any Sutler that Entertains them after Night fall shall have his Liquor Spilt – & he shall be Drummed out from the Garrison – This Order to be read to the Companys at Roll Calling & Communicated to the Sutlers –

18th Tuesday Fair – Moved into the Lower Room & Staid in the Fort all Day –

Wednesday Fort Edward 19th Sept. 1759
– Parole Montresor –

Capt. of the Day for to Morrow Capt Williams – For Guard Lt Scott – To Visit the Barracks Ensn. Freeman the Bridge & Blockhouse No. 4 to be Releiv'd to Morrow – the Battoe party Goes to Morrow – if the Day be fair the Wood Cutting party Continues; they are to Cord & Split all the Wood they have Cut as they are to Change Next Day –

19 Wednesday Do. staid in Fort all Day[27]

Thursday Fort Edward: 20th. Sept. 1759
– Parole Whitehall –

Capt. of the Day for to Morrow Capt. Whiting – for Guard Ensn. Freeman; To Visit the Barracks Lt. Stiles – the Royal Blockhouse Island & Blockhouses No. 1 & 3 to be Releivd to Morrow –

20 Thursday Do. – Settled Accompts with the Officers

Friday Fort Edward 21st. Sept. 1759
– Parole Jamaica –

Capt. of the Day for to Morrow Capt. Luse For Guard – Lt. Stiles To Visit the Barracks Lt. Henshaw The Bridge & Blockhouse No. 4 to be Releivd to Morrow the Battoe & Wood Cutting partys continue the Wood Cutters to Cord all they have Cut. Capt. Luse Lt. Scott Ensn. Freeman & Lt. Henshaw & Mr. Washington Comissary for the Crown to Inspect some provision Said to be Damnified at 11 ºClock to Morrow Morning –

21st Friday Do. Wrote a Letter home by Mr. Herrod of Sutton.

---

[27] This second entry for Sep. 19 is between the two entries for Sep. 20 in the original text. It is given in its proper order in this volume.

Saturday   Fort Edward 22d. Sept. 1759
– Parole Bermudas –

Capt. of the Day for to Morrow Capt Whiting – For Guard – Lt. Henshaw – to Visit the Barracks – Ensn. Baker. The Royal Blockhouse Island & Blockhouses No. 1 & 3 to be Releiv'd to Morrow No Battoe or Wood Cutting Party's –

22d Saturday   Do. Visited the Barracks Inspected Some provision said to be Damnified, Condemn'd 7 Barrs. of Flow'r 1 Tearse of Bread: 2 of Beans &c.
Fort Edward 22d. Sept. 1759
W. Henshaw

Sunday Fort Edward: 23d. Sept. 1759
– Parole St. Christopher –

Capt. of the Day for to Morrow Capt. Whiting – for Guard Ensn. Baker – To Visit the Barracks Ensn. Force the Bridge & Blockhouse No. 4 to be Releiv'd to Morrow. No Battoe or Wood Cutting partys – a Serjt. Corpll. & 24 Privates to parade at 7 ^{O}Clock to Morrow for Fatigue they are to take 3 Battoes; they are to Cut & Carry Wood from the Furthest part of the Wood above the Fort to the Hospital & to be very Careful they do not hurt the Battoes –

23d Sunday Do. Dismiss'd the Guard. Nothing Extraordinary this Guard –

Monday Fort Edward 24th Septr. 1759
– Parole Guardaloop –

Capt of the Day for to Morrow Capt Luse – For Guard Ensn. Force; To Visit the Barracks Lt. Gibbs the Royal Blockhouse Island & B: Houses No. 1 & 3 to be Releiv'd to Morrow – A serjt. Corpll. & 30 privates to parade at 8 ^{O}Clock to Morrow for Fatigue   they are to Repair the Road across the Creek & to Carry 8 Hatchets & 8 spades with them –

24th Monday Do. Dismiss'd the Guard Reports brought in   Nothing Extraordinary –

Tuesday Fort Edward 25th. Sept. 1759
– Parole Providence –

Capt. of the Day for to Morrow Capt. Williams – For Guard Lt. Gibbs –To Visit the Barracks Lt. Stiles – the Bridge & Blockhouse No. 4 to be Releiv'd to Morrow – all the Vents in the Fort to be Swept to Morrow a Sub. Serjt. Corpll. & 24 Privates to parade Early to Morrow Morning to Repair the Roads betwixt this & Fort Miller they are to Begin at the first bad steps & work Downwards for this Duty Lt. Scott the Battoe party goes to Morrow for this Duty – Ensn. Freeman.

25th Tuesday Do. Lieut. from the 4 Mile Picquet Came to see us –

Wednesday Fort Edward 26th. Sept. 1759
– Parole Grandterre –

Capt. of the Day for to Morrow Capt Whiting For Guard Lt. Scott – To Visit the Barracks Lt. Henshaw the Royal Blockhouse Island & Blockhouses No. 1 & 3 to be Releiv'd to Morrw. A Subaln. Serjt. Corpll. & 24 Privates for the Roads to Fort Miller: they are to Begin where the party this Day left of & work Down wards; for this Duty Lt. Stiles – the Officer & Battoe party Continues – A Return to be Giv'n in this Night or Early to Morrow of all the Men in the Garrison that have Been Bred Sailors –

26th Wednesday Do. Lt. Holliston from the ½ Way Brook Came to see us

Thursday Fort Edward 27th. Sept. 1759
– Parole Bassaterre –

Capt. of the Day for to Morrow Capt. Luse – For Guard Lt. Stiles – To Visit the Barracks Ensn. Baker the Bridge & Blockhouse No. 4 to be Releiv'd to Morrow a Subaln. Serjt. Corpll. & 24 Privates for the Roads For this Duty Lt. Henshaw —

27 Thursday: Do. Nehemiah Gale came Sick from the Lake was Carried to the Hospital on the Island; Omitted

Visiting Barracks 12 Men Draughted out of the Garrison to Man the Brig at Crown point set out to Day –

Friday Fort Edward 28th. Sept. 1759 – Parole Windsor –

Capt. of the Day for to Morrow Capt Williams – For Guard Lt Henshaw – to Visit the Barracks Ensn. Force – the Royal Blockhouse Island & Blockhouses No. 1 & 3 to be Releivd to Morrow – for the Battoe party to Morrow Ensn. Baker – for the Roads – Lt. Dayton – a Garrison Court Martial to set at 10 ºClock to Morrow –

Capt. Luse Pressident
Ensn. Freeman   Lt. Stiles   } Members
Ensn. Force   & Lt. Gibbs

the Prisoners to be Acquainted & all Evidences to attend –

28th Friday Do. – Went with the Working party on the Roads – Cause way'd Each side of the 2 Mile Bridge

**Saturday Fort Edward 29th. Sept. 1759
– Parole Hampton Court –**

Capt. of the Day for to Morrow Capt. Whiting – for Guard Lt. Dayton – To Visit the Barracks Lt. Gibbs – the Bridge & Blockhouse No. 4 to be Releiv'd to Morrow – the Battoe party Continues & they are to take Care they Dont break the Battoes & if any are Broke through Carelisness the Expence of Repairing will be Kept of their Wages – the Officer that Commands the party is to Report if any Battoes is hurt; for the Road party to Morrow Ensn. Force –

29th Saturday Do. A flying Report that Genll. Wolfe has taken Quebec Releivd the Main Guard.

**Sunday Fort Edward 30th. Sept. 1759
– Parole Northampton –**

Capt. of the Day for to Morrow Capt. Luse – For Guard Ensn. Force – to Visit the Barracks Lt Scott the Royal Blockhouse & Island & Blockhouses No. 1 & 3 to be Rel[d].

to Morrow the Battoe party Continues For the Roads to Morrow Lt. Gibbs.

30th Sunday, Do. Dismiss'd the Main Guard; Nothg. Extraordinary. Went to the Island to Visit the Sick in the Hospital –

1st Octo. Monday Do. – Jno. Allen of Sutton in Capt. Baldwins Compy. Deceas'd this Day about Daybreak Priz'd his Cloathing 14/ L[egal] M[oney] Saml. Gordon Fetched my Waistcoat & Breeches from Albany –

Monday Fort Edward 1st. Octo. 1759
– Parole Winchester –

Capt. of the Day for to Morrow Capt Williams; For Guard Lt. Gibbs – To Visit the Barracks Lt. Stiles the Bridge & Blockhouses No. 1 & 3 to be Releivd to Morrow the Battoe party Continues – For the Roads Lt. Scott –

Tuesday Fort Edwd. 2d. Octo – 1759
– Parole Herenhousen –

Capt. of the Day to Morrow Capt. Whiting For Guard Lt. Scott – To Visit the Barracks Lt. Henshaw the Royal B[lock] H[ouse] Island & B[lock] Houses No. 1 & 3 to be Releiv'd to Morrow the Battoe party Continues – For the Roads Lt. Stiles – 2d Tuesday Do. Went a Hunting N[othing] Remarkable

Fort Edward Octo. 3d. 1759 – Parole Mendon –

Capt. of the Day for to Morrow Capt. Luse, For Guard Lt. Stiles, To Visit the Barracks Ensn. Baker the Bridge & Block house No. 4 to be Releiv'd to Morrow – the Battoe party Continues A Garison Court Martial to set Imediately

Capt Williams Pressident
    Lt. Henshaw   Lt Dayton   } Members
    Ensn. Baker   & Ensn. Force   }

the Prisoner to be Acquainted & all Evidences to Attend

3d. Octo. Wednesday   Moffit Try'd for Striking & Kicking "Poll" Jones –

$$\begin{array}{r}\text{H[enshaw?]}^{28}\ldots\ldots\ldots 150\\ \text{B[aker?]}\ldots\ldots\ldots\ldots 400\\ \text{D[ayton?]}\ldots\ldots\ldots\ldots 200\\ \text{F[orce?]}\ldots\ldots\ldots\ldots 100\\ \text{W[illiams?]}\ldots\ldots\ldots 250\\ \hline 5\,|\,1050\,|\,210\ \text{S}\end{array}$$

Thursday Fort Edward: 4 Octo. – Parole Frankfort –

Capt. of the Day for to Morrow Capt. Whiting For Guard Lt. Henshaw To Visit the Barracks Lt. Dayton the Battoe party Continues – the Royal Blockhouse Island & Blockhouses No. 1 & 3 to be Releiv'd to Morrow for Fatigue 1 Serjt. 16 privates they are to take two Battoes with them & Carry Firewood for the Hospital. 4th Thursday Do. Nothing Extraordinary.

Friday   Fort Edwd. Octo. 5th 1759 – Parole Menen –

Capt. of the Day for to Morrow Capt. Whiting for Guard – Ensn. Baker To Visit the Barracks Ensn. Force the Bridge & Block house No. 4 to be Releiv'd to Morrow the Battoe party Continues – a serjt. & 16 Men to Carry Wood to the Hospital

5th October at Fort Edward 1759 Friday Releiv'd the Guard Rainy [Timothy] Woodbridge Esqr. Capt. Lt. of the 4 Mile post to see us. A Set Down.[29]

Saturday Fort Edwd. Octo 6th. 1759 – Parole Brussels –

Capt. of the Day for to Morrow Capt Luse; for Guard Lt. Dayton To Visit the Barracks Lt Gibbs the R. Block House Island & B. Houses No. 1 & 3 to be Releiv'd to Morrow; the Battoe party Continues; a serjt. & 16 p[rivates] to Carry Wood to the Hospital.

---

[28] This account may be between these officers and Ryan and Spear, the sutlers with whose accounts Henshaw was engaged the following week. The expense may have been in part for the banquet to Timothy Woodbridge.

[29] A rough term for banquet, given evidently in honor of the visit of Capt. Lt. Woodbridge.

6th Saturday Fair. Dismiss'd the Guard Mr Woodbridge Gone to the Lake a set Down at Nt.

Sunday: 7th. Octo. Fort Edward 1759 – Parole Venango –

Capt. of the Day for to Morrow Capt. Williams – For Guard – Ensn. Force – To Visit the Barracks Lt. Scott – the Bridge & B[lock] H[ouse] No. 4 to be Releiv'd to Morrow – the Battoe party Continues. A Serjt & 12 Men to Carry Wood to Hospital. 7th Sunday Do. Staid in Fort –

Monday Fort Edward 8th Octr. 1759 – Parole Fort Miller –

Capt. of the Day for to Morrow Capt Whiting for Guard Lt. Gibbs – To Visit the Barracks Lt. Stiles the R[oyal] B[lock] House Island & B Houses No. 1 & 3 to be Releivd to Morrow the Battoe party Continues – A Serjt. & 22 Men to take 5 Battoes & Cut & Carry Wood to the Hospital to Morrow.

8th Monday Very Warm Staid in Fort Settling Accompts between Ryan & Spear sutlers in partnership

Tuesday Fort Edward 9th Octr. 1759 – Parole Presque Isle –

Capt. of the Day for to Morrow Capt. Luse – For Guard Lt Scott To Visit the Barracks Lt. Henshaw the Bridge & Block house No. 4 to be Releiv'd to Morrow – the Battoe party Continues – A Serjt. & 16 Men to Carry Wood to the Hospital.

Tuesday 9th. Octr. Do. Warm Setling Accompts between Ryan & Spear N[othing] Extraordinary

Fort Edward: 10th Octo. 1759 – Parole Saratoga –

Capt. of the Day for to Morrow Capt Williams;– For Guard Lt. Stiles To Visit the Barracks Ensn. Baker; the R B House Island & B Houses No. 1 & 3 to be Releiv'd to Morrow the Battoe party Continues & they are to Carry the Sick they will be Delivered to them upon the Island – A Serjt. & 16 to go Early to Morrow Morning with the 18

Men that Came from Albany – & he is to Deliver them to the Commanding Officer at Lake George –

10th Wednesday Do. It has been very Warm for 4 Days past Sent a Lettr. home by [John] Holton of Sutton, Lt. Worthington Came Down with 40 Invalids this Day Setling Accts. between the Sutlers

Fort Edward 11th. Octo. 1759 – Parole Dantzick –

Capt. of the Day for to Morrow Capt Whiting – For Guard Lt. Henshaw To Visit the Barracks Lt. Dayton the Bridge & Block house No. 4 to be Releiv'd to Morrow – the Battoe party Continues & are to [bring] Down all the Sick that Can have Room to Morrow. A Serjt. & 16 Men to Cut & Carry Wood from the Lower Bridge with the two Battoes prepar'd this Day

11th Thursday Do. Lt. [John] Worthington set of with the Invalids – A party from our Hospital Joyn'd him; Mr. Shaw went wth him Finish'd Setling Accompts Between Ryan & Spear

Fort Edward 12th. Octr. 1759 – Parole Lemerick –

Capt. of the Day for to Morrow Capt. Luse – For Guard Ensn. Baker To Visit the Barracks Ensn. Force the R. B. House Island & B. Houses No. 1 & 3 to be Releiv'd to Morrow the Battoe party Continues A Serjt. & 16 Men to Carry Wood to the Hospital

12th Friday Rainy – Mr. Furbush & the Jersey Chaplain set out this Morning with 100 Invalids – Releiv'd the Main Guard

Saturday Fort Edward: 13th. 1759 – Parole Brunswick –

Capt. of the Day for to Morrow Capt. Williams – for Guard Lt Dayton To Visit the Barracks Lt Gibbs the Bridge & B. House No. 4 to be Releivd to Morrow A Serjt & 16 Men to Carry Wood to the Hospital –

13th Saturday Rainy all Day. Dismiss'd the Guard [Wind] N. E.

Fort Edward 14th. Octo. 1759 – Parole Fife –

Capt. of the Day for to Morrow Capt. Whiting – For Guard Ensn. Force To Visit the Barracks Lt. Scott the R. B. House Island & B[lock] houses No. 1 & 3 to be Releivd to Morrow; the Battoe party Continues – A Serjt. & 16 Men to Carry Wood to the Hospital

14 Octo. Sunday Fort Edward 1759 Took a Walk out very pleasant

Fort Edward 15th Octr. 1759 – Parole Herbertshur –

Capt. of the Day for to Morrow Capt. Luse – For Gd. Lt Gibbs To Visit the Barracks Lt. Stiles the Bridge & B. House No. 4 to be Releiv'd to Morrow; the Battoes go to Morrow – A Serjt. & 16 Men to Carry Wood to the Hospital – 15th Monday Do. Walk'd to the 4 Mile post

Fort Edward 16th Octo. – 1759 – Parole Quebec –

Capt. of the Day for to Morrow Capt Williams For Gd. Lt Scott – To Visit the Barracks Lt. Henshaw the R: B: house Island & B: house No. 1 & 3 to be Releiv'd to Morrow the Battoe & wood Cutting Partys Continue –

16th Octor. at Fort Edward Tuesday Cold Morng. heard the News of Quebec being taken – Genll. [James] Wolfe & Colo. [Robert] Monkton[30] Kill'd – Genll. [Louis Joseph Marquis de] Montcalm & the 1st. & 2d. next in Command with 1500 Kill'd & made prisoners Went up to the Great Falls to see them – struck across to the half way Brook from thence home –

Wednesday Fort Edward 17th Octobr. 1759 – Parole Townsend –

Capt of the Day for to Morrow Capt Whiting For Guard – Lt. Stiles – To Visit the Barracks Ensn. Baker the Bridge to be Releiv'd to Morrow 1 Subn. 2 Serjts. & 80

---

[30] This report so far as it concerned the death of Col. Monckton was incorrect. Monckton was seriously wounded at this time but recovered, later becoming a Lieutenant General in the British army on Apr. 30, 1770. He died in England, May 3, 1782.

privates to parade at 8 ºClock To Morrow to Cut & Carry Wood to the Hospital – the Battoe party makes a part of that Number they are to take 8 Battoes – for this Duty Lt. Dayton

17th Wednesday, Fair & pleasent – Capt. Paine set out for home he came here yesterday – Visited the Barracks &c

Fort Edward 18th. Octobr. 1759 – Parole Hague –

Capt. of the Day for to Morrow Capt. Luse – for Guard Lt. Henshaw; To Visit the Barracks Lt. Dayton the Royal Blockhouse & Island to be Releiv'd to Morrow – 1 Sub. 1 Serjt. 2 Corpll. & 50 privates to Cut & Cord Wood below the Bridge – For this Duty Ensn. Force A Serjt. & 20 Men to Repair the Roads across the Creek Both parties to Parade at 8 ºClock

18th Thursday – Do. Staid in Fort all Day Nothing Remarkable at Fort Edward – all's Well

Fort Edward 19th Octo. 1759 – Parole Ardoch –

Capt. of the Day for to Morrow Capt. Williams For Guard Ensn. Baker To Visit the Barracks Ensn. Force the Bridge to be Releiv'd to Morrow the Battoe party to go for provision to Morrow – A Serjt. Corpll. & 30 Men to Cut wood & to parade at 8 ºClock –

19th Friday Do. Releivd the Main Guard heard that Genll. Amherst had taken one & Sunk [other] Vessels in the Lake

Fort Edward 20th. Octobr. 1759 – Parole Aberdeen –

Capt. of the Day for to Morrow Capt. Whiting – For Guard Ensn. Force To Visit the Barracks Lt. Gibbs – the Royal Block house & Island to be Releiv'd to Morrow – an Officer & 80 Men to parade at 8 ºClock to Cut Wood the Battoe party makes a part of that Number – who are first to Carry the Straw over to the Island – Capt. Stirling[31]

---

[31] Captain Stirling here mentioned is probably the William Alexander, Lord Stirling of later days.

The Orderly Book of Lieut. William Henshaw. 245

Expects that Every 20 Men will Cut 13 Cord of Wood & the Officer is to make Report of the same for this Duty Lt. Scott –

20th Octo. Saturday Fair & pleasent Dismiss'd the Guards N. Extr^y. Timo. Woodbridge Esqr. & Lt. [Jacob] Tilton Commander at the 4 Mile Picquet to see us

Fort Edward 21st. of Octo. 1759 – Parole Oxford –

Capt. of the Day for to Morrow Capt Luse – For Guard Lt. Gibbs – to Visit the Barracks Lt. Scott the Bridge Guards to be Releiv'd to Morrow; the same Number of Men to parade to Morrow as to Day to Cut Wood – For this Duty Ensn. Freeman

21st Sunday Do. Very Warm Heard the Court had Voted to keep the Massachusetts Troops in pay till the 1st. of Decr. at the Desire of the Genrl. if the Service Requird it –

Fort Edward 22d. Octobr. 1759 – Parole Boscawen –

Capt. of the Day for to Morrow Capt Williams – for Guard Lt Scott – to Visit the Barracks Ensn. Freemn the Royal Blockhouse & Island to be Releiv'd to Morrow – the Wood Cutting party continues For this Duty – Lt. Stiles –

22d Monday – Do. Tarry'd in Fort all Day Very hard Rain at Night

Fort Edward 23d. Octo. 1759 – Parole Cambridge –

Capt. of the Day for to Morrow Capt Whiting – For Guard Ensn. Freeman To Visit the Barracks Lt. Stiles the Bridge Guard to be Releivd to Morrow the Wood Cutting party goes to Morrow if the Day be Fair – for this Duty Lieut Henshaw –

23d Octo. Tuesday Rain F Edwd. 1759 Serjt. Toy Return'd from Crown point

Fort Edward Octo. 24th. 1759 – Parole Farquhar –

Capt. of the Day for to Morrow Capt Luse – for Guard Lt. Stiles – To Visit the Barracks Lt. Henshaw the Royal

Blockhouses & Island to be Releiv'd to Morrow the Battoe party goes to Morrow for this Duty Ensn. Baker

24th Wednesday Cold – a Report that the Army is Return'd to Crown Point Went With a party of 30 Men to Cut Wood – Cut & Corded 51½ Cord &c

Fort Edward 25th. Octo. 1759 – Parole Erskine –

Capt. of the Day for to Morrow Capt Williams; For Guard Lt. Henshaw; To Visit the Barracks Ensn. Baker; the Bridge Guards to be Releivd to Morrow; A Sub: 1 Serjt. 2 Corplls. & 42 Privates to go to Fort Miller for provision; for this Duty Ensn. Force; A Serjt. Corpll. & 24 privates to take 2 Battoes & Cut & Carry Wood to the Hospital to Morrow

25th. Thursday. Cloudy. Thanksgiving this Day in the Massachusets Province – Eleven Officers Din'd together. Pl. Pug. Rt Pok. & Mutn. Roe Dr. Cabg. Caro. Turk.[32] Visited the Barracks

Fort Edward: 26th. Octo. 1759 – Parole St. Andrews –

Capt. of the Day for to Morrow Capt Whiting – For Guard Ensn. Baker – To Visit the Barracks Ensn. Force the Royal Blockhouse & Island to be Releiv'd to Morrow – A Sub. 1 Serjt. 2 Corplls. & 37 Privates to go to Fort Miller for provision with 8 Battoes to Morrow – for this Duty Lt. Gibbs – A Serjt. Corpll. & 30 privates to Cut Wood at the East End of the Bridge to Morrow –

26th Friday – Fair – Releiv'd the Guard – Nothing Material

Saturday Fort Edward 27th. Octo. 1759
– Parole Dumbferline –

Capt. of the Day for to Morrow Capt. Luse – For Guard Ensn. Force To Visit the Barracks Lt. Gibbs – the Bridge Guards to be Releiv'd to Morrow – A Sub: 1 Serjt. 2 Corplls. & 45 Privates to go with 8 Battoes to bring up Provision –

---

[32] Plum Pudding, Roast Pork and Mutton, Roe Deer, Cabbage, Carrot and Turkey.

The Orderly Book of Lieut. William Henshaw. 247

they are to carry Down 5 Battoes besides which are to be left at Fort Miller to be Repaird; the Officer to Oblige the Men to put in 15 Barrels in Each Battoe for the Future; for this Duty – Lt. Scott – a Serjt. Corpll. & 24 Men to Cut Wood to Morrow; the Serjt. to take Care that the Men Split Wood into such pieces as One Man may be Able to Load it.

27th Saturday Do. Dismiss'd the Guard – took a Ride with Lt. —— as far as the 4 Mile Picquet – Capt. Richardson Came from Crown Point –

Sunday Fort Edward 28 th Octo. 1759
– Parole Greenock –

Capt. of the Day for to Morrow Capt. Williams; for Guard Lt. Gibbs To Visit the Barracks Lt. Scott the Royal B House & Island guards to be Releiv'd to Morrow – the Battoe party goes to Morrow – for this Duty – Ensn. Freeman – A Serjt. Corpll. & 24 Privates to Cut Wood to Morrow–

28th Sunday Do. Capt. Richardson set out for home Wrote a Lettr. to B[rother] Denny

Fort Edwd. 29th Octo. 1759 – Parole Levingstone –

Capt. of the Day for to Morrow Capt Whiting – for Guard Lt. Scott – To Visit the Barracks Ensn Freeman – the Bridge to be Releiv'd to Morrow the Battoe party Goes to Morrow For this Duty Lt. Stiles A Serjt. Corpll. & 24 privates to Cut Wood As the time for which the provincial Troops were Inlisted is Near Expired the Companys are to be Acquainted at Roll Calling that his Excellency Genl. Amherst finding it to be Absolutely Necessarry for the Good of the Service to Keep the Troops some time Longer, to put the Important post of Crown point in a Respectable Footing has wrote to the Several Governments Acquaint'g them therewith & Desiring a longer Provision to be made for the troops & they being Satisfied with the Necessity thereof, have ordered that the provincial Troops shall Remain till the 1st. of Decr. if his Excelly. finds it Necessary, & it is Expected that none in the Garison as they have Behaved so Well During the Campaigne will think of Deserting the service of their Country or Officers while the Regts. they Belong to do Remain at Crown point & his Excellency Genl. Amherst is Detirmind to punish with the Utmost Severity any Man that is Catched Attempting to Desert or Inticing others to Desert –

29th Monday Fort Edward 29th. Octo. 1759 Cold Chilly Day

Fort Edwd. 30th. Octo. 1759 – Parole Fort Stanwix –

A Garrison Court Martial to set Immediately, Capt Whiting Pressident
Lt. Gibbs Lt. Henshaw } Members
Ensn. Freeman & Ensn. Baker }

The Prisoners to be Acquaint'd & all Evidences to Attend –

Capt. for the Day for to Morrow Capt. Luse; for Guard Ensn. Freeman To Visit the Barracks Lt. Stiles the Royal Blockhouse & Island Guards to be Releiv'd to Morrow the Battoe party Continues for this Duty Lt. Henshaw – A Serjt. Corpll. & 24 Privates to Cut Wood – Yesterdays Orders to be Read to the Company at Roll Calling, & they are to be paid soon for their Battoe Service.

30th Tuesday Cold Set on a Court Martial to try 2 of the 80th for theft[33] Had a Bayonet made for my Gun the Troops are Determin'd to Desert the 1st. of Novr.

Fort Edwd. Octo. 31st. 1759 – Parole Ipswich –

Capt of the Day for to Morrow Capt Williams; for Guard Lt. Stiles To Visit the Barracks Lt. Henshaw the Battoe party & 24 Privates From the Garison to Cut Wood for the Garison for this Duty – Ensn. Baker –

31st Wednesday. Cold – Went with a party of 56 Men to Cut Wood Cut & Corded 37 Cord Capt Fulcome Came from the Lake Report they Expect the Provincials will Desert to Morrow

---

[33] See record of Court, under this date. Ante p. 155.

The Orderly Book of Lieut. William Henshaw. 249

Thursday Fort Edward. 1st Novr. 1759
– Parole Massachusetts –

A Garrison Court Martial to set Imediately, Capt. Luse Pressident

Lt Dayton   Lt. Scott
Lt. Gibbs   & Ensn. Freeman } Members

The Prisoners to be Acquainted & all Evidences to Attend

Capt. of the Day for to Morrow Capt. Whiting; for Guard Ensn. Baker; to Visit the Barracks Ensn. Force the Royal Blockhouse Bridge & Island to be Releivd to Morrow A Sub 1 Serjt. 2 Corplls. & 45 Privates to go with 8 Battoes to Morrow for provision to Fort Miller for this Duty Lt. Dayton –

1st Novr. Thursday Fort Edwd. 1st. Novr. 1759 This Morng. the Officers in the Garrison up by Dawn of Day to stop the Men in Case they should Attempt to Desert; at 8 °Clock, 18 or 20 of the New Jersey Regt. March'd out of the Barracks with their Firelocks & Haversacks: 6 or 7 was stop'd before they got out of the Sally port, 3 or 4 Officers Headed the Rest & Drove them into the Fort One was Whip'd Imediately: 3 or 4 more Confin'd but Soon after Releas'd – A party of our Men took about 20 of Colo. Willards Regt. that Deserted from the Lake Sent them back by a party of our Men: Lt. Stiles Commanded them as soon as they Ariv'd at the Lake they was Imediately sent over the Lake to go to the Genll .–

Friday Fort Edward: 2d. Novr. 1759 – Parole Conerscorp –

The two Companys of the Massachusets Force to March to Morrow to Joyn their Regts at Crown Point. The Bridge & Island to be Releav'd Early to Morrow Morng. by the Jersey troops – A Sub. Serjt. 2 Corpll. & 20 Privates of the Royal Highlanders to Releive the Guards in the Fort at 8 °Clock to Morrow Morng. – For this Duty Lt. [James] McIntosh[34]

---

[34] At this point the Orderly Book ceases, as Henshaw remains no longer at Fort Edward and the post is under the charge of another than his regiment. The Journal continues until November 26th.

2d. Friday. Cold Chilly Weather; this Afternoon a Compy. of the R[oyal] H[ighland] Regt. Ariv'd at Fort Edwd. they Brought Marching Orders from the Genll. for us to March to Crown point & Joyn our Regts. &c –

3d Saturday Our Troops set out for Crown point that were Left in Garrison; about 9 ᴼClock Ensn. Baker & myself left to settle the Battoe Accompts with Mr. Campbell, & Return a Number of Arms that was Left by Dead & Sick men. Set out for Fort George about an Hour before sun set Arivd at the Lake at 11 ᴼClock at Night, Rainy all Day & Night –

4th Sunday. Very Cold Hail, Snow & Rain – Went on Board the Battoes at 10 ᴼClock the Wind very tempestuous the Lake Rough. Ariv'd at the Landing at Colo. Willards Camp at 9 ᴼClock at Night – Lodg'd with Capt. [Valentine] Jones & Lt [Samuel] Dunlap the Soldiers Encampd in the Wood, 36 Miles from Fort George to the Landing –

Colo. Willards Camp at the Landing: Monday 5th Novr. 1759 – Set out at 11 ᴼClock Stop'd at the Mills 2 Miles from the Landing: Cross'd the Lake through the Mill pond; Came to Ticonderoga 2 Miles from the Mills went to Genll. Lymans House Staid an Hour & set out in the Road that our Troops Cleard to Crown point Provided one Batteau to Carry our Baggage; Encamp'd in the Woods about 4 Miles from Carillon Snow in the Forenoon Rain in the Afternoon & all Night

Provincials Camp in the Woods Between Ticonderoga & Crown point Tuesday 6th Novr. – Set out at 7 ᴼClock Came to our Baggage Boat at the Lake Stop'd & Refresh'd Ourselves, then set out & Came to Majr. [Francis] Balls Encampment Ariv'd at Colo. [Joseph] Ingersol's Encampmt 2 Miles & ½ from Crown point 12½ from Ticonderoga there Join'd our Battalion – a Very Pleasant Day – Snow in the Night. Lake Champlain Runs Near North from Carilon to Crown point, then Runs N East

7 Novr. Camp Near Crown point Wednesday Fair – Join'd in a Mess with Lt. [Nathaniel] Ingersol Lt. Bond

& Ensn. Fuller. Set out for Crown point; went & Viewd the Old & New Fort Went to Brigadeer Ruggles Returnd again at Sunset Spent the Evening with Colo Ingersol; was Warn'd for Fatigue for to Morrow. Report that our Troops will be Discharg'd next Sunday – News that Majr. [Robert] Rogers is Come into No. 4. with his party, Lost but 1 Man

Thursday 8 Novr. Camp Near Crown Point – Went on Fatigue with a party of 20 Men to make a Glassee & Clear Brush from the Fence that Runs from the Lake to the Bay Inclosing 5000 Acres of Land, 3 Miles from the Point & 2 Miles from the Lake to the Bay as the fence Runs – Cloudy Day

9th Friday Do. Camp Near Crown point The Invalids of the 1st. Battn. of Colo. Ruggles Regt. went of to Day; Colo. Ingersol Lt. Ingersol Capt. Cox & Ensn. Ward. Colo. Whiting with 500 Invalids set off from the point – Colo. Salstonstall takes the Command at this Encampment – At Evening a party of Invalids set out through the Woods by No. 4 – Officers of the 1st. Battalion Capt. Robinson & Ensn. Seagraves A Field Officer Commanded the party that went: 3 or 400.

10th Camp Near Crown point Saturday: Kings Birth Day, Went to Crown Point the English Flag Hoisted in the New Fort, the Grenadiers Drawd up & Fir'd three times – a Band of Musick Follow'd them. Towards Evening the Regiments Draw'd up & Fir'd – the Cannon all Discharg'd at the New Fort & Great Rejoyceing throughout the Camp on that Ocasion

11th Sunday, at Camp; F[air] Pleasent Weathr. Staid in Camp all Day –

12th Monday Do. Colo. Babcocks Regt March'd by No. 4 Went to Crown Point; One of the Light Infantry Hang'd for theft; the Kings Oxen Sold by Lots

13th Tuesday Do. Colo. Worcester [David Wooster's] Regt. March'd by No. 4: the Sail of Oxen 20 for a Lot, Sold for

22 to 60 & 70 £ Currency, a Lot Went to Capt Whitings Encampment from there to the Point

14th Novr. 1759; Wednesday. at Camp Near Crown Point Fair & pleasant; Walk'd to Crown Point; this Morning Colo. [Nathan] Whitings Regt. March'd off by the way of No. 4.

15th Camp Near Crown Point Thursday Rainy Went on Fatigue Clearing a Road from the Block House North of the Massachs. Point to the Lower B. House by the Bay: a Flag of Truce [was] Brought in – Capt Trott & Capt – — of the Rangers Came into Camp: Our Battn. Packing up their all's for a March: Made Ready – staid in Camp all Night – very Rainy

16th Friday. up at 4 °Clock; Rainy Bad Weather for a March 1st. Battn. set out for the Point; Went & Settled the Battoe Acctt. with Colo. Robinson Set off From Crown point an Hour after the 1st. Battn. set off – Overtook them at the place Where they Encamp'd at, 4 Miles Distance From the point. Return'd again to Crown point in Persuit of our Baggage which was left Behind; Ensn. Sellon & I got Information that the Guard on the East Side of the Lake had taken it; Determine to persue it in the Morng. Lodg'd at Capt Baldwins Rainy Night –

17th Novr. 1759, Saturday. Crown point. Rose at Day Light – Breakfasted with Capt. Baldwin, Went to Majr. Monypenny & Inform'd him of the Loss of our Baggage; he Orderd the Releiving Guard to search the Old Guards packs; Searched But Did not find them – then I Look'd about the Old Logs & found two Spoons & a Rasor hid under a Log. the Guard went & Assisted me in Searching for the Baggage & Found it all Conceal'd in a Valley. Ensn. Sellon Went over to the Point – in his Absence Found our Baggage. Capt. Baldwn. Nixon & Majr. Ball Went by us some time ago (it being 12 °Clock) at the East side of the Lake Opposite to Crown point – Colo. Schuyler Regt. Sail'd to day Set off from here at ½ after 2 °Clock Encamp'd at Dark about 17 Miles from the Lake without any Fire. Cloudy Day

18th Novr. Fair Sunday Ensn. Sellon & I set out at Day Light; Overtook a party of 15 Men Belonging to Colo. Whiting & [the] Worcester [Wooster] Regt. about 12 ºClock Found a Hampshire Lad in the Woods whose Name was Edward Lynds of Somersworth in N Hampshire. He was most Dead with Scurvy Itch & Cold – had been in the Wood 4 or 5 Days. He said he could not move. I Gave him some Chocolate to take which Refresh'd him but could by no Means persuade him to try to Move, till I threatened him which made him Cry. He walk'd 4 Miles, where I Incamp'd – Gave him hot Chocolate for Supper he is Exceeding Thankful for my Forcing him along

19th Novr. Monday Fair – Set out at Break of Day; the Lad that I took up in the Woods, I Committed to the Care of a Serjt & 12 Men of the Conecticut. After I had seen him washd & Scowr'd from Head to Foot then Ensn. Sellon & I Travell'd apace to Joyn our Regt – Came to Otter Creek; Travell'd 3 or 4 Miles by it & Encamp'd. Rainy Night

20th Tuesday Cloudy – Set of at Dawn of Day – Cross'd Otter Creek at 11 ºClock 7 Miles from our Encampment Last Night, Wrote this at the Foot Bridge 37 Miles from here to No. 4; 45 from here to Crown point. Travelled 5 Miles & Encamp'd A Rainy Afternoon & Night; Lt. Gibbs I overtook—[35]

21st Wednesday: Cloudy – Set out at Break of Day. Overtook several of our Compa. at 10 ºClock; – the Brigadeer at 12 had spraind his Ankle Cross'd a Terrible Mountain, Just at Dark a Mile over & very Steep Encamp'd at the Foot of the Mountain; 18 Miles From Last Nights Encampment & 15 from No. 4: Got 3 Pints of Chocolate for supper, have Been without Provision & Fair'd hard this 2 or 3 Days the Regts. Provision all Gone 3 or 4 Officers sent Forward to Get Provision & Meet the Men & take Care of the Sick.

---

[35] Dashes at this point in the original indicate omissions. Possibly other persons overtaken were in mind; if so, these entries may have been made at a later date when their names were forgotten.

Camp in the Woods. 22d. Novr. 1759 Thursday Fair – Set out at Day light Ariv'd at the Height of Land by Sun rise. Arriv'd at No. 4 at 3 °Clock in the Afternoon Went & Lodg'd at Mr Putnams 1 & ½ Miles from the Ferry up the River in a Little Picquet Fort.

23d. Novr. at No. 4 Friday Do. Went to the Old Fort this Morng. – a Great Many of our Men Gone home; Made a Billeting Roll Draw'd Meat 1 lb p Man – Bread None – Returnd & Lodg'd at Mr Putnams Picquet.

24th Saturday No. 4 or Charlestown – Fair Went to the Old Fort: 40 Men Detach'd from our Regt. to go Back & bring in the Sick Officers Lt. Macfarlin & Joy [Daniel McFarland and David Joy] Draw'd Meat No Bread in the town Set of at 8 °Clock Went & Lodg'd at Major Bellowses at No 3 or Walpole 10 Miles from No. 4: Paid the Men the Billeting Money: 3/ Sterling p Man

25th Sunday Fair at No. 3 – Draw'd One Day's Allowance of Meat & Flow'r Set of at 8 °Clock Stopt at No. 2 or Westmorland 8 Miles from No 3 from there to Upper Ashavillet or Keen 8 Miles From there to the Town 4 Miles Supp'd at the Tavern from there to Swansey 4 Miles Stop'd & Lodg'd at Mr. Carpenters

26th Monday Snow & Rain – Set out from Swansey – Came to Winchester: 12 Miles – from there to Mount Geace & Pecquage 14 M[iles]. Lodg'd at Lt Dexters (from there Cross'd the River & Came to Petersham from there to N Rutland & Lodg'd at Capt Craiges)[36]

Tuesday 27th Novr. 1759 at Pequage – Set out from Lt. Dexters Cros'd the River into Petersham 7 Miles; From there to Capt. Craiges at New Rutland 10 Miles a Fair Day

28th Wednesday – Fair Set out from Capt. Craiges Came to Rutland 5 Miles Parted with Lt. Martin & Nixon From there Home at Leicester at 2 °Clock 10 Miles &c &c &c.

---

[36]These words are crossed out in the original text.

INDEX.

INDEX.

A

Abbott, Edward, 75, 76.
Abercrombie, James, 60, 61.
Abert, Gerrit, 87, 88.
Adems, Robert, 105.
Albany, Dutch Church at; account against John Bradstreet, 82, 90.
Alexander, William, 58, 244n.
Allen, James, 58, 172 and note.
Allen, John, 183, 215, 239.
Allen, Thomas, letters to, 40.
Amherst, Sir Jeffrey, 21, 63, 64, 65, 72, 85, 86, 94, 155, 161, 213, 217, 244, 247, 248; letters, 66, 68, 69, 70, 71; letters to, 12, 62, 67.
Andrews, Rev. William, 40.
Apthorp, Charles Ward, 62, 65, 72.
Appy, John, 63, 64.
Arnot, Hugh, 79, 81, 86.
Ashley, Noah, 143.
Askwith, Samuel, 145.
Atkins, John, 145.
Atkinson, Theodore, 139.

B

Babcock, Henry, 190, 251.
Bagley, Jonathan, 138, 140, 149, 150.
Bailey, John, 160.
Richard, 172n.
Baker, Elijah, 201, 202, 204, 205-249.
Baldwin, Jeduthan, 151, 153, 155, 183, 185, 189, 252.
Josiah, 183.
Ball, Francis, 158, 198, 250, 252.
Ballard, John, 183.
Balneaves, Patrick, 81.
Barbut, Theodore, 173.
Bardwell, Ebenezer, 154.
Barnard, Selah, 147.
Barrington, Capt., 171.
Barritt, William, 162.
Barron, William, 163, 165.
Barrons, Oliver, 164.
Baxter & Humphrey, 79.
Bayard, William, 71, 72.
Bayley, William, 88.
Baylie, Richard, 172 and note.
Beckwith, George, 212.
Beckworth, John, 172 and note.
Belknap, William, 163.
Bellows, Jesse, 161, 254.
Benoit or Benneway, Vincent, 85.
Bergstrom, J. G., 69.
Bernard, Francis, 162, 165, 166.
Berry, Ephraim, 141.
Samuel, 163, 164.
Blair, Gov. John, letter to, 31.
Blanchard, Abner, 183.
Bleecker, Anthony, 88.
Henry, jr., 88.
Jan James, 107.
Bliss, Luke, jr., 159.
Moses, 186.
Blunt, Andrew, 183.
John, 183, 203.
Bogle, John, 183, 188, 195.
Bolster, Isaac, 183.
Bond, Nathaniel, 183, 203, 250.
Bone, John, 70.
Boscawen, Edward, 171.
Bostwick, David, letter to, 11.
Bouquet, Henry, 13, 18, 19, 20, 21, 71, 91.

Bowman, ——, 232.
Bowyer, Richard, 173.
Braddock, Edward, 10, 138, 144, 171ff.
Bradford, James, 144.
Bradstreet, John, argument in support of land claims, 103–131; commission, 58; letters, 12, 16, 17, 18, 19, 20, 21, 24, 25, 57–97; mentioned, 13, 14, 17, 187, 192.
Bradstreet, Samuel, 68.
Brattle, William, 151.
Bray, Edward, 187.
Breck, Robert, 186n.
Brereton, Percival, 173.
Brewer, Josiah, 153, 154, 209, 215, 217, 220, 221.
Brown, Adam, 73.
    Ezekiel, 165, 166.
    John, 145.
    Samuel, 143.
Brown, see also Bruyn.
Browning, William, 16, 18, 72, 73.
Bruyn, Jacobus, 125.
Buckhanon, Francis James, 173.
Buffington, David, 82.
Bull, John P., 143.
Burbank, Abijah, 186.
Burk, John, 135, 143, 144, 146, 147, 149, 150, 151, 152, 153, 154, 157, 158, 159, 160.
Burket, Thomas, 190.
Burt, Eleazer, 143.
Burton, Daniel, 40.
    George, 198.
    Ralph, 173, 176.
Butler, John, 68, 93, 105.
Butrick, George, 87.
Butterfield, Leo or Leonard, 165, 185.
Byerly, Frederick, 87.
Byram, Benjamin, 165, 166.

C

Campbell, Alexander, 17.
———, John, 18, 20, 74, 201, 250.
Canada, Peter, 190.
Caner, Rev. Henry, 40.
Cannon, John, 160.
Carleton, Sir Guy, 27.
Carns, John, 69.
Cartwright, Thomas, 59.
Carver, Jonathan, 225.
Cary, James, 83.
Carye, Lucius Ferdinand, 88.
Catlin, John, 150.
Cawey, Eleazer, 85.
Chandler, John, 166, 185.
    John jr., 148.
    Rev. Thomas Bradbury, 38.
Charles, Joseph, of Samuel Whiting's Conn. Co., 198.
Cheever, Ezekiel, 162.
Chipman, Robert H., 141.
Choat, John, 139.
Christie, Gabriel, 63.
    John, 79.
Chulmley, Robert, 173.
Church, Edward, 218.
    Josiah, 151.
Clark, Joel, 66.
Clarke, Thomas, 135, 136, 137, 138, 139, 142, 146, 148.
Claus, Daniel, 14.
Clew, Lawrence, 86.
Cobb, Silvanus, 164.
Coburn, John, 193.
Cockburne, John, 193.
Collins, James, 60.
Collyson, Francis, 77.
Comyn, Peter or Pieter, 61, 85, 89.
Condie, Adam, 96.
Cooke, John, 83.
Connecticut, claim to Western land, 11.
Conway, Henry S., 24, 48.
Cope, John, 173.
Cornbury, Edward Hyde, Lord, 106, 107, 111.
Cory, Benjamin, 164.
Cosby, Gov. William, 121.
Cotton, John, 166.
Coventry, George, 62, 64, 67, 68, 95, 96, 189, 193.

Index.

Cowart, Joseph, 173.
Cowper, ——, 222.
Cox, Ebenezer, 185, 251.
Crawford, William, 204.
Cresap, Thomas, 25.
Crimble, Waterhouse, 173.
Crippen, Joseph, 91.
Crogan, George, 21, 22, 25, 32, 33, 34, 37, 38, 39, 50, 52, 104.
Crombwell, Major, 197.
Crow, Richard, 173.
Crown Point, diary of soldier at, 156; reports regarding, 217, 218; camp near, 250ff.
Cummings, Solomon, 183.
Curry, Donald, 153.
Curtis, Zacheus, 154.
Curwen, Samuel, 154.
Cusick, James, 145.
Cutler, (a sutler), 208, 214, 221.
Cuyler, Abraham, 70, 93.
Cornelius, 16, 67, 81, 83, 86.

D

Daly, Richard, 78.
Danks, Benoni, 149, 155, 161, 165.
Davis, Edward, 166.
Tristram, 157.
Dawson, Henry, 74.
Day, Luke, 158.
Dayton, Elias, 201, 202, 204–249.
Deare, Thomas, 145.
Degarius, John, 74.
Degrov, Michel, 79.
DeLancey, James, 35, 39, 65, 142.
Oliver, 32.
Demaris, Capt., 174.
Demler, George, 83.
De Normandie, Daniel, 61, 64, 145.
Denny, Samuel, 185, 224n, 247.
William, 147.
Desertion, orders regarding, 187, 190, 213, 247.
Detroit, expedition to, 11, 16, 33 34; fire in 1763, 71; troops for in 1764, 72; supplies in, 76; negotiations at, 19, 76.

Dewey, Paul, 151.
Dexter, Lieut., 254.
Dickey, David, 165.
Dimuck, Gideon, 157.
Dinwiddie, Gov. Robert, 171, 175.
Disney, Daniel, 172.
Dixson, Thomas, 165.
Dobson, Robert, 173.
Dod, Major, 193.
Doolittle, Capt., 213.
Doricke, Levi, 193.
Doughty, Rev. John, 40.
Douglass, William, 57.
Douw, Abraham, 72, 88.
Dowes, William, 187, 194.
Dowlar, Henry, 83.
Dox, Samuel, 83.
Dubell, John, 88.
Dunbar, John, 173.
Thomas, 171, 176.
William, 172.
Duncan, Alexander, 16, 75.
John, 84.
Duncan, see Dunkin.
Dunham, Daniel, 84.
Dunkin, John, 183.
Dunlap, Samuel, 204, 250.
Duyce, Mathias, 155.
Dwight, Joseph, 143.
Dyer, Eliphalet, 11.

E

Edgell, Benjamin, 153.
Edmiston, William, 173 and note.
Edwards, Benjamin, 165, 166.
Eells, Edward, 206.
Egan, John, 145.
Elgar, Thomas, 158.
Ellison, John, 14.
Elmer, Samuel, 153.
Emerson, Moses, 144.
Emery, Ambrose, 163.
Nathaniel, 163.
Richard, 141.
Emott, John, 145.
Etherington, George, 83.
Eyre, William, 18.

F

Fairservice, James, 58.
Falconer, Thomas, 172n.
Farley, Samuel jr., 164.
Farmar, Robert, 22.
Farrington, Thomas, 162, 163, 164, 166.
Faulkner, Thomas, 172 and note.
Feather, John, 84.
Fellows, John, 151.
Ferguson, William, 204.
Finney, Francis, 155.
Fire Arms, regulations, 192, 194, 227.
Fitch, Eleazer, 193, 212.
Flag or Flagg, Asa, 159.
  Benjamin, 186.
  Zechariah jr., 164.
Fletcher, Levi, 162.
Flower, John, 84.
Floyd, Hugh, 164.
Floyer, Scob, 174.
Fluree, John, 84.
Fonda, Adam, 88.
  Douw, 83, 85.
  Jellis, 68, 81, 82, 88, 93.
  Peter, 79.
Forbes, John, 195.
Force, Ensign, 201, 202, 203, 205–249.
Forsey, (a sutler) 202.
Forster, William, 165.
Fort Edward, conditions at, 81, 155, 166, 200; orders issued at, 195–249; troops stationed at, 152, 199.
Fort Miller, 219.
Fort Williams, account for building of, 143.
Foster, Thomas, 155.
France, illegal commerce with, 160; influence upon Indians, 11, 13, 16, 25, 27, 34, 82, 150, 219. French inhabitants of Nova Scotia brought to Massachusetts, 145; victory at Fort Duquesne, 144, 171ff.
Franklin, Benjamin, 23; letters, 10; letters to, 24, 48.
Franklin, William, 31; letters to, 23, 24, 29, 33, 34, 47, 48, 52.
Frazer, Simon, 22.
Freeman, Ensign, 201, 202, 204–249.
Fulcome, Capt., 248.
Fuller, Andrew, 150.
Fuller, Ensign, 251.
Funnel, Pomp, 183.
Furbush, ——, 242.
Furnace or Furness, Capt., 185.

G

Gage, Thomas, 23, 47, 62, 64, 65, 72, 90, 91, 172, 191, 218; letters from, 80; letters to, 12-22, 24, 30, 32, 33-39, 62, 63, 74-82, 84-87, 89, 92, 94.
Gage, Henry, 82.
Gale, Abijah, 183.
  Levin, 31.
  Nehemiah, 183, 220, 237.
Galland, John, 29, 30.
Gamble, James, 71.
Garfield, Benjamin, 183.
Gates, Horatio, 174.
  Sippio, 183.
Gay, Jotham, 155.
Gethins, Richard, 172.
Gibbs, Joshua, 153, 201, 203–249.
Gibson, Ephraim, 162.
Gilman, Peter, 140, 141.
Gladwin, Henry, 15, 16, 23, 70, 173.
Glen, Cornelius, 81, 93.
  Henry, 85.
  John, 68, 70, 94; letters, 25, 29, 63, 64, 74, 77, 82, 83, 84, 85, 86, 88, 89, 93, 96.
  John jr., 84.
Goffe, John, 159.
Goldthwait, Thomas, 164.
Googins, Joseph, 183.
Gordon, Lord Adam, 47.
  Robert, 173.

Index. 261

Gordon, Samuel, 239.
  Ensign, 201.
Graham, Charles, 190.
Gordon, 196, 197.
Grant, Allan, 82, 85.
  James, 188, 190, 191; 197, 199.
Gray, Harrison jr., 159, 160.
  Robert, 174.
Green, Thomas, 163.
Gridley, Isaac, 146.
  Richard, 141.
Griggs, Lieut., 214.
Gwynn, Anthony, 60.

H

Hale, Robert, 9, 10, 136, 137, 138, 139, 140, 141, 143, 148, 162, 166.
Halket, Francis, 172.
  James, 172.
  Sir Peter, 171, 172, 176.
Hallowell, Benjamin jr., 59, 148, 162.
Hamilton, John, 174.
Hancock, Thomas, 64, 67.
Handsard or Hansard, John, 173 and note.
Hardenbergh, Johannes, 94, 106, 112, 113, 119, 126.
Harriman, Nathaniel, 163.
Harris, John, 158.
  Samuel, 190, 191.
Harrison, Thomas, 173.
Hart, John, 173.
Hartt, Ralph, 60.
Hatfield, William, 183.
Hathorne, John, 173.
Hawks, Gershom, 159.
  John, 157, 194.
Hawley, Joseph, 151.
Hay, Jehu, 23, 33, 34.
Haynes, Midshipman, 174.
Hemstreack, Jacob, 88.
Henshaw, Benjamin, 194, 227, 231.
  Daniel, 153, 220, 224.
  Jonathan, 152.
  Joseph, 210, 220.

Henshaw, William, Account Book 161; appointment as Lieutenant, 151; letters, etc., 152, 153, 154, 155, 160, 162, 166; Journal and Orderly Book, 179-254.
Herres, Valentine, 150.
  William, 150.
Herrod, ——, 235.
Heywood, Thomas, 157.
Hicks, Whitehead, 82.
Higgins, Cornelius, 216.
Hill, Launcelot, 78.
Hillsborough, Wills Hill, Earl, 31, 32.
Hind, Richard, 40.
Hinshelwood, Archibald, 155.
Hitchcock, Luke, 186.
Hoar, Jonathan, 146.
  William, 58.
Hobson, Samuel, 172.
Hogan, William, 80.
Holden, John, 190.
Holliston, Lieut., 237.
Holman, Jonathan, 152.
Holton, John, 242.
Hooker, Silas, 183.
Hovey, Daniel, 183.
How, Samuel, 183.
Howard, Nathan, 183.
  William, 18, 221.
Howath, Lieut., 174.
Hubbard, Thomas, 136, 137, 142, 146.
Hudson "of Hoosek", 228.
Hull, James, 183.
Hunt, Alexander, 60.
  Samuel, 199.
  William, 163.
"Huron Andrew," 34.
Hutchinson, Israel, 150.
  Thomas, 138, 139, 152.
Hyde, Edward, Lord Cornbury, 106, 107, 111.

I

Indians. attacks by, 15, 38, 82; lands of, 52; treaties with, 16, 18, 19, 31, 36, 78, 118, 167; trade with, 17, 26, 36, 77.

Ingersol, Nathaniel, 183, 204, 250, 251.
　Thomas, 186.
Ingersoll, Joseph, 151, 153, 156, 185, 192, 196, 198, 201, 250, 251.

J

Jaquet, Peter, 145.
Jeffreys, James, letter to, 32.
Jennison, William, 157.
Johnson, Andris or Andrew, 83.
　Guy, 14, 34, 35, 37, 38.
　James, 183.
　John, 35, 38, 88.
　Thias, 183.
Johnson, Sir William, 9, 10, 12, 16, 17, 19, 74, 92, 104, 124, 138, 142; letters from, 11, 12, 13, 14, 15, 17, 19, 21-40, 47, 48, 50, 52, 94; letters to, 10, 74.
Jones, Cornelius, 186.
　Jacob, 153.
　John, 77.
　Valentine, 221, 250.
Joy, David, 193, 254.

K

Kempe, John Tabor, 27.
Kendrick, John, 73.
Kenfield, George, 153.
Kennedy, Primrose, 172n.
　Quinton, 172.
　Robert, 59, 60.
Keppel, Augustus, 144, 171, 174.
Keppel Manuscripts, 169ff.
Killoran, Bartholomew, 59.
Kimball, Major, 199.
King, Thomas, 20, 38, 39.
　William, 151.
Kirkwood, James, 59.
Knaggs, George, 145.
Knap, John, 165.
Knight, Benjamin, 158.
Knoeb, Gerrit, 87, 88.
　Jacob, 87.

Knower, John, 204.

L

Lackey, William, 183, 187, 188.
Lake, Ephraim, 16.
Lake, see also Leake.
Lamb, Anthony, 73.
Lamson, William, 194.
Lane, Edmund, 149.
Lansing, Philip, 187.
Larkin, George, 158.
Lascells, Peregrine, 174.
Lawnson, Henry, 86.
　Isaac, 86.
Lawrence, Gov. Charles, 144, 155, 171.
　John, 145.
Leake, Robert, 161, 188, 195.
Learnad, Elijah, 183.
Learned, Jeremiah, 152.
Lee, John, jr., 141.
Le Hunte, George, 58, 77.
Lessley, Matthew, 172.
Levens, Abel, 183.
Lewis, Andrew, 31.
Line, William, 145.
Littler, William, 172 and note.
Livingston, James, 79.
　Philip, V. B., 11.
　William, 11.
Lock, Robert, 172n.
Lords of Trade, letter to, 25.
Loring, Joshua, 12, 62, 65, 67, 68, 72, 73, 94.
Lothrop, Benjamin jr., 69.
Lott, Abraham jr., 142.
Louder, —— of Boston, 192.
Loudoun, John, Earl of, 58, 61, 147.
Lovejoy, Daniel, 186.
Lovewell, Zacheus, 207n.
Lowder, Ensign, 221.
Luke, John, 75.
Luse, Zephaniah, 201, 202, 203, 205-249.
Lyman, Phineas 193, 212, 250.
Lynd, Samuel, 214.

Index.   263

Lynds, Edward, 253.
Lyttleton, William H., 213.

M

McClean, Allen, 189.
McCloud, William, 173.
McComb, John, 64.
McCuller, Patrick, 173.
McDaniel, Jacob, 163.
    Malcolm, 190.
McDonald, William, 77.
McDonnel, Allen, 23.
McDougall, George, 75.
    John, 145.
McFarland, Daniel, 254.
McGee, Thomas, 18.
McIntosh, George, 84, 96.
    James, 249.
McKay, Charles, 83.
McKee, Alexander, 22, 23.
McKeen, Robert, 73.
McKellar, Peter, 173.
McLeod, Norman, 33.
    William, 173.
McMartin, Peter, 190.
McNeal, John, 174.
McNeill, Hector, 174n.
McTaggart, Peter, 60.
McTavish, Andrew, 22.
Macvicar, Duncan, 73.
Mainor, Capt., 185.
Maisonville, Francis, 38, 39.
Maitland, Richard, 81, 87, 88.
Malcolm, Joseph, 141.
Man, ———, 215, 222.
Marsh, Ebenezer, 183.
    Moses, 159.
    Perez, 143.
Martin, Aaron, 183.
    Adam, 183.
    John, 204.
    Samuel, 77.
    William, 96.
Mason, Abel, 183.
Mather, Samuel, 161.
Maturin, Gabriel, 80, 90, 91, 93.
Maxwell, Thomas, 165, 166.

Maxwell, William, 71.
Merrick, John, 186.
Meserve (Meservey) Nathaniel, 60, 61.
Middagh, George, 66.
Miller, John, 74.
    Richard, 174.
Moffett, Thomas, 155.
Moffit, Aquilla, 183.
    Joseph, 183.
Moncel, Henry, 193.
Monckton, Robert, 243 and note.
Moneypenny, Alexander, 189, 191, 252.
Monier, John, 83, 95.
Mongomery, see Montgomery.
Monroe, see Munroe.
Montcalm, Louis Joseph Marquis de, 243.
Montgomery, Alexander, 195, 198, 200, 206, 207.
Montgomery, Richard, 20.
Montour, Andrew, 15.
Montreseur or Montresor, John, 13, 16, 173, and note.
Moore, Gov. Henry, 23, 31, 92, 94, 95, 96, 105, 124.
Morris, Robert Hunter, 10.
    Roger, 172, 175.
    Thomas, 18, 20, 21.
    William, 173.
Mortier, Abraham, 61, 62, 63, 64, 65, 66, 67, 68, 69, 71, 72, 73, 94.
Morton, ——— "of Glascow", 186.
Moseley, Richard, 40.
Muffett, Thomas, 153.
Mugford, James, 60.
Munn, John, 154.
Munroe, Rev. Harry, 40.
Murphy, Edmond, 158.
Murray, Gov. John, 94.

N

Nartloo, or
Nartlow, Francis, 172 and note.
Neilson, Samuel, 145.
Nelson, Samuel Nicols, 155.

Newell, Andrew, 59.
Newhall, Jonathan, 148.
Niagara, defense of, 17, 75, 80; Indian conference at, 19; surrender of, 219.
Nichols, ———, 223.
Nicolls, William, 142.
Nixon, John, 185, 193, 252.

O

Occom, Samson, 11.
Ogilvie, William, 69.
Okeman, John, 165.
Oliver, Andrew, 146, 151, 152, 162.
Orde, Thomas, 173.
Orme, Robert, 10, 144, 171, 172, 174.
Osborne, John, 136, 141, 143.
Otis, James, 58, 62.

P

Paine, Samuel Clark, 185, 188, 194, 213, 244.
  Timothy, 159.
Pallisser, Sir Hugh, 175.
Parker, John, 159.
Parkman, Moses, 163, 164.
  William, 183.
Parks, Amariah, 183.
Partridge, Oliver, 147, 154.
Patrick, William, 143.
Patterson, Alexander, 95, 96.
Patton, John, 150.
Peirce, Benjamin, 159.
Penington, George, 172.
Penn, John, 14, 19, 30, 31, 34.
  Richard, 28, 31.
  Thomas, 28, 31, 35.
Pepperrell, Sir William, 58, 136, 141, 148, 149, 214.
Peronie or Peyroney, 174, 176.
Peters, Elias, 193.
  Rev. Richard, 27.
  William, 83.
Petty, Aaron, 153.
Peyroney, see Peronie.
Phillips, Jonathan, 183, 186, 211.

Phips, Spencer, 146.
Phyn & Ellice, 97.
Pierce, Benjamin, 151.
Pitcher, Solomon, 84.
Pitt, William, (Lord Chatham,) 65, 160.
Plaisted, John, 141.
Polson, William, 174n.
Pomeroy, Seth, 143.
Pomroy, Benjamin, 214.
Pond, Eliphalet, 148.
Pontiac, 18, 21, 23, 24.
Poor, John, 194.
Pottinger, James, 172 and note.
Poulson, William, 174.
Pownall, Gov. Thomas, 10, 138, 142, 148, 150, 151, 152, 154.
Pratt, Abraham, 183.
Preston, William, 172.
Prideaux, John, 195, 198.
Putnam, Ebenezer, 183, 254.
Putnam, Tarrant, 166.
Pynchon, Joseph, 150.

Q

Quin, William, 83.
Quincy, Josiah, 138.

R

Rackley, William, 165.
Ray, Christian, 186.
Rea, Richard, 74.
Reed, Benjamin, 186.
  John, 59, 60.
  Capt., 185.
Rice, ———, 218.
Richardson, Benjamin, 194.
  Philip, 143, 145, 247.
Riggs, Joseph, 145.
Riky, John, 64.
Robbins, Ichabod, 183.
Roberts, Asa, 183.
  Benjamin, 39, 74.
Robertson, James, 72.
Robinson, Beverly, 73, 78, 195, 198, 199, 251.
  DeLancey, 94.

Index.

Robinson, Thomas, 33.
Rogers, Robert, 31, 69, 94, 167, 211, 217, 251.
Roggers, David, 190, 191.
Rose, Samuel, 190.
Ross, Robert, 173.
Royan, Robert, 145.
Rugg, John, 153, 154.
Ruggles, Timothy, 140, 146, 151, 152, 153, 156, 157, 158, 159, 185, 189, 193, 194, 198, 202, 210, 222, 251.
Rutsen, Jacob, 107, 122.
Ryan & Spear 240n; 241, 242.

S

St. Clair, Arthur, 71.
St. Clair, see also Sinclair.
Salmon, John, 145.
Saltonstall, Richard, 196, 251.
Sargent, see Sergeant.
Saturday, Jacob, 161.
Schermerhorn, Jacob W., 88.
Schuyler, Abraham, 93.
 Peter, 193, 199, 252.
 Philip, 65, 67, 88, 89, 92, 95, 96.
Scott, Charles, 201, 203, 204–249.
 John, 162.
Seagraves, Ensign, 251.
Sellon, John, 252, 253.
Sergeant, Thomas, 185.
Seydam, Hendrick, 145.
Shaddock, ——, 186.
Shaw, ——, 242.
Shelburne, William Petty Earl, 26, 27, 80, 90, 95.
Sheldon, Ebenezer, 143, 154.
Shirley, William, 14, 61, 145, 150, 171; letters from, 9, 10, 58, 135, 136, 137, 138, 140, 141, 142, 144; letters to, 9, 57, 58, 139.
Shirley, William, *Secretary to Genl. Braddock*, 172, 175.
Shuckburgh, Richard, 121.
Shumway, Peter, 183.
Simpson, Andrew, 172 and note.

Sinclair or St. Clair, Sir John, 19, 20, 145, 172, 176.
Sinewood, William, 81.
Smallman, Thomas, 22, 23.
Smedley, ——, *of Mansfield, Conn.*, 231.
Smith, Aaron, 209.
 Adam, 25, 86.
 Ephraim, 153.
 Robert, 173.
 William, 11.
Smyth, Edward, 84.
South Carolina, Governor of, 213, 234.
Spann, Theodore Augustus, 149.
Sparks, William, 173.
Spendelow, Lieut., 174, 175.
Splitdorff, Carolus Gustavus de, 174.
Staats, Samuel, 82.
Stanley, Thomas, 158.
Stanniford, Jeremiah, 60.
Stanwix, John, 61.
Star, Jonathan, 146.
Stebbings, John, 145.
Stedman, John, 70, 73, 74, 83.
Steel, ——, 224.
Stephens, Adam, 227, 231.
 James, 92.
Sterling, Robert, 173.
 Thomas, 22.
Stevens, Adam, 174.
 John, 94.
Stevens, see also Stephens.
Stevenson, John, 69.
Stewart, Robert, 174.
 Walter, 174.
Stiles, Jacob, 162.
Stiles, see also Styles.
Stirling, Capt., 244.
Stone, Joseph, 166.
 William, 174.
Stout, Jonathan, 64.
Stowell, Cornelius, 151, 156.
Strange, Robart, 92.
Streeter, John, 183.
 Jonathan, 183.

Streeter, Samuel, 183.
　Zebulon, 183.
Strong, Samuel, 91.
Strubble, Christopher, 14.
Styles, Amos, 201, 202, 204–249.
Sumain, Simon, 174.
Susquehanna Company, 12.
Sutlers, orders regarding, 188, 197, 208, 230, 234; see Brewer, Josiah; Cutler; Forsey; Ryan & Spear; Taylor, Ezra.
Sutton, Daniel, 145.

T

Talbot, Midshipman, 174, 175.
Tannott, Thomas, 60.
Tapley, John, 165.
Tatton, Charles, 172.
Taylor, Eldad, 186.
　Ezra, 187, 194.
　Othniel, 157.
Teedyuscung, (Indian), 15.
Ten Broek, John, 145.
Thompson, Joseph, 159.
Ticonderoga, capture of, 216, 217; fortifications, 220.
Tilton, Jacob, 245.
Titcomb, John, 140.
Torrance, Thomas, 160.
Town, David, 183.
　Elijah, 183.
　Moses, 183.
Townsend, George, 216.
　Robert, 172.
Toy, Sergt., 245.
Treby, John, 172.
Trott, Capt., 252.
Trotter, Matthew, 84.
Tucker, Ebenezer, 183.
Tyce, Nathaniel, 73.
Tyng, John, 162, 163, 164, 165, 166.
Tyron, William, 96.

V

Valleau, Isaiah, 145.
Van Alstyn, Martin, 84.

Van der Bogart, Jykeris, 86.
Van Driessen Petrus, 93.
Van Duerson, Abraham, 145.
Van Eps, Abraham, 84.
　Jean Baptiste, 88.
Vanhorne, David, 11.
Van Schaick, Goose, 66.
Van Schoonhoven, Guert, 83.
Van Slyke, Garret, 88.
Van Valkenburgh, Isaac, 91.
Van Vleck, Teunis, 86.
Van Vordt, Jacob, 88.
Van Vrank, Nicholas, 87, 88.
Vaughan, John, 80, 83, 87.
Vedder, Albert, 93.
　Jacob, 88.
Vrooman, Jan, 88.

W

Wadleigh, Joseph, 60.
Waggoner, Edmond, 174 and note.
　John, 174 and note.
Waldo, Samuel jr., 151.
Walker, John, 155, 162, 165.
　Josiah, 183.
　Phineas, 183.
　Thomas, 31.
Wall, James, 190.
Walmough, Capt., 164.
Walsh, Hunt, 149.
Walsham, John, 173.
Warburton, Hugh, 174.
Ward, Josiah jr., 158, 251.
Warner, Ichabod, 158.
Washington, George, 144, 171, 172, 175, 177.
　Commissary for the Crown, 208, 235.
Watkins, Ephraim, 183.
　Ward, 204.
Watts, John, 35, 39.
Wayne, Anthony, 97.
Webb, Daniel, 154.
Welles, Samuel, 139.
Wells, Simeon, 143.
Welsh, William, 60.
Wendell, Jacob, 157.

Index.

Wentworth, Benning, 139, 140, 141; letters from, 9, 138; letters to, 9, 10, 137.
Westerlo, Eilardus jr., 82, 90.
Wethered, Samuel, 162.
Wharton, Samuel, 29, 48.
Wheeler, Daniel, 193.
Wheelock, Eleazer, 31, 40.
Wheelwright, Nathaniel, 71, 72.
White, Jonathan, 145.
White, see Whyte.
Whiting, Charles, 185n, 251.
John, 185n.
Leonard, 152, 153, 154, 155, 162, 163, 164, 185, 201, 202, 204–249, 252.
Nathan, 185n, 206, 252.
Whitmore, Edward, 67.
Whitney, Ebenezer, 183.
Whyte, Alexander, 74.
Widman or Wideman, William, 173 and note.
Wilkins, John, 34, 70, 71.
Willard, Abijah, 152, 159, 185, 204–249, 250.
Joseph, 135, 142.
Josiah, 136.
Nahum, 157, 161.
Williams, Elijah, 143.
Ephraim, 142, 143.
Israel, 135, 143, 144, 150, 151, 154, 158, 159.
Job, 185, 200, 202, 203, 204–249.
John, 91, 193.

Williams, Stephen, 143.
Thomas, 143.
William, 91.
Williamson, Adam, 173.
Wilson, George, 60.
John, 70.
Wimple, Andrew, 85.
Winepress, William, 69, 79.
Wingfield, William, 59.
Winslow, John, 141, 146, 148.
Wolfe, James, 154, 234, 238, 243.
Wood, Draper S., 25, 92.
Woodbridge, John, 11.
Thomas, 60.
Timothy, 148, 240, 241, 245.
Woodroff, Jonathan, 145.
Woods, Henry, 166.
Woodward, Henry, 174.
Wooster, David, 251, 253.
Worster, Ebenezer, 119, 128, 131.
Henry, 118, 120, 128.
Worthington, John, 149, 158, 159, 193, 242.
Wouter Dance (Indian), 25, 26, 29, 93.
Wright, John, 174.
Wyer, David, 154, 204.
Wyman, Daniel, 183.
Wyncoop, Jacobus, 145.
Wyoming Valley, settlements in, 11, 12, 35.

Y

Young, George, 199.

www.ingramcontent.com/pod-product-compliance
Lightning Source LLC
Chambersburg PA
CBHW050133170426
43197CB00011B/1824